To Kate, Ffreya and Kit

... In the brightest day and in the darkest night –
amidst your happiest scenes and gloomiest hours –
always, always...
Sullivan Ballou

UNDEFEATED
The Story of the 1974 Lions

Rhodri Davies

y Lolfa

First impression: 2014
Second impression: 2014

The publishers wish to acknowledge the support of
Cyngor Llyfrau Cymru

Cover design: Y Lolfa
Cover photograph: Colorsport

ISBN: 978 184771 931 7

Published and printed in Wales
on paper from well-maintained forests by
Y Lolfa Cyf., Talybont, Ceredigion SY24 5HE
website www.ylolfa.com
e-mail ylolfa@ylolfa.com
tel 01970 832 304
fax 832 782

CONTENTS

Foreword
by Gareth Edwards

THERE ARE SOME questions which never go away, and some answers which are not easily given. Who was the best – Benny or Barry? Who were the greatest Lions, those who beat the All Blacks in 1971 or those who defeated the Springboks in 1974? And when it came to '74, should we even have been in South Africa at all? These are the difficult conundrums I have lived with since the Seventies.

I've pondered all these questions, and many more besides during the intervening years, and admit that different circumstances have at times led to different answers. Now, forty years down the line, seems like a good time for a re-appraisal, and for a definitive assessment.

These are the very questions that Rhodri Davies has asked – and answered – in *Undefeated*. Reading it made the tour of 1974 come alive again in my mind. Back then I was in the thick of it and often couldn't really appreciate just what it all meant. This time around I have the best seat in the grandstand, close enough to the action to feel every nuance (and punch) but far enough away to see the bigger picture. It was a tour that created many myths. Finally here is the reality.

We'll gather again this year, on the fortieth anniversary of the only undefeated Lions tour in modern history. We'll be greyer, we'll be slower and, sadly, we'll be fewer. But the rekindling of old fires, the tall tales retold, and the toasts to absent friends will bond us together like the brothers we are.

There's been a persistent feeling among members of the tour party that the 1974 Lions never got their historical due. Whether because of the political issues which dogged us, or purely down to rugby politics, the Lions of 1974 have sometimes been seen as the 'poor relations'. Hopefully, this book will change any lingering perception of that being the case. The players – myself included – have been honest and frank, and have been rewarded with an historical memoir that does justice to the side's unparalleled achievements.

Immerse yourself. Then make up your own mind about just how good the Lions of 1974 really were.

Introduction

ARTHUR BENNETT WAS a pioneer, a pathfinder. He toured
South Africa in 1974, not as a player but as a fan. He was
a travelling Lions supporter before such a thing existed. I
know this, as I know the hows and whys of his journey, and
know about some of the adventures he undertook along the
way, because I was lucky enough to spend a night in Arthur's
company one evening in June 2009. He had managed to make
it on to another Lions tour, back to South Africa, thirty-five
years later, and that night in the Five Flies restaurant in Cape
Town was long, loud and happy.

The following day, 23 June, Arthur and his gang, six mates
from Senghennydd and Caerphilly in south Wales, visited
a Stellenbosch winery. They had saved steadily for years in
order to make the trip, and they weren't going to miss a thing.
That afternoon too was long, loud and happy if memory serves
me correctly, and was followed by a visit to the legendary
Newlands Stadium to watch the Lions take on the Emerging
Springboks in a midweek match.

The night was wet, the game was awful, but the gang of six
– as always – had the best time imaginable. Back on the tour
bus, and waiting for the obligatory head count before leaving
for their hotel, Arthur was taken seriously ill. He died within
minutes, there in the shadow of Newlands Stadium.

In the aftermath I spent some time with his shell-shocked
friends, at times stoic and at times overcome with emotion. I
was proud to be in their company, as I was glad – lucky in fact
– to have met and spent a little time with Arthur.

He is still missed, and remembered with love by friends and family. So this book is for them – for Arthur Bennett – trailblazer, for the 'Sneggy' boys who kept him with them in their hearts and kept on touring, and for every fan who follows his team to the far-flung corners of the earth.

It's also for every wife, like Sheila Bennett, who understands, and lets them follow their dream.

Rhodri Davies
29 March 2014

Prologue

Over the Hills and Far Away

We all shall lead more happy lives
By getting rid of brats and wives
That scold and bawl both night and day –
Over the Hills and far away.
Over the Hills and O'er the Main,
To Flanders, Portugal and Spain,
The Queen commands and we'll obey
Over the Hills and far away.

Courage, boys, 'tis one to ten,
But we return all gentlemen
All gentlemen as well as they,
Over the hills and far away.
Over the Hills and O'er the Main,
To Flanders, Portugal and Spain,
The Queen commands and we'll obey
Over the Hills and far away.

George Farquhar, *The Recruiting Officer* (1706)

THEY WERE UNCONQUERABLE, unsurpassed, inspirational, the team of all the talents. They ventured into the heart of darkness, and emerged – as none before – as champions. They took the record books and tore them apart, rewriting, page by glorious page, their own illustrious history. They forged an iron will, a self-belief and a self-reliance borne of isolation. They became a band of brothers which decades, age, infirmity – even death – could not tear apart. They set

11

the bar so high that no-one who followed could ever hope to emulate them – possibly to imitate – but never to scale those same heights. They achieved what was thought to be impossible, and in so doing passed into legend. They were the immaculate, immortal Lions... of 1971.

And therein lay the challenge facing any and all who followed. Carwyn, Gerald, Barry and the rest did something no-one had done before, and something that quite possibly no-one would ever be able to do again. Well in one sense no-one ever did. No Lions team since has won a series in New Zealand, and the legend of '71 remains untarnished. In fact it grows with every passing year, with every passing tour. But the British and Irish Lions of 1974 faced an even sterner test. They too entered the belly of the beast, very much alone, seemingly friendless – yet this particular beast was given a mauling it never forgot. The Lions of '74 didn't imitate, didn't emulate, but set their own benchmark. They fought, clawed, scratched, and eventually soared their way to the top of rugby's Mount Olympus. In the process they eclipsed even the mighty achievement of the gods who'd gone before.

They were the Undefeated.

CHAPTER 1

For the Sake of Argument

'Comparisons are oderous.'
William Shakespeare, *Much Ado About Nothing*

'Tell your story as you ought, Seor Don Montesinos, for you know very well that all comparisons are odious, and there are no occasions to compare one person to another.'
Miguel de Cervantes, *Don Quixote*

IF COMPARISONS ARE sometimes odious, if they are often meaningless, if they are almost always pointless, then they are also intermittently inevitable – and besides, boy are they fun! So as long as the Lions continue to tour, and continue to have a place in rugby's consciousness, then comparisons will be made, debates will rage and arguments will be laid out. Which was the best ever Lions player, or party, or tour?

Recent generations will argue the case for their own vintage, since there have been three winning tours as well as a number of near misses over the last quarter of a century. The rough-house, rabble-rousing Lions of 1989 for example, who harried and bullied their way to an unlikely series victory in Australia. Or the Lions of 1997, who went to South Africa as unfancied minnows, and came back as giant killers.

Or even the most recent tourists, the non-vintage Lions of 2013. Carried on the mighty shoulders of Adam Jones and given bite by the record-breaking boot of Leigh Halfpenny they had character to spare, and needed every last ounce of it.

They put 35,000 red-clad, stadium-rattling fans, and millions more at home through two and a half matches of gut-wrenching, bottom-clenching torture against an equally under-powered Australian side. They went into the Third Test at one apiece and under intense pressure, especially after coach Warren Gatland had dropped Lions legend Brian O'Driscoll for what amounted to a career defining clash. They then proceeded to win the Third Test once, then almost lose it, before going out and winning it all over again in the final half-hour of that final match of the tour. They cut loose to such an extent that they posted the highest ever Lions Test match score, winning by forty-one points to sixteen. In so doing, they too ensured their rugby immortality.

There were others. The 1993 Lions who almost ambushed New Zealand, the 2009 side who could – and quite possibly should – have beaten South Africa, and the 2001 tourists who threw away a series in Australia.

But previous generations tell tales of better sides, who kept the flame alive in tougher times, through harder tours, and came desperately close to toppling the hegemony of the southern hemisphere. The Lions of 1955 actually drew a series against the Springboks, the Lions of '59 scared the life out of the All Blacks, and almost came home with an historic series win. A look through either of those squads is to glance at greatness. They too were genuine Lions legends.

But with all due deference to those Lions past and present, when it comes down to the best of the best, the choice always comes down to two... 1971's conquerors of New Zealand or 1974's destroyers of South Africa.

How many batted an eye on reading the names Carwyn, Gerald and Barry a few minutes back? How many wondered who they were? How many wondered about their surnames? The fact that Carwyn James, Gerald Davies, Barry John and plenty more are known to rugby's worldwide fraternity simply by their first names says pretty much everything you need to know about their standing and their achievements.

But there is no doubting the greatness of their immediate successors either. The biggest question is whether they should have gone to South Africa in the first place.

All that went before – the adventurers, the pioneers, the whipping boys and the nearly men – were merely preparing the way. All that came afterwards owe their very existence, their chance to climb the mountain, to those two parties of extraordinary men. The fact that the prospect of a new Lions adventure still captures the imagination today is in no small measure down to the lasting impression made by the tours of the early Seventies. We are still enjoying their legacy, and quite possibly, for better or worse we are still basking in their reflected glory.

For the British and Irish Lions are, in the twenty-first century, an anachronism, a throwback. In an age where players are not only professional, but where the very best are millionaires, the Lions should in theory have gone the way of that other grand old rugby institution, the Barbarians. Once, an invitation to play for and to tour with the black and white hoops was an honour, a chance to take centre stage in some of the rugby calendar's most prestigious occasions. But the Barbarians have long since given up their exalted place at rugby's top table, and exited to the periphery.

Some might argue to the contrary, citing the Barbarians' match against the Lions themselves in Hong Kong at the beginning of the 2013 tour as proof of their lasting longevity and appeal. Fair enough, but even that game was far from being a sell-out, and if the ambition these days is simply to be a pre-tour warm up and a moneymaker for someone else's blockbuster then things have changed drastically.

There was a time when a Barbarians match was in itself the highlight of a tour.

The Barbarians are now, sadly, relegated to the role of appetizer as opposed to the feast itself. And yet the Lions not only endure, but prosper, enjoying fanatical support from the tens of thousands of happy tourists who travel south with them these days, bringing a holiday mood and much needed revenue to their southern hemisphere hosts.

Why do they travel? Why do the Lions still matter so much? Yes, there is money to be made, and in some ways everything always comes back to the money. The Lions are big business: hosts, players and to a lesser extent the home unions all benefit from their existence, and as long as that scenario remains, the Lions will continue to tour.

But for the players it has never really been about the money. Amateur or professional, when it comes to being asked to represent the British and Irish Lions, there is an element of the 'band of brothers' mentality at work, and this is just as relevant to supporters. It's a coming together of traditional, tribal foes to take on an even greater – a far more menacing – enemy. It's a time when neighbouring rivalries are put aside for the common good.

Former Lions describe rugby tours to the southern hemisphere as 'going off to war'. Lions history has forever been a tale of isolated, disparate groups forced together far from home, forced to bond, to live cheek to jowl, to work together and for one another. To paraphrase the old military adage, they endure long periods of boredom punctuated if not by moments of sheer terror, then by extreme pressure, and no little excitement.

The only other modern-day equivalent in terms of sport – especially over recent decades – is golf's biennial centrepiece, the Ryder Cup. Anyone, fan or player, who has walked the fairways of the Belfry, the K Club or the Celtic Manor, immersed in that familiar feeling of bonhomie, knows that nothing else on earth can engender a similar sense of being European as taking on the Americans in one of sport's greatest rivalries. That most individual of sports becomes a team bonding exercise, a chance to play for something bigger than oneself. When the challenge entails heading over the Atlantic, into the bear pit of the USA's overt patriotism, the stakes are raised again. And that, despite the fact that a number of Europe's finest these days live and ply their trade in those very same United States.

The Ryder Cup has been known to make even the most fervent Eurosceptic shed a tear. It's surely the only instance where continental Europeans – Spaniards, Italians and Germans – are seen as Brothers in Arms by Little Englanders.

Politics, economics, geography, downright xenophobia damn it, all crumble in the face of a small white ball and a big blue flag with golden stars on it. If only those sentiments lasted more than a long weekend once every two years. And just as Europe's finest golfers feed off the huge galleries, the fervent, sometimes fevered support and the baying of the opposition's partisan crowds, so the pick of Britain and Ireland's rugby talent relishes nothing more than the chance to don the Lions' red in a far-flung corner of the rugby empire.

They feel duty-bound and honoured to answer the call. They aren't tramping after Wellington through the Iberian Peninsula, but they are off on a campaign into dangerous, hostile territory nonetheless. And as opposed to a tour with their individual countries – with the honourable exception of England, that is – campaigning with the Lions affords the unique opportunity for players to travel in expectation as well as hope.

Scots, Irish and Welsh have a genuine chance of mixing it with, and even of upsetting, the very best. They are on a level playing field – in theory at least – and know that winning with the Lions is the highest achievement to which they can aspire. Even England's World Cup winners of 2003 admit in their more honest moments that travelling with the Lions is something else.

Martin Johnson inspired the 1997 Lions to a two-one Test series victory in South Africa, and led them to a two-one Test defeat in Australia four years later. He then returned to

Australia with England in 2003 and became the only northern hemisphere captain to lift the William Webb Ellis trophy as a world champion.

Interviewed during the 2013 Lions tour to Australia, he came close to defining the indefinable and putting the Lions into perspective. Ironically, it wasn't the series win that stayed with him, but the defeat, when Justin 'The Plank' Harrison stole a throw from under Johnson's nose to deny the Lions a last-chance grab for glory in that deciding Third Test in Sydney.

Johnson's summation went like this: 'Nobody remembers a Six Nations or Tri-Nations from twelve years ago, but everyone remembers a Lions series... I played in over eighty matches for England and I can't remember all of them, but I recall every minute of every game I played for the Lions. It is a very special experience. I was walking the dog the other day thinking about that final line-out we lost in 2001. It lives with you.'

Not the victory, mind you – one of the precious few – but the heartbreak. And that was twelve years down the line.

Like Johnson, Andy Irvine has known both the smiles of celebration and the scars of defeat as a Lions tourist. A player on three amateur Lions tours, he was also chairman of the Lions committee during the 2009 tour to South Africa, and manager of the 2013 tour to Australia. As such, he is uniquely placed to compare the values and traditions of old with the reality of twenty-first-century Lions rugby. He can certainly appreciate the glaring disparity in certain aspects. Yes, the players are rich beyond the wildest dreams of generations past. Yes the circus of big business, sponsorship, hospitality and tourism are now as much a part of Lions life as the rugby itself.

But Irvine is convinced that the tour still has meaning, especially for the players. He has worked hard to make sure that is the case, along with his friend and colleague Gerald Davies. The Welshman was tour manager in South Africa in 2009, before swapping roles with Irvine. He began the process of refocusing on certain lost values and experiences, establishing a core ethos aimed at rekindling the flame: 'Things hadn't gone too well in 2005, and I believed that we could benefit by bringing something of the amateur era into the professional game. I talked to former players, current players, coaches and media men... The general view was that a Lions tour was different to any other. There were things that we needed to do socially, culturally, in the countries we visited – it encompassed the whole ethos of touring... You needed not only to be good rugby players, you needed to be good people.'

Those who went on the 2009 and 2013 tours certainly benefited from a touch of the old school mentality, a mindset which Irvine continued to insist upon during the last tour: 'I do feel very strongly that we must keep up as many of those traditional amateur attitudes on tour as possible – an ambassadorial role, visiting schools, taking coaching sessions with kids and local clubs. I think that's really important even in this modern era, that we still have some of these old values. And I think that's why the Lions are respected now and will be respected in future.'

But we're talking about the first generation of rugby playing millionaires. It's a different age, and it's a different game. Do those core values still have meaning? Does a Lions tour itself still have meaning? Yes, says Irvine: 'I think it does. I think that's what differentiates it that wee bit from the norm... You ask those young guys – those young lads who went to Australia. I think to a man they'll say they loved every minute of it, and that it was the highlight of their career.'

Again, Davies sings from the same born-again Lions song-sheet: 'I was fully aware that they were professional players, they got paid to do the job. I told them that I was from an amateur era, but that there were players on the tours that I went on who were thoroughly professional in their outlook. Professionalism isn't a case of having a contract and being paid. Professionalism is an attitude of mind. In my era we had players who were disciplined, hard-training, focused and aware of what it took to be a winner. I tried to convey this to them, and to convey just how the Lions were different to anything else... You talk to any players from those last two tours and ask what it meant. They'll tell you without exception that it was the most extraordinary rugby experience of their lives. I have talked to them – and that's the answer I get time and time again.'

In fact, when those young men are asked by independent parties, they tend to vindicate Irvine and Davies's positivity. Ben Youngs accomplished something special with the Lions of 2013. Not only did he contribute to the winning of a series, he did so in tandem with his brother Tom, a feat not seen since the Hastings brothers came back victorious from Australia in 1989. In the immediate aftermath of the 2013 victory, Ben wrote his regular column for *The Times* newspaper. He compared playing for England alongside his brother to playing for the Lions: 'England was special, but for the Lions together? That blew it out of the water.'

Jamie Roberts is a two-time Grand Slam winner with Wales, and a two-time Lion. He emerged from the 2009 tour of South Africa not just as the player of the series, but also as a global star, forming an axis with Brian O'Driscoll that rivalled the legendary Matthews/Williams, Dawes/Gibson, and Gibbs/Guscott partnerships of tours gone by. By the time he went on the 2013 tour, Roberts had emulated Jack Matthews in another vein, having qualified as a doctor before getting on the plane.

He left for Australia as the fulcrum of Warren Gatland's battleplan for demolishing the Wallabies. The plan was working just fine too, until Roberts was injured against the New South Wales Waratahs a week before the First Test. While he made the most of a bad lot, and found time to jam with the touring Manic Street Preachers, the Lions struggled on without him. Struggled, that is, until his return for the Third and final Test, in which Roberts scored the try that crowned a remarkable, record-breaking forty-one points to sixteen win.

He is now plying his trade with a genuine European juggernaut, Racing Metro of Paris, and a very lucrative trade it is too. Along with fellow Lion, and Ireland outside-half Jonathan Sexton, Roberts is one of that country's highest paid players, which makes him one of the world's highest paid players. Conservative estimates put their earnings in the region of £500,000 a year. So how does this archaic, romantic, relic from an age gone by – a Lions tour for goodness sake – get inside the minds of players at the top of rugby's rich list? How does Lions selection make them raise their game to new heights? Easily enough, as it turns out.

Roberts is that rare combination – charming, intelligent, articulate and level-headed. When I asked him to explain his affinity with the Lions, this was his response: 'I was only two years old when the Lions won in Australia in 1989, and I was ten when they won in South Africa in '97. And yet I could tell you all about those tours, and the ones before, because as current players it's a part of our legacy. And yes, the game has changed – beyond measure in lots of ways – but the Lions remain the pinnacle for any British and Irish player. Playing for my home town Cardiff was an honour, then getting picked for my country was huge... still is. But being asked to represent all four countries, to be chosen to keep company with the very best – against the very best – is the ultimate. And I know that's true of all the other boys as well – no matter which nation they're from. Being a Lion marks you out. It makes you unique.'

Especially if you win. That's the one caveat Irvine adds to the mix – if all Lions are equal, some are more equal than others: 'One thing I would say, it does make a difference to win the series, because you then become one of the serious elite. And make no mistake there's a big, big difference... But I know there have been some super internationalists over the years who just haven't been good enough to be selected for the Lions. I think the lads themselves, those who make it, appreciate how important it is and how much of an accolade it is to play at that level.'

So that's why the Lions endure, that's why they continue to travel south against the odds of probability and professional sport – and that's why the fans follow. Of course, the fact that supporters are afforded that opportunity these days is down largely to the curtailed duration of modern-day tours. We are talking weeks not months, the beginning of June to the start of July in the case of the 2013 Lions. It was not always thus.

The original tourists – not officially Lions – but the first assorted squad of rugby players to leave the British Isles for a journey into the southern hemisphere and into the unknown, were RL Seddon's touring party, which set out for New Zealand and Australia in 1888. Twenty-two players, mostly English, on a voyage of discovery which lasted from March to November, three of those nine months being spent at sea. The tour is mainly notable today for a few extraordinary elements: one player, Harry Eagles, apparently played in every match on tour, all thirty-five of them in the union code, more again in Victoria under local 'Aussie' rules.

The party also had to endure its very own tragedy. Tour captain Robert Seddon didn't make it home – he was drowned in an accident on the Hunter River in New South Wales on 15 August, just over halfway through the tour. He was buried locally in Maitland, a new captain was elected and the tour went on.

The 1888 tourists played no Test matches. The subsequent 1891 tour to South Africa included three Tests, all victories for the side from the British Isles. In fact, all twenty matches were won by the touring side but, as befits the Victorian Age, theirs was considered very much missionary work. The Test matches counted in statistical terms though, and 1891 is acknowledged as the first Rugby Football Union sanctioned tour.

And so the Lions were born, although not in name for some

decades yet. The Boer War, The Irish War of Independence and two World Wars changed everything, not just rugby's landscape, but the idea of touring to the southern hemisphere, the Lions ideal itself, survived the horror and the upheaval. If the Lions legend reached its apogee in 1971, fully eighty years after the first 'official' tour – there had been great players, excellent teams, and successful tours in the intervening years.

Robin Thompson's 1955 expedition to South Africa and Ronnie Dawson's 1959 party to Australia and New Zealand in particular did much to raise the profile and standing of British and Irish rugby.

They played with class and style, and they played to win – something they achieved with enough regularity to impress their uncompromising hosts.

The 1955 party, which included such notables as Jeff Butterfield, Tony O'Reilly and Cliff Morgan actually won two Test matches in South Africa to draw the series. Uncompromising flanker Clem Thomas was one of the tour's stars despite missing the opening stages with appendicitis. He later wrote the seminal *The History of the British and Irish Lions* in which he summed up the '55 tour's success perfectly: 'They played some of the most direct running rugby ever seen, unsurpassed until those great Lions teams of 1971 and 1974.'

The 1959 tourists, comprising a number of the same stars and including one Sydney Millar of Ballymena making his first Lions tour, ran the All Blacks desperately close in two of their four Tests, and won another. Outscoring New Zealand by four tries to nil in the First Test in Dunedin, only to lose by a point to Don Clarke's six successful penalty kicks at goal told its own story – and that story of near misses and could have beens was the story of the tour. Llanelli and Wales full-back Terry Davies was one of the tour's stars, and one of four Lions chosen among *The New Zealand Rugby Almanac*'s players of the year. He recalls that the Lions of '59 were plain unlucky, played some great rugby and suffered especially due to the ridiculous bias of home referees. His best recollection was in fact not rugby related at all: 'New Zealand in those days switched off the lights at six o'clock – everything closed. So they had this thing called the six o'clock swill, where all the workers knocked off at five, raced to the pub and got as many down them as they possibly could before closing.' Not that the Lions needed a second invitation to imbibe when the occasion arose, and that despite the fact that their expenses worked out at ten shillings – fifty pence per day – for the whole trip. Suffice to say that Davies left Llanelli weighing around 12 stone, and came back tipping the scales at over 13 – it wasn't down to training.

The Sixties were a decade of hard lessons, but they were hard lessons learnt.

The Lions toured South Africa in 1962 and 1968, with a tour to New Zealand in between in 1966. They played twelve Test matches against the All Blacks and the Springboks on those three tours, and won none of them.

Progress of a fashion came with the recognition that the Lions, at the very least, needed a dedicated coach if they were going to compete properly. The first, John Robbins of Wales, was appointed for that 1966 tour, with the title of assistant manager.

As for the players, well Millar himself, Willie John McBride, Mike Gibson, Delme Thomas, Ray McLoughlin, Rodger Arneil, John Taylor, Bob Hiller, John Pullin, Gerald Davies, Barry John and Gareth Edwards all took the knocks and suffered the defeats of those tortuous tours to South Africa and New Zealand during the Sixties.

All would play their part in the successes of the following decade. If the chance came again, if the circumstances were right, they would be ready.

CHAPTER 2

Out of the Shadow of the Long White Cloud

'Sort of desolate, decayed, the smell of – I don't want to dramatise it – death, you know. That's what it feels like, no-man's-land. And it's not a nice place to be.'

Anton Oliver, New Zealand hooker

THOSE WORDS WERE offered up from the depths of despair, after a World Cup quarter-final defeat against France at the Millennium Stadium in 2007. And if Oxford graduate Oliver did so in a more cerebral fashion than some hookers, he still perfectly summed up how New Zealanders feel about their rugby, and just how they feel about losing. That emotion hasn't changed across the decades, and to be fair, All Blacks players don't have to experience those depths too often. But in the summer of 1971, the All Blacks lost... and then they lost again, badly.

And yes – it felt like death.

The side that beat them, the Lions of 1971, was based fairly and squarely around that year's Grand Slam winning Welsh side. Their season and their accomplishments are remembered in the main for two epic matches. Gerald Davies's arcing sprint for the line in the dying minutes gave Wales the chance of snatching a win in Scotland, but it took John Taylor's nerveless touchline conversion to get them there. For drama – for an example of what in Mexican boxing terms is known as 'cajones' – Taylor's effort was unbeatable. And all in front of Murrayfield's open terraces, seemingly populated by tens of thousands of travelling, euphoric, bobble-hatted Welshmen.

The Slam itself was sealed with another historic victory, the first for Wales in Paris for fourteen years, at the Stade Colombes. JPR Williams and Gareth Edwards pre-empted the scrum-half's glorious effort for the Barbarians two years later with their very own two-man effort, Williams sprinting three-quarters of the length of the field and finding Edwards steaming up on his outside for the try. Barry John clinched it after a heel against the head late in the second half. Was there ever a man who held a rugby ball – two handed – as though it were such a priceless treasure, as though it were his very own precious commodity? That ghosting, gliding effort was according to John's autobiography: 'The best try I ever scored,' and there were plenty of candidates.

But his own memory of that encounter may well have been clouded by another decisive intervention earlier in the game, a last-ditch try saving tackle – not John's forte by his own admission – on the imposing Frenchman Benoît Dauga. It helped Wales to its first Grand Slam since 1952, but left John bloodied, broken nosed and somewhat concussed. With that as a memento, and the Grand Slam under his belt, he was unsure about touring at all with the 1971 Lions.

His only previous experience as a Lions tourist had ended early due to an injury suffered in the First Test against South Africa in 1968. He had also toured New Zealand with Wales in 1969, and been helpless to stop a comprehensive walloping. All these aspects conspired to make John a very reluctant tourist, but there was one person to whom John just couldn't say no.

Carwyn James was one of John's heroes, more than that, since he came from the same village, Cefneithin in the Gwendraeth Valley of Carmarthenshire. Carwyn the player would have been an idol, Carwyn the man would always command the utmost respect where the younger man was concerned. They knew each other, they understood each other, and they trusted each other. Carwyn was coaching the Lions... he would let Barry do his own thing, he would give him the space he needed, it was to be Barry's show.

John toured, and became immortal.

* * *

Administrators in most walks of life don't get much credit. If they do things right after all they go unnoticed, and this is equally true of rugby's blazers. So credit where it's due to the Four Home Unions tours committee, who had the vision and the courage to pick a man who had never – and would never – coach his national side.

Since tour manager Doug Smith was a Scotsman, tradition dictated that the coach needed to be from one of the other Home Unions. The choice of James was made somewhat easier by the fact that the incumbent Wales coach, Grand Slam winning Clive Rowlands, had turned down his Union's offer of candidacy. That left another well-respected Welshman, Roy Bish, as well the RFU's candidate Martin Underwood, and IRFU's Roly Meates. Luckily the one about the Englishman, the Irishman and the two Welshmen turned out not to be a joke, but an inspired piece of thinking. They got their man absolutely right. James and the equally impressive Smith gelled into a well-balanced and like-minded management team. Charm, diplomacy and a hard edge when needed were allied to sharp rugby minds – the '71 Lions were blessed as much by their leaders as they were by talent.

True, Carwyn James never coached Wales, and therein lies a great 'what could have been'. But he certainly knew how to beat New Zealand, not only with the Lions of '71 but with Llanelli and the Barbarians in subsequent years. As Gareth Edwards put it later, Carwyn was the man who 'took coaching to new levels'.

Brian Clough took over from Don Revie at Championship-winning Leeds United in 1974 and departed forty-four days later. In the immediate aftermath, and during a live television interview alongside Revie (no, it wouldn't happen these days), Clough attempted to explain his methodology at Elland Road. Referring to Leeds' much maligned style of play – and sportsmanship – Clough stated that: 'I want to win the league, but... to win it better.' There was winning, and there was winning the right way. James subscribed to that mentality too. For him, for the most part, it was 'a thinking game'.

Carwyn, whose personal demons, physical afflictions and emotional travails would take their tragic toll over the decades to come, was still immersed in his love for the game during the early Seventies, and still imbued with an ambition to prove things could be done differently. Charismatic, intellectual, political, if he'd have succeeded in his attempt to win the seat of Llanelli for the Welsh National Party Plaid Cymru in the general election of 1970, the Welsh political landscape might just have been changed forever. His failure meant that rugby's landscape was changed forever – Welsh politics' greatest loss, but British rugby's greatest gain?

He charmed, cajoled, prompted and yes, at times, bullied his players to previously unknown heights. The one reply, almost a mantra when former players are asked about what set James apart is 'man management'. Despite maintaining his distance for the most part, he was as likely to impart wisdom over a cigarette or a decent glass of wine as he was on the training field. He treated his players like men, he let them find their own answers, and yet managed to steer them in exactly the direction he wanted to take.

Geoff Evans, the erudite London Welsh second row who toured with the '71 Lions, and later went on to manage the Welsh rugby team, summed up the coach's knack of getting the best out of his players when I asked him what made James so special: 'He knew that each one of us needed to be treated as individuals, some of us would need an arm around our shoulders, others a proverbial rocket... He'd look around the training field and decide to do so-and-so with one, this and that with another... and nothing at all with Barry.'

John himself concurs entirely with that view: 'He knew that a rugby ball in my hands every day would kill me. He knew me well enough, so he let me be... I never really thought about it too much at the time. I was doing what came naturally, and I did it very well. A match was just another day at the office for me.' But he was still enjoying his office job at that stage, revelling in the freedom afforded by his classy, accommodating team-mates, and his understanding coach.

So Wales provided the coach in James, the captain in John Dawes, the talisman in John and the vast bulk of the touring party.

Yet the Welsh had a reputation – still have a reputation – well-earned during the dreadful, nightmarish Nineties, but long held nonetheless, of being poor tourists. Prone to cliques, homesickness and at times boorishness, they have seldom done themselves justice on summer tours to the southern hemisphere. The Triple Crown winning squad which toured New Zealand in 1969 had a good number of those stars who would go again with the Lions two years later, they were obviously a supremely talented bunch. But that tour proved a huge disappointment.

They were still suffering from the effects of a long, non-stop journey when they played their first match within days of touching down, and they played the All Blacks themselves less than a week later. There was no time to acclimatize, no time to prepare – it wasn't a case of not being able to recover, they simply never got going in the first place. New Zealand legend Don Clarke, who after all knew a thing or two about destroying touring teams, was by that stage a sports journalist. He covered the tour with a deepening sense of disappointment, and according to John called this Welsh party: 'The worst touring side he had ever seen in New Zealand.'

So seeing thirteen Welshmen named in the original

Lions party for 1971 (Geoff Evans would eventually make it fourteen) and a Welsh captain in John Dawes must not have had the All Blacks quaking in their boots. In fact, they may just have been guilty of a touch of pre-tour complacency.

That sense of confidence would not have been lessened either by the result of the Lions' first tour match – a defeat to Queensland in Brisbane. Queensland coach Des Connor (not O'Connor as he's been described in the past, although his punch-line was pretty funny as it turned out) was not impressed. These Lions were: 'Hopeless... undoubtedly the worst team ever to be sent to New Zealand.' Bold talk. And once again the effects of the long, energy sapping journey south weren't factored into the equation. The Lions lost only one more match throughout the whole tour.

What followed would shake New Zealand to its core.

The statistics tell some of the story, but as all good Lions tourists tell it, statistics, like the best kind of swimsuit reveal much, but not all. Twenty-six matches were played between 12 May and 14 August, twenty-three of which were won. They lost two and drew one – the final Test – and came home as history makers.

The tour of 1971 is without a doubt the most analysed, discussed and written about in Lions history. Start watching footage of those epic encounters and you will immediately become immersed, mesmerised. John Dawes, one of seven London Welshmen in the party, struck all the right notes as captain, and proved the perfect foil to John and Gibson's strokes of genius in midfield. Doug Smith – having got the right man for the job of coach – proceeded to get everything else right too, including the now famous prediction that the Lions would win two Tests, lose one and draw one.

Yes the Welsh contingent, the Davieses – Gerald and Mervyn – Barry John and Gareth Edwards are rightly celebrated, but they also brought out the best in other budding stars. David Duckham came into his own, Mike Gibson seized his chance of winning with the Lions after the misery of the Sixties. And, of course, Willie John McBride, on his fourth Lions tour, finally found himself playing with a side worthy of his own immense passion.

They played twenty-four matches in New Zealand, twenty of which were non-Tests in name, but they offered the sternest of challenges to any touring team nonetheless. The names themselves are enough – Waikato, Wellington, Otago, Canterbury, Taranaki, Hawke's Bay, Auckland. From plane to coach to hotel to training pitch to match day cauldron, from Saturday to midweek to Saturday, the Lions bestrode New Zealand and took on all comers.

The bloodbath against Canterbury is still spoken of today. Delme Thomas toured with three Lions parties, in 1966, '68 and '71, and saw pretty much everything along the way. He recalled that fixture in Christchurch as simply: 'The dirtiest match I ever played in... It just wasn't safe to be out there on the field.' It was dubbed 'The Game of Shame' by *The Christchurch Press*, while the tabloid *Truth* claimed afterwards that: 'New Zealand rugby has become a grotesque and wounded bull.'

Two Test props – Sandy Carmichael and Ray McLoughlin – were battered out of the tour, other Lions lost teeth, everyone lost tempers, and New Zealand rugby lost its dignity. Most importantly Canterbury lost the match, and the Lions went into the First Test in Dunedin battle hardened and mentally prepared. Watching the battle from the safety of the stands, John and James were more interested in the form and positional play of Canterbury full-back and All Black totem Fergie McCormack than they were in the flying fists. One word in Welsh passed between the old master and the young apprentice from Cefneithin, *'diddorol'*... 'interesting'... It was enough.

* * *

If you talk to Gareth Edwards about the First Test against New Zealand back in 1971, he'll tell you how there were times when he wanted to count the number of All Black players on the field, because he was convinced they had more than fifteen. He never had time to draw breath, let alone to start totting up jerseys. The Lions were swamped by the men in black, and that they had no real right to be in the game at all. But thanks to a charge-down try from Scotland's Ian McLauchlan, the prop forever more known as 'Mighty Mouse', they managed to hang on in there. A superb, tormenting display of kicking from John: 'He may as well have had the ball tied to his boot on a piece of elastic' according to Edwards, helped to keep the All Blacks at bay, and somehow the Lions came away with a victory by nine points to three.

Fergie McCormack's days as an All Black were over, the gauntlet had been well and truly thrown down.

And it was picked up with an eager appetite for revenge. The All Blacks knew by now that these Lions were different to those who had travelled south before. They knew too that they faced a very real challenge to their home supremacy. They always like a challenge do New Zealanders.

Gareth Edwards had to be replaced because of injury during the course of that First Test – he'd struggled physically, and continued to struggle in terms of confidence for the next few weeks. Neither he nor his back row could do very much to stop opposite number Sid Going from inspiring the All Blacks to a 22–12 win in the Second Test in Christchurch.

It looked comprehensive, it sounded depressingly familiar, but decades later another piece of Lions legend is repeated time and again by those who sat in the losing dressing room post-match. Yes, the Lions had lost, but coach James had seen enough to convince himself – and his players – that they had the beating of New Zealand overall. Gerald Davies had scored two tries – one, involving a counter-attack from deep led by JPR and Gibson, which is still ranked among the greatest of all time to this day. The Lions realised that when they played as they could, when they played to their full potential, their illustrious opponents had no answer. Now all they had to do was find a means of playing to their full potential when it mattered most. At one win apiece with two to play, it was, in tour terms, do or die.

Prior to the Third Test, the Lions had to endure another physically bruising encounter at Hawke's Bay. They dealt with it with what was, by now, a customary aplomb, by playing rugby of the highest calibre, by using their unsurpassed rugby skills to eviscerate, to completely embarrass their hosts, and by fighting their own corner physically when they had to.

Second row Geoff Evans recalls local prop and hard man Neil Thimbleby in particular putting himself about that day to the extent that Evans's fellow London Welshman Mike Roberts, playing opposite Thimbleby in the front row, turned to his mate before one scrum and said simply: 'Right Evs, stand by your beds.' In Evans's own words: 'The scrum packed down... the scrum erupted.' Roberts had made his point. And the Lions made theirs, by twenty-five points to six.

July 31, 1971 was a red-letter day in Lions history. It was the day that the red jersey became a mythical thing – possibly the day that the Lions really took a permanent hold on the public's imagination. The scoreline was 13–3, impressive enough, but in no way a true reflection of what was achieved in Wellington.

Gareth Edwards was finally fully fit and ready for the fray, another player who would go on to Lions greatness, Gordon Brown came in for his first Lions Test, and the uncapped Derek Quinnell was drafted in on the blind-side to 'take care' of Sid Going. Ray 'Chico' Hopkins, that fine scrum-half who understudied Edwards so well, had to play the role of Going in training throughout the previous week, much to his chagrin. But the preparation worked. By game-time Sid might still have been Going, but the defensive gaps were all gone. John Pullin, immovable and imperturbable at hooker, remembered the Third Test years later: 'We hammered them that day. We had seen it coming about eight weeks previously when we had thrashed Wellington on the same pitch 47–9, and now it had all come together for us.'

Gerald Davies scored yet another crucial try, before Edwards showed the world – and opposite outside-half Bob Burgess in particular – what he was all about, with a hand off, caught in an ageless snapshot, that lifted the New Zealander off his feet. John was on his team-mate's shoulder to take the pass and score under the posts.

It was also the match which gave the Lions forwards their historical due. They would never subdue the All Blacks – Meads, Lahore, Kirkpatrick and the rest were legends in their own right. But the likes of John Taylor, Mervyn Davies, McBride, John Pullin and the unsung props, Sean Lynch and Ian McLauchlan, would hold their own and then some; they would cause enough problems, and crucially, win enough good ball for their backs to shine.

Quinnell is Barry John's brother-in-law, and he spoke for all when he described it as a privilege to be able to play his part, to help set John and the Lions' match winners free: 'Just to be able to watch first-hand as the class of '71 worked their magic.'

The Lions should have won by more. They simply crushed the All Blacks – and the win put them two-one up with one to play. They were history-makers, they would draw the series at least. But that wasn't enough – they still had to finish the job.

The last few provincial matches summed up the tour in many ways. The Ts and Ws (Tuesdays and Wednesdays) were magnificently led by Bob Hiller, and the fact that they didn't lose a game in New Zealand not only kept the first fifteen on their toes, but did wonders for morale. It became, according to Geoff Evans, a 'badge of honour', and a responsibility in itself. They didn't want to let anybody down, and a defeat would have done just that. Willie John McBride captained the side – something he had never done in three previous tours – during one of the final matches. John Bevan, the young man mountain, scored a seventeenth tour try to equal Tony O'Reilly's record from 1959.

The last weeks of any long journey are invariably the most difficult – it is impossible to stop thoughts from wandering – and from turning towards home. But with the 'dirt-trackers' keeping the tour's momentum going to the very end, and with history there to be made, the management trio of Smith, James and Dawes ensured that the focus was maintained.

The Fourth Test – the tour's final fling – would take place in Auckland fully three months after their inauspicious opener in Brisbane. For those present, looking back now, there is a sense if not of disappointment, then of a missed opportunity. A win would have been the perfect denouement to the tour, it was what the 1971 Lions deserved. But on a nerve-shredding, emotion sapping afternoon, they had to settle for a draw.

It ended fourteen apiece. Peter Dixon, back on the blindside, scored the Lions only try – and the match is remembered mainly for JPR Williams's drop goal struck from a distance – within yards in fact of the halfway line. Reacting to a teasing Bob Hiller's assertion that he could never be considered a complete, all-round full-back until he'd dropped a goal, Williams took up the challenge. As Hiller put it: 'JPR was the best full-back I have ever seen in a Lions jersey. And if I was picking an all-time Lions XV, he would be the first name on the team sheet. Mind you, I was a better kicker than him.' According to his London Welsh team-mate Geoff Evans: 'JPR couldn't ordinarily kick the skin off a rice pudding, but he'd told us pre-match that he'd do it, and he did do it. The iconic raised hand towards the grandstand was a salute to his fellow players... Told you so!' His effort eased the pressure just when they needed it.

And boy was there pressure. Even Barry John felt it that day, choosing the safe option and at times the wrong option: 'With the clock ticking and history beckoning, all I wanted was to get over that finishing line... yes at times I played it too safe.'

It was understandable.

New Zealanders never quite got to grips with John, either on the field or in terms of the bigger picture. Many in New Zealand felt greater admiration for Mike Gibson, but then again he was a player they could recognise – a player after their own hearts. All Blacks legend Colin Meads spoke for many of his countrymen with this assessment: 'Gibson was as near to the perfect rugby player as I have ever seen in any position. He was the real king of those Lions – and I say that with great respect for Barry John.' If Gibson was a player New Zealanders could hope to emulate, there was none of that in Barry John. Delme Thomas put it succinctly when he told me years later that: 'The All Blacks just didn't understand Barry… They couldn't fathom how he could do the things he did – then again not many could.' He made it look so easy, and yet it took its toll. Within a year, he had walked away from rugby for good.

John, and the Lions held on for the draw and the series win – the scenes at the end still get emotions racing when recalled over forty years later. Delme Thomas made it onto the field from the replacement's bench – it was, he says now from the comfort of his arm chair, 'one of the greatest days of his life', possibly only bettered by leading his beloved Llanelli to victory over the All Blacks the following year.

Pre-match, Gerald Davies had mentioned to his closest friend Gareth Edwards that he would love to get his hands on a match ball – being stuck out on the wing at game's end afforded little opportunity to bag a souvenir. During the melee at the final whistle Edwards can be seen in grainy archive sprinting after that very gift and tucking it up his jersey – that was his first thought – and it was presented with glee to Davies in the changing rooms afterwards.

But after the initial euphoria had washed over them, and the emotion drained away, they sat there side by side trying to come to terms with what they'd accomplished. Edwards turned to Davies and said in Welsh: *'Ni 'di gwneud e… ni 'di ennill y gyfres.'* They'd done it – they'd won the series. Affirmation came by way of a nod, a pause and a shrug of the shoulders... then the words: 'So what?' It wasn't flippancy, or a lack of appreciation – if anything it was the opposite. Davies had grown up in the Carmarthenshire village of Llansaint, listening to his father's tales of watching the mighty All Blacks at Stradey Park. He was more aware than most of what they represented: 'Beating them on their own patch, knowing how much they meant to my father, and how much he relished the idea of beating them, was the fulfilment of a dream.'

'When Alexander saw the breadth of his domain, he wept for there were no more worlds to conquer.'

Not the words of Aristotle, Plutarch or Cicero, though they could have been. Those words are uttered by uber-terrorist Hans Gruber, played with suave menace by Alan Rickman in 1988's *Die Hard*. They could just as easily have been written for those magnificent British and Irish Lions of 1971. Their conquest left them utterly spent.

If the aura of New Zealand rugby had been comprehensively shattered by the Lions of '71, then the effort involved in destroying that myth was in itself shattering. They were physically, emotionally, psychologically drained by achieving their ultimate dream. According to John, the magnitude of the tour, of what they'd accomplished together, combined with the minimal numbers, meant that an unbreakable bond was forged: 'There were only thirty-five of us... away from home for three and a half months. We didn't need three buses to load everybody on like Clive Woodward. We were entirely dependent on each other... That's what brought us together – it's lasted to this day.'

The reference to the Lions tour to New Zealand in 2005 is interesting. All in all Woodward took fifty-one players and twenty-six backroom staff on the eleven-match (discounting the warm up against Argentina at the Millennium Stadium), five-week tour. With the best will in the world, bonds were much more difficult to form on that disastrous trip.

Derek Quinnell was lucky enough – and talented enough and powerful enough – to beat the All Blacks four times, with the Lions in Test matches in 1971 and 1977, with Llanelli in 1972 and with the Barbarians in 1973. That's some record – but nothing could beat that first success: 'When you looked about that dressing room, you knew that the players around you were definitely as good as – and probably better than – the players in the next room. It gave you huge confidence.'

They came home to a welcome that Quinnell likened to 'Beatlemania'. The Lions of '71 were the pin-up boys of a rugby generation. And, since their achievement in New Zealand has never been equalled, they remain so – somewhat surprisingly perhaps – more than four decades later.

That says everything about their legacy.

* * *

So, 1971 had Carwyn, all lilting mysticism and romance, but with a winner's pragmatism and man management skills which were decades ahead of their time.

Yet 1974 had Syd Millar, himself a veteran of three Lions tours as a player and renowned as a steely warrior. He had an eye for detail and the capacity to take the pressures of the world on his own shoulders so as to keep them away from his players. For that he was loved and admired by all.

Ah yes, but 1971 had Barry, 'The King', who destroyed New Zealand's full-back Fergie McCormack on the basis of a chat with his Cefneithin companion and coach. Barry's wafting, weaving magic, Barry who showed his contempt for Hawke's Bay's thuggery by sitting on the ball in midfield. Barry at his peak against the best.

And yet '74 had Phil, all cut, thrust, and jink – a bob to Barry's weave.

If The King was majestic, the pretender was mercurial. He topped Barry by beating the All Blacks three times, marshalling his home town Llanelli to the greatest day in their history in 1972, instigating the greatest try of them all for the Barbarians in 1973, and captaining the Lions to a win in the Second Test of their 1977 tour. Bennett was at the height of his powers during the tour of '74, and inspired all around him.

But wait – 1971 had Gerald, who showed his own contempt for Hawke's Bay's tactics not with his fists as many of his forwards did, and not by sitting on the ball like his fly-half, but by scoring four dazzling tries in one match – tries of the highest calibre, tries that tore his opponents apart with razor-like precision and speed. He did the same in the Tests – and staked his undisputed claim to a place among rugby's legendary figures.

And yet '74 had JJ – again no surname required. He had represented Wales as a sprinter at the 1970 Commonwealth Games in Edinburgh, and this tour was the one that established his rugby reputation forever as a try scorer par excellence. He broke records, he made an art form out of a seemingly impossible skill to master – a chip and a chase. Look at his tries – at crucial times in crucial matches – and marvel. He took on the mantle and ran... ran like the wind.

And on we go: 1971 had Gareth... 1974 had... Gareth... hang on a minute!

Yes, the incomparable Edwards, as well as JPR Williams, Mike Gibson, Gordon Brown, Mervyn Davies, Ian McLauchlan, Sandy Carmichael, Fergus Slattery and, of course, Willie John McBride all came aboard again in 1974, a little older and a little wiser. It could be argued that maybe six of that number – Edwards, Williams and Brown included – raised their game even further in South Africa, and performed to an even higher standard than they had in 1971. But all, to a greater or lesser degree, would play their part in the epic that followed.

And this time, equally importantly, McBride was to be captain.

CHAPTER 3

Never Surrender

'Here a question arises: whether it is better to be loved than feared, or the reverse. The answer is, of course, that it would be best to be both loved and feared. But since the two rarely come together, anyone compelled to choose will find greater security in being feared than in being loved.'

Niccolò Machiavelli, *The Prince*

LOVED OR FEARED, or both? When it comes to Willie John McBride it's a very good question. Was he loved? Unequivocally – by the players who followed him to South Africa in 1974, and by a fair few more besides. Was he feared? Unequivocally, by his opponents – be they rugby men or politicians – and by his own men too at times. Phil Bennett is among those who feel that McBride captured the essence of a true leader, of Machiavelli's perfect Prince back in 1974: 'Without a doubt. We were more afraid of him than the Afrikaners truth be told. We knew that he'd never take a step back, there was an aggression, a grim determination at times. It could frighten you. "There is no escape" he'd say, and you knew he meant it... But we were also afraid to let him down, because there was this huge respect. Yes, you could call it love I suppose.'

Before you start thinking that this is an outside-half talking, a man prone to sentiment or romance, let me point you in the direction of Fran Cotton, front row hard man, a prop who pushed, pulled and punched his way to glory alongside McBride in 1974: 'When it comes to Willie John, you've just got to understand how much respect there was. He'd been there, he'd done it, he knew. He led by example, always in the vanguard, leading the troops. At the end of the day I don't think love is too powerful a word. The players simply loved and adored him.'

Maybe those players making their first Lions tour were more impressionable, maybe they were younger, maybe they needed leading. Not all of the 1974 squad will confess as much. Some veterans who also toured with the 1971 Lions blanch at such talk. They remember the qualities of that tour's captain, John Dawes, a man very much admired by those who played under him and respected by those who know him. But even Gareth Edwards, who yields to no man in his admiration for Dawes, can see that McBride engendered a special kind of loyalty: 'I'm not detracting from John Dawes here at all. John was a fantastic leader of men, and did a wonderful job in New Zealand. But you're talking different tours and different men... Willie John by that time had become more than a player. He was something of an icon really – and he was certainly seen as a father figure by a number of those guys. And we were going into a war, don't forget. Metaphorically speaking, it was a rugby war. And if you had to follow anybody over the top of a trench and out into no-man's-land, it was going to be Willie John. He was that imposing, that influential a figure by 1974. So yes, it's easy to see why he was so loved. You just had to be there to understand.'

This is possibly the first instance where the tours of 1971 and 1974 diverge, where there is a marked difference in attitude or in recollection. There were firm friendships forged in 1971 too, there was respect in abundance, and a lasting affinity. But when it comes to the British and Irish Lions of 1974, it seems as though love was all around. Then again, so was a fair dollop of fear as well as an excess of loathing.

William James McBride is big enough to take it all in his stride. He is still a big man, still imposing despite being well into his seventies. Of course big is a relative term, at just under 6' 4", and just over 16 stone he would today be the perfect fit for a Lions centre. Yet for McBride the term 'big' is an understatement of some proportion. In Lions terms, in rugby history, William James, known globally as Willie John, is a colossus.

He was born on 6 June 1940, two days after the final evacuation of Britain's beleaguered and decimated Expeditionary Force off the beaches of Dunkirk in France. Two days after Winston Churchill's immortal rallying cry to the nation: 'We shall go on to the end. We shall fight in France, we shall fight on the seas and oceans, we shall fight with growing confidence and growing strength in the air, we shall defend our island, whatever the cost may be. We shall fight on the beaches, we shall fight on the landing grounds, we shall fight in the fields and in the streets, we shall fight in the hills; we shall never surrender.'

Now McBride would be the first to insist that he is no Churchill, and yet in purely rugby terms, he comes pretty close. Players never seriously compare their sport with warfare – when they use terms such as 'war' and 'battle', they are figurative uses. Even when referring to games of unparalleled violence, as McBride witnessed during a number of Lions tours, players appreciate that their battles are nothing in the grander scheme of things.

Yet they fight nonetheless, for their team-mates, their brothers in arms, their survival – and if George Orwell was right to describe sport as 'war minus the shooting', then McBride would be the first to appreciate a stirring speech made in times of trouble. He would always be the first over the top, and there would be no better man to lead his troops into a rugby war.

That June date of birth has an even more prescient historical meaning. McBride celebrated his fourth birthday on the very day that an armada of Allied ships appeared off the beaches of Normandy and launched the biggest invasion force ever assembled for an amphibious assault. D-Day, sixth of June 1944. Who suits that date better than William James McBride?

He was born into a farming family near the village of Toomebridge, on the shores of lovely Lough Neagh, about twelve miles from the town of Ballymena. He lost his father – also William James – early, and found rugby late. Both events had a profound effect on his life: 'I grew up without a father. I was only four years of age when it happened, so I just about remember him... I remember the day he died. Luckily my mother was a very strong woman, I had an older sister and there were four of us brothers too. But they were tough years because we lived on a farm. There was no machinery, just horses and we all had our jobs to do.'

There was no history of sport in the family, and no time for sport on the farm. Young William James didn't play the game which made him famous until he was seventeen years old: 'For the simple reason that I was needed at home in the evenings, and on weekends. There wasn't much time for anything else, in truth.'

His first sporting steps were actually taken with a pole, rather than a ball in hand: 'Believe it or not, one of the first sports I took up was pole-vaulting, and because I was always quite determined, I won the Ulster School Championships twice. I look back on that with great pride, in fact.'

It was his first taste of sporting success – more would soon follow. Having turned his hand to rugby, his progress was meteoric: 'I was initially enticed to get involved on the basis that I was just a big guy and the school needed bodies. But I went through from the school Thirds to the Firsts and then to the Ulster Schools team quickly enough. That was all after I turned seventeen, so I only played for a year or so at school. The amazing thing when I look back now is that I was playing in a Test for the Lions just four years later.'

Raised an Ulster Protestant, in the heartland of Ulster Protestantism, he was well-versed in the history of the 'Troubles'. Except that the 'Troubles' were far more than history during McBride's formative years – the Troubles were an everyday reality. He saw the worst of Northern Ireland's bleakest decades and experienced first-hand the terror of the Republican bombing campaign in Belfast. He worked near the city's Grand Central Hotel – by then used as an army barracks – and wrote about an attack on that building in his memoirs: 'The ground shook as though an earthquake was happening… I was thrown against a brick wall and to the ground… when I got outside my offices, I was confronted with an awful sight. The Grand Central Hotel… had completely disappeared.'

The experience left McBride appalled and disgusted. Ulster's civil war bred men for whom politics seemed merely an excuse for perpetrating evil: 'No accountability, no conscience, no feelings, nothing at all from killers who might as well have been emotionally dead in terms of the pain and anguish they had dealt out to their victims.'

Bloody Friday – 21 July 1972 – was even worse, a day when McBride saw: 'Scenes of chaos and destruction I never want to see again in my life… Those who thought they had escaped one explosion fled directly into the path of another, to be blown to pieces or horribly maimed.' McBride's sister worked in a Belfast hospital, and had to deal with the immediate aftermath of the carnage. It left mental as well as physical scars on those who survived. It also left McBride himself with a certain mindset in regard to seeing the bigger picture. It was, he remembered: 'A brutal reminder that in the overall scheme of life, rugby football came very low down in the order of importance.'

Forty years later, those years – Northern Ireland's most turbulent and horrifying – still bring a tinge of bitterness to that soft Ulster brogue: 'They were unbelievable, terrible times, and people forget that now. Having to go through all that, seeing the death and the destruction, going to people's funerals, one after the other, living with the scars. They were horrible years, and for what?'

And yet the game he loved had its own role to play. Since

rugby union was – and is still – one of the very few things that binds the island together, Unionist and Republican, North and South, Protestant and Catholic, to be an Ulsterman, and a proud one at that, playing for Ireland brings its own questions, its own compromises. It forces an immediate appreciation of this unique world where sport and politics collide. Vilified by local Loyalists for firstly playing for and subsequently accepting the captaincy of Ireland, he then had to suffer the indignity – and fear no doubt – of having armed guards posted outside his hotel door at the Shelbourne Hotel, Dublin, during match-day weekends. This for fear of being a Republican paramilitary target.

Why did he put himself, and his family through it? 'It's the old thing in life. You do things because you believe that they're right. You have principles and you stick to them.'

So McBride carried on regardless, as he always did if he felt something was right. Whatever the thoughts of others, whatever the opposition, whatever the consequences, McBride was his own man. That very mindset, the hard-headed determination to go his own way because that's what he felt he should do, would prove essential again when the call to arms came for the ultimate rugby test. His decision to captain a Lions tour to South Africa lost McBride the respect of a number of principled, honest, decent people. Some of the anti-apartheid campaigners who abhorred his stance back then still do to this day.

By 1974, McBride was a veteran of four Lions tours already, those of 1962 and 1968 to South Africa, as well as the 1966 trip to New Zealand and of course the famous 1971 tour to the same country. He had to be persuaded by Carwyn James to accept the invitation in '71: 'I remember Carwyn came over and it was one of those moments that hits you. I'm in my seventies now and it was one of those moments that stays with you. He came to Belfast, we had lunch and he said that he wanted to talk to me about my experiences in New Zealand, who I'd seen, what I'd thought. Also in terms of the Five

45

Nations Championship, who were the people I thought could stand up to the All Blacks? Who could be counted on when we were up against it? Now I thought that was a wonderful way to approach things... Here was a man talking to the players – coaches didn't normally do that in those days. So we had this chat and needless to say his plan was working because I was finding all this very exciting. And then he reels me in. He says; "I heard a rumour that you're not available." And I'm saying; "I've got to give my career some attention, I need to move on at the bank, and besides I'm tired of losing." And he just sits back, takes a puff of his cigarette and says to me; "But I'm not going to lose... and I need you." And you know, nobody had ever said that to me before. It makes you sit up when somebody says that. So thankfully, I left the meeting and pretty much made up my mind that I was going.'

It was a lesson McBride took on board as captain in 1974: 'That need to make people feel important, to make them feel you needed them, was something I learned then and there, and I carried it with me to South Africa.'

James had convinced him not only of his integral value, but also that this tour would be different. McBride had played two Tests in South Africa in 1962 and lost, he'd played three in New Zealand in 1966 and lost. He'd played all four in South Africa in 1968... lost three and drawn one. Nine Test matches for the Lions – not one win. No wonder he needed persuading in 1971.

But that tour changed British rugby forever, and in the process changed McBride too. For the first time in three-quarters of a century a side showed what could be accomplished by the British and Irish Lions, what a collective will to succeed could achieve.

In the aftermath of Ray McLoughlin's enforced exit from the tour after breaking a thumb during the Canterbury melee, McBride had emerged as pack leader in 1971. If he decided to take up the challenge one more time in 1974, he was the prime candidate to lead the party.

He was, in fact, recommended for the post by none other than Doug Smith, whose opinion carried considerable weight. He was also Ireland's captain in 1974, appointed by none other than Lions coach Syd Millar. Since the Welsh axis of James as coach and Dawes as skipper had worked so well in 1971, the fact that McBride and Millar were like-minded Ballymena boys meant that the Ulsterman was an obvious choice for any number of reasons.

Not that he was everyone's favourite, or indeed the only outstanding candidate. Gareth Edwards had captained Wales during that season's Five Nations campaign, Ian McLauchlan had led Scotland and John Pullin did the honours for England. All three were Lions Test match stars during the victorious series of 1971, and in the intervening years Pullin had also led England to historic victories in both South Africa and New Zealand. Those milestone victories in Johannesburg in 1972 and Auckland in 1973 had set a unique benchmark.

In playing terms, Edwards was by far the stand out name, but he would already be burdened by the weight of expectation and the pressure of having to manage the Lions' on field game plan in South Africa. As undoubted star turn, the responsibility of captaining the Lions as well would be just too much.

There was another option which some observers thought might just fit the bill. Ireland's Mike Gibson was also a veteran of the 1971 tour, indeed one of its shining lights, and he was a well-respected figure. But although he was an outstanding candidate in some ways, Gibson was far from ideal in others. Firstly he had been Ireland's captain before McBride's appointment, secondly he was a back, and thirdly his availability as a tourist was uncertain due to the timing of his professional law exams. Millar's vision of how to take on and beat South Africa was formed on two losing Lions tours during the Sixties. Gibson had accompanied him on one, but McBride had accompanied him on both, sharing the grunts' workload, sharing the cuts and bruises, sharing

47

the humiliations. Theirs was also a shared philosophy. Willie John got the nod.

But at thirty-three years of age, and after being cajoled into touring in 1971, was there any uncertainty this time around? 'It sounds silly in respect to the doubts I had before going in '71, but there were no qualms at all about '74. Syd Millar and I were from the same club, I'd grown up with him really. And now he was national coach of Ireland, and I was captain. So Syd got picked to coach the tour to South Africa, and I got an inkling early on that I might be asked to captain the side. Now I'd lost there twice before, and felt that this time around we could turn that on its head. And I thought: "Wouldn't that be a nice way to finish?"'

Clive Rowlands captained Wales to a Triple Crown, coached Wales to a Grand Slam, and managed the Lions on a victorious tour to Australia in 1989. In 1974 he headed the Four Home Unions selection committee for the Lions tour as the WRU's representative. He felt the decision in regard to the captain was an easy one: 'There was never going to be anyone else – and it was absolutely the right call – Dawes in '71, McBride in '74, Calder in '89, Johnson in '97 – who else could have led those tours? They were all unique men.'

Other seasoned rugby men held similar opinions. JBG Thomas, that doyen of Welsh rugby journalism and experienced Lions press pack campaigner wrote in his post-tour book *The Greatest Lions* that: 'There was only one man... It simply had to be the "Big Fella" from Ballymena... Thus the captain was selected far earlier than anyone realised.' And thus contended the author, McBride was a member of a triumvirate, along with manager Alun Thomas and coach Miller, which pretty much dictated exactly who they wanted to take on tour.

This scenario was radical thinking for its time, but McBride himself confirmed Thomas's version of events when we spoke about the pre-tour decision making process: 'Syd and I had long chats, of course. Syd knew what and who he wanted, but we bounced things off each other. He'd naturally ask about guys – either guys we'd been up against or guys he was pondering over. There was tremendous work done by Syd before the selection of that team to be fair.'

Clive Rowlands also confirmed that: 'We knew pretty much who Willie wanted – and didn't want, going into the decision making process.'

If McBride was an obvious Lions captain to most, not every seasoned rugby man was convinced. *The Daily Telegraph*'s John Reason saw the decision as something of a betrayal. Like JBG Thomas, Reason had travelled with the 1971 Lions to New Zealand, and felt privileged to have seen them first-hand. He wrote in glowing terms about their triumph in the immediate aftermath of the tour, in one of the definitive Lions books, *The Victorious Lions*. He followed it up with *How We Beat The All Blacks – The 1971 Lions Speak*, an insightful account of the tour and of rugby thinking in general. A number of players from the '71 tour imparted their own thoughts that time around, and talked a lot of sense in the process.

So Reason was close to that party, and to its coach.

John Reason toured with the 1974 Lions too, and again wrote about the experience in another post-tour book, *The Unbeaten Lions*. This time though his tour report was anything but glowing. A rugby man to the core, his arguments were often well thought out and measured, but even forty years later there are certain Lions whose hackles rise at the very mention of 'that book'.

If Reason was unhappy with the choice of Willie John McBride as captain of the 1974 Lions, it was because he saw that choice as a statement of intent – a statement which scuppered any prospect of open attractive rugby from the very off. According to Clive Rowlands, he went so far as to contact the management and selectors in order to lobby on behalf of his friend Gibson. Those efforts didn't go down well, and probably didn't help the Irish centre's cause either.

Reason contended that if Gibson had been made captain,

both David Duckham and Gerald Davies could have been persuaded to tour on the basis that they might just have seen some ball. Any chance of building on the scintillating brand of rugby played by the Lions of '71 was therefore a non-starter, purely on the basis of McBride's selection as captain.

As it was, a number of Lions who did travel to South Africa told me privately that they were disappointed by Mike Gibson's attitude when he did finally join the tour party as a replacement in 1974. One went so far as to say that he would have made a 'disastrous captain'.

In fact some of those 1974 Lions feel that the politics of the pen were as damaging to their cause as the politics of apartheid.

The fact that neither Gerald Davies nor Mike Gibson were included in the party meant that for the first time there was no Oxbridge element to the squad's make up. Just a rag tag bunch (Ripley and Ralston excluded) led by a couple of Irish rogues. The souring of relations between the Lions' leadership and certain elements of the press began early, and would never recover.

This might explain some of the negativity surrounding the 1974 Lions, though not all.

Reason's first-hand experiences during the New Zealand tour of 1971 and the South Africa tour of 1974 make for a fascinating contrast, as do his opinions on the merits of the respective squads, different playing philosophies, and results. In layman's terms, there was no comparison for Reason – the '71 Lions were by far the better side, and theirs was by far the more praiseworthy achievement.

These are arguments to be revisited later, especially the relative strength or weakness of South African rugby at that particular juncture, and the quality of rugby played by the '74 Lions. But a quick look at the try scoring statistics might just answer a few questions as to whether TGR Davies and DJ Duckham would have enjoyed playing with these rugby 'philistines'. One hundred and seven tries were scored in twenty-two matches – forty-four of those tries from wing and full-back. 'TGR' and 'Dai' could have had the time of their rugby lives if they had decided to join the tour of '74.

If ever you want to cut to the chase and put Lions matters into perspective, the best bet is to head straight for the wit and wisdom of Ian McLauchlan – hero at the coal face in 1971 and 1974: 'They called '74 a forwards thing. Rubbish. Tommy Grace scored fourteen tries, JJ Williams thirteen tries, Andy Irvine eleven. It was classic rugby.' In fact, Grace scored thirteen, Williams twelve and Irvine five, but McLauchlan had a point.

His fellow Scotsman Ian McGeechan was even more pointed in his autobiography *Lion Man*: 'John Reason published a book in which he played down our achievements, devalued our victory... Anyone who took to the field on that tour knew how wrong he was... They [South Africa] could play all right. The South African back division in 1974 was every bit as good as the New Zealand backs in 1971, and the idea that there is any such thing as an easy Lions tour of South Africa is almost too ridiculous for words.'

In reality, Gerald Davies's decision not to travel owed more to political than rugby principles anyway, and more again to issues of geography and employment.

Having played for the Lions in South Africa in 1968, he had seen apartheid first-hand. His conscience had been pricked even further in subsequent years, and he was undoubtedly uncomfortable at the prospect of a return visit: 'There was a nagging doubt at the back of my mind. I had been there with Cardiff, I had been with the Lions and I was simply uncomfortable with apartheid... It was on my conscience yes, I had a colleague [in college] at Loughborough who was referred to as a Cape Coloured back home in South Africa. In college we'd go to the pub, chat, live a normal existence. But in his own country that couldn't happen. When I went to South Africa in '68 I couldn't even see him at our hotel. We ended up meeting in a garden.'

But Davies's decision was also influenced by more practical concerns. He had just accepted a role with the Sports Council for Wales – a public body – in Cardiff. The added pressure of a change of direction from teaching and a relocation back to Wales after six years in England all contributed to his reticence: 'I was about to move back to Wales, I was married, we needed to look for a house, I couldn't leave my wife for two and a half months not even knowing where we were going to live.'

Simply put, it was hardly the ideal time to disappear.

The same was true of David Duckham, who'd endured a tough Championship – at times productive and at others disheartening. He had given away a last minute penalty against Scotland at Murrayfield that season – it had cost his side the match. Even though he'd scored vital tries against France and Wales during the same campaign, confidence mattered, and Duckham's was lacking. As Fran Cotton recalls, the winger had his own personal issues in 1974: 'David did go through a difficult spell in his career during that time where he felt that he was under enormous pressure all the time. I don't know why, but that's definitely what it felt like for him. I don't think he ever really rediscovered his early Seventies form after that.'

When I asked Willie John McBride about Duckham's absence, his response was more straightforward. If fit, the Englishman would have travelled: 'Duckham and I are great mates. He was injured, he had a recurring hamstring problem, and the thing in his mind was that if he went to South Africa he'd simply break down because of the hard grounds. So he told me he was staying at home.'

So in reality the choice of captain, and the potential style of play, were neither here nor there in terms of either Davies and Duckham's decisions.

As for the uncompromising philosophy which so appalled certain journalists, well it's a safe bet that even Carwyn James in his more pragmatic moments would have appreciated such thinking. It was James, after all, who'd been credited with the equally blood-thirsty rallying cry: 'Get your retaliation in first.' Millar and McBride were preparing to take on the unrivalled might of the Springboks, and as McBride kept reminding his players, there was no escape, and they could take no prisoners.

When John Reason described the difference between the approach in 1971 and 1974, he was describing a difference not just in geography, but in rugby mentality, in rugby heritage and in respective rugby upbringings: 'The 1971 tour embraced the aspirations and the philosophies of Llanelli, London Welsh and Wales... The 1974 tour embraced the aspirations and the philosophies of Ballymena, Ballymena and Ireland. There was a world of difference between the two concepts of the game.'

But that discounted the simple fact that James and Dawes were backs, whilst Millar and McBride were forwards. That in itself must have had a certain influence on their respective approaches. And what of Plato's truism about necessity being the mother of all invention? Carwyn James coached some of the most breathtaking rugby teams ever to grace the field of play, but he also knew how to win ugly, and was more than happy to do just that when the rare occasion demanded.

Take another look at the First Test in Dunedin in 1971, or indeed Llanelli's victory over the All Blacks at Stradey Park the following year, if in any doubt.

The 1971 Lions never got the better of their opponents upfront, thus in practical terms they had to utilise their backs to the utmost to stand any chance of winning the series. Yes, there was a philosophy, hand-reared in Cefneithin by way of Old Deer Park, but it also made perfect sense under the circumstances to play to their strengths.

Come 1974, perfect sense under the circumstances meant making the most of the huge talent, physical strength and unrelenting combativeness available among the forwards.

But that philosophy in no way ignored the class and guile available behind.

McBride bridles at the notion that Millar's Lions – his Lions – didn't play the game the right way: 'Syd knew the game inside out. He played a simple game because it was effective, there was no need to over-complicate. He lectured things that we still lecture today – "Get your scrum right". The team that scrummages best is the team that usually wins, just look at the 2013 tour. So that was the basis of our success. But we had far more than that to offer, we played unbelievable rugby, stunning stuff behind. John Reason said that we played Ballymena rugby. Well by God if we could play that kind of rugby in Ballymena I'd be a proud man.'

Clem Thomas, another superbly articulate chronicler of Lions tours and Lions history, was positive about both the tough approach and the back play of the tour of '74: 'It is entirely true to say that McBride's Lions were a great side, because of a huge determination to win through a highly organised forward effort; but then, after all, both the captain and the coach were forwards. That is not to say that they did not possess backs who showed tremendous quality, illustrated by the incontrovertible evidence of the huge number of points scored... They were certainly more than merely a forward-orientated team.'

Essentially it came down to this. The Springboks were uncompromising in the extreme. Quite simply they would win at all costs, but preferably by bullying the opposition into submission. In order to defeat them, the Lions would have to take the same approach and then some. That was coach Syd Millar's starting point in preparing for his greatest challenge.

* * *

John Sydney Millar is, like McBride, a proud Ulsterman and Irishman, and his Lions record stands up there with the very best.

Born six years and a couple of weeks before McBride (they would both celebrate birthdays whilst on tour), Millar won thirty-seven caps for Ireland, and played forty-four times for the Lions, on both the tight- and loose-head.

Over the course of three separate Lions tours, he made a grand total of nine Test match appearances. Two of those tours were to South Africa, in 1962 and 1968, and he'd also played there with Ireland in 1961, making him something of an expert.

By 1974 he was coach of Ireland, but by no means favourite for the post of Lions coach.

The man with the outstanding record (as he'd been in 1971) was Clive Rowlands, but he was handicapped by the choice of fellow countryman Alun Thomas as manager, and – by his own admission – he was at a disadvantage in terms of being a touch outspoken. Another candidate was Englishman John Burgess, who had coached North West Counties to their famous win over the All Blacks in 1972. He may well have been the favoured option as far as the Four Home Unions committee was concerned, but his candidacy came to nothing because he wasn't allowed to take the requisite time off work.

That narrowed the options considerably. Syd Millar was by then coach of Ireland as well as being a seasoned and hugely respected former Lion, experienced in the ways of South African rugby. He was well-liked by all and known as a tough, well-organised leader. He was announced along with Alun Thomas as Lions coach and manager respectively, during the summer of 1973.

Alun Thomas was, by that stage, a rugby administrator and businessman based in west Wales, but he'd been some player himself in days gone by. Versatile enough to play at fly-half, centre and wing for Wales during a thirteen-cap international career at the beginning of the Fifties, he was at centre on that famous November day in 1953 when the Cardiff club made history by beating the All Blacks.

By 1955 he was playing for Llanelli, and playing well enough to be selected for that year's Lions tour to South Africa as a full-back. His Test chances went west through injury and a bad case of jaundice, but experience counted nonetheless. He was back in South Africa less than a decade later, as assistant manager to DJ Phillips on Wales's first ever international tour overseas.

A firm advocate of the need for coaching, and a firm believer in Millar's methods, Thomas would have his hands full during the year ahead – especially in dealing with the political maelstrom which threatened to suck the tour under. Viewed as an honorable, reliable servant to the game, he was awarded the role of president of the Welsh Rugby Union for the 1985–6 season.

Back in 1974 though, he was a true sign of the times. From the 'pre-coach' days of the first half of the twentieth century, to the junior roles taken on by Lions' assistant managers in the late Sixties, the role had developed and the dynamics had changed. Carwyn James and Doug Smith were essentially a partnership of equals, but by 1974 the coach's role had become the important one – Millar, not Thomas – was the leader of this Lion pack. From that day to this, the coach of the Lions party has always been the de facto leader.

If the choice of Alun Thomas was seen as sensible, then the choice of Millar was soon vindicated too, since Ireland went on to win the Five Nations Championship of 1974.

And their partnership worked right from the off. Thomas sent all his players a letter after they'd been selected. It included not only his congratulations, but guidelines on protocol and behaviour, a request for personal stories which he could share with the squad in the weeks ahead, and even suggested reading material in order to understand both the Lions and the South African experience.

He sent an update on the different interpretations of rugby's laws in South Africa.

He expressed a hope that he could: 'Scrounge a pair of

Dunlop Greenflash Shoes' for each player, and he invited anyone having last minute doubts in light of the apartheid issue to phone him for a chat before making any decision.

He also included an interview which gave an insight into the coach's way of thinking, an interview which Millar had given to none other than John Reason. The Irishman's words would later be held up as an example of his wrong-headedness:

'Winning a series in South Africa is much more difficult than winning a series in New Zealand' said Millar. He went on to explain that the Lions of 1959 – his first tour – came desperately close to defeating the All Blacks, whereas he'd never had the same experience in South Africa.

He likened conditions in New Zealand to those at home: 'The grounds are the same. The grass is the same. The mud is the same. The wind is the same. The rain is the same. The matches are all played at sea level. A New Zealand winter is like a mild winter in Britain. Once you become used to the time change, you might just as well be playing in Britain.'

Whilst acknowledging that: 'Provincial rugby in New Zealand must now be of a higher standard than it is in South Africa,' Millar also pointed out how playing in that country brought its own problems, its own specific challenges. The sun shone, the air was thinner, there was 'the overriding problem of altitude', the ball bounced differently, the grounds were hard and the tackling harder. Injuries were more prevalent as a consequence. It was, quite simply, 'a different game'.

Those pre-tour thoughts on what lay ahead summed up how generations of Lions tourists have viewed those two ultimate rugby challenges, a Test series in New Zealand and a Test series in South Africa. Few were better qualified than Millar to voice those opinions.

Even decades later and with the rugby world changed immeasurably, those thoughts indicate a serious thinker – a man who's been there and done it – and spent plenty of time mulling it over.

He puts a tour to New Zealand and a tour to South Africa into context – other rugby men who've had similar experiences concur with the majority of his views.

Clive Rowlands puts it bluntly: 'South Africans think in an entirely different way to New Zealanders. Back then an All Black pack wanted the ball in their hands going forward. South African forwards didn't necessarily care about the ball, they just wanted to kill you as you got your hands on it. They also had great backs, but up front – the likes of Marais and Ellis – they were big men who knew how to handle themselves. They wanted to dominate you as a person, get inside your head, but also get you by the balls... Well Syd matched their mentality and then some. And he was right to do it that way.'

But others, John Reason included, dismissed Millar's pre-tour assessment as outdated, claiming that the analysis was based on the past not the present, and that South African rugby had deteriorated massively in the years prior to the 1974 tour:

'The Springboks turned out to be so poor that it did not matter who the Lions chose as captain or who they chose in their team. British rugby could have won the series with any one of three or four teams. The only issue at stake in the selection of the 1974 Lions was the fundamental one of producing the best team available and therefore of doing justice to Britain's best players. That justice was not done.'

Strong words. And again Clive Rowlands speaks for many in disagreeing: 'Justice not done? They devastated the Springboks, absolutely devastated them.'

In fairness there was some basis for questioning the strength of South African rugby during that particular period, not least the evidence supplied by England's successful tour in 1972. They went through a seven-match fixture list, including Natal, Northern Transvaal and Western Province and ending in a Test match, unbeaten. And England had been coming off the back of a Five Nations whitewash that season! As Neville Leck of *The Cape Times* wrote in the aftermath their triumph, they arrived: 'The most derided and underestimated tour team of all time... they were neither a great team... nor were there any really great individual match-winners among them.' And yet: 'South Africa never stopped underestimating England until it was too late – so they came, they saw and they conquered.'

Poor organisation within South African rugby, increasing international isolation and important Springbok retirements all added to the downward spiral. According to Reason in *The Unbeaten Lions*: 'When Syd Millar said that winning a series in South Africa was harder than winning a series in New Zealand, he could not have been further from the truth, but he was taking out a sensible insurance policy.'

Yet Millar only had to point to the history books. One look at the lack of planning and organisation on previous Lions tours, at those countless talented squads filled with excellent players, who were poorly led, who underestimated the challenge ahead, and who paid the price, must surely have vindicated the Irishman's pre-tour cautiousness. The British and Irish hadn't won a series in South Africa since 1896, the days of Queen Victoria. History wasn't on their side.

In fact, support for Millar's methodology came from the unlikeliest of sources. Before a match had been played, John Dawes – captain of the 1971 Lions, soon to take over from Clive Rowlands as Wales coach – talked about what lay ahead. Even the Prince of Old Deer Park, leader of rugby's carefree cavaliers, was sure that a little bit of 'roundhead' would be needed this time around: 'You have to build on a solid foundation before you start playing fifteen-man rugby... I think this tour is going to be a lot tougher than our 1971 New Zealand trip.'

Another 1971 veteran agreed, and still defends Millar's approach to this day. There are few who think more deeply about their rugby – and about presenting their thoughts in public – than Gareth Edwards. He feels that the 1974 Lions coach was right on the money, whereas a number of sceptics were out of touch: 'It was daft. People didn't have access to television coverage so couldn't really appreciate the quality or the hardness of the players you were up against, the physical demands on your own players, the effect of altitude. All those ingredients that made a tour to South Africa as difficult as possible. You played them in their own back yard, on their bone hard pitches, Transvaal, Northern Transvaal, Free State, where the flight and bounce of a ball was completely different, where thin air played a huge part in everything, especially the physical impact on your body. All that was going on – so we knew it would be hard.'

Millar decided that the only way to beat South Africa was at their own game. First and foremost they had to be matched in the set-piece, and they had to be matched for physicality.

Ian McIntosh is one of the game's most respected figures. He pitted his wits against the Lions of 1974, and went on to coach the Springboks themselves. He is now a selector for the South African national team. These are his thoughts on the debate about Millar's methodology: 'Reason was wrong on two counts. Firstly, there is no such thing as a weak South African team on home soil – history proves that. The All Blacks had never achieved what the Lions did in 1974, and wouldn't for decades to come. Secondly, Millar was damn right – the only way to beat the Springboks was to take them on up front first and foremost. Then use those great backs.'

As it happened, Millar – a former prop – had exactly the right expertise to bring about that eventuality. He was also confident that he had the right tools at his disposal to get the job done. So it now fell to the coach, the manager, the skipper, and the Four Home Unions selection panel to decide on just who would be best placed to implement their plans. Which players would carry the hopes and expectations of British and Irish rugby on their shoulders in the arduous months ahead? And exactly whose shoulders would be broad enough to cope not just with the pressures of South African rugby, but with everything else that was coming their way?

CHAPTER 4

Until Lambs Become Lions

*'The relationship between the Welsh and the English
is based on trust and understanding. They don't trust us
and we don't understand them.'*
Dudley Wood, RFU Secretary 1986

THROW IN THE Scots and the Irish, whose historical antipathy towards the English was often based more on suspicion and hatred than trust and understanding, and it made for a potentially explosive mix. In fact Caledonian and Hibernian hostility sometimes made Anglo/Welsh relations look like the most cosy of 'ententes cordiales'. So when deciding on just who would make the grade in terms of playing personnel, both for the tour in general and the Test matches in particular, coach and captain were determined that they would need one thing above all else... characters.

And there were none bigger than Bobby Windsor. The two-time tourist captured the essence of the Lions experience in his autobiography *The Iron Duke*, co-written with Peter Jackson: 'On Lions tours, the best men in the world are the English. Englishmen are like oaks, strong, dependable types who never let you down. Really good blokes to have around you, on and off the pitch.' From dependency in a tight spot, Windsor forged friendships that lasted a lifetime with men he was brought up to mistrust and dislike. All Lions tours do that, but successful ones particularly so.

Considering that so many of them were still playing – and in many cases still at the top of their game – it came as something of a surprise that only eight players who'd travelled successfully with the Lions of 1971 were selected as tourists just three years later (Gibson's arrival eventually brought the total to nine).

The list of absentees was mighty impressive. Barry John, destroyer of New Zealand, and John Dawes, skipper and steady hand on the '71 tour, had both retired. Two other stalwart Welshmen, Gerald Davies and John Taylor, decided not to travel – Taylor outspokenly expressing his opposition to the apartheid system. There was no David Duckham, and there was no Mike Gibson, ruled out of the start of the tour by legal exams.

There were some big names missing up front as well, notably Derek Quinnell of Wales. His raw power and size had been invaluable in New Zealand and he could well have played a similar role in South Africa. But Quinnell had only managed two matches for Wales in the previous months, both at lock, and was struggling for fitness: 'I had broken a collar bone playing for Llanelli against Pontypool in a Cup quarter-final beforehand, and couldn't guarantee that I'd be ready. I was put on stand-by, but incredibly for South Africa the Lions were very fortunate with injuries. They almost had a full complement throughout, so I wasn't needed.'

There were also some prominent props who didn't make the trip. Sean Lynch and Ray McLoughlin of Ireland and Claude Brian 'Stack' Stevens of England all missed out for a variety of reasons. Age was a factor in at least one instance, as was the inability to commit to another tour.

Among the highest profile absentees were flanker Peter Dixon and hooker John Pullin of England. Dixon was at that stage the last man to have scored a try for the Lions, but it was Pullin's omission which truly surprised observers.

He'd been the Test match hooker in South Africa in 1968, he'd been the Test match hooker on the winning tour of 1971, and he had already captained England to victories in both South Africa and New Zealand post '71. Surely he should have been one of the first names pencilled in?

Willie John McBride remembers Pullin's absence differently from others, explaining that the West Country's most famous farmer had too many commitments at home: 'John was farming at the time, and just wasn't available. His father had been ill, and John had to take on a lot more in terms of farm duties from what I remember.'

So would he have gone? Would his availability have made a difference to the decision-making process?

'Yes, it probably would. But there were a lot of choices like that to be made. I just remember having a chat to him about it and him explaining that he couldn't go.'

Fran Cotton, Pullin's front row international colleague, was surprised that the hooker didn't make the trip: 'I don't think any of us expected him not to go. He'd gone with the Lions in '68, he'd starred in '71. He was a very good player. So it was an enormous surprise.'

Cotton himself did go, despite missing England's only win of the 1974 Five Nations campaign, that final match against Wales. Of the eight England forwards who played that day, the three Lions, Stevens, Pullin and Dixon were left behind, while the other five – prop Mike Burton, locks Roger Uttley and Chris Ralston and back-rowers Tony Neary and Andy Ripley all made it onto the plane.

Irrespective of their lack of Lions pedigree, that made for six uncompromising citizens who knew first-hand how to win Test matches in the southern hemisphere.

So, whereas the 1971 party had a distinct Welsh lilt, the tour of '74 – besides its Irish leadership – was a much more eclectic affair, comprising of nine Welshmen, eight Englishmen (Alan Morley made it nine later in the tour) seven Irishmen (eight after the belated arrival of Gibson), and six Scots.

They would be men of character – mean characters

at times – and they certainly weren't picked simply as ambassadors.

McBride felt that had been the case too often in the past: 'Gentlemen, middle-class Englishmen. I didn't want us going as diplomats and nice chaps – I'd been on too many poor tours before where that had been the case.'

The party (with pre-tour international caps) in full read like this:

Manager – Alun Thomas (Wales)
Assistant Manager/Coach – Syd Millar (Ireland)

Full-Back
Andrew Robertson Irvine – Heriot's F.P. and Scotland (10)
John Peter Rhys Williams – London Welsh and Wales (28)

Wing
Thomas Oliver Grace – St Mary's College and Ireland (8)
Clive Frederick William Rees – London Welsh and Wales (1)
William Charles Common Steele – Bedford and Scotland (14)
John James Williams – Llanelli and Wales (6)

Centre
Roy Thomas Edmond Bergiers – Llanelli and Wales (10)
Geoffrey Williams Evans – Coventry and England (9)
Ian Robert McGeechan – Headingley and Scotland (10)
Richard Alexander Milliken – Bangor and Ireland (8)

Outside-Half
Phillip Bennett – Llanelli and Wales (15)
Alan Gerald Bernard Old – Leicester and England (11)

Scrum-Half
Gareth Owen Edwards – Cardiff and Wales (36)
John Joseph Moloney – St Mary's College and Ireland (12)

Hooker
Kenneth William Kennedy – London Irish and Ireland (41)
Robert William Windsor – Pontypool and Wales (5)

Prop
Michael Alan Burton – Gloucester and England (7)
Alexander Bennett Carmichael – West of Scotland and Scotland (35)
Francis Edward Cotton – Coventry and England (11)
John 'Ian' McLauchlan – Jordanhill and Scotland (22)

Second Row
Gordon Lamont Brown – West of Scotland and Scotland (21)
William John McBride (Captain) – Ballymena and Ireland (57)
Christopher Wayne Ralston – Richmond and England (18)
Roger Miles Uttley – Gosforth and England (8)

Flanker
Thomas Patrick David – Llanelli and Wales (2)
Stewart Alexander McKinney – Dungannon and Ireland (8)
Anthony Neary – Broughton Park and England (22)
John Fergus Slattery – Blackrock College and Ireland (21)

No. 8
Thomas Mervyn Davies – Swansea and Wales (29)
Andrew George Ripley – Rosslyn Park and England (16)

Even if a considerable sprinkle of stardust had been lost, there was still a hardcore of '71 veterans who did travel again in '74, and almost all stepped up their game, relishing the added responsibility of leading and educating the 'greenhorns'.

This applied in particular to Dr John Peter Rhys Williams. First capped at the age of nineteen, Williams was twenty-five years old and in his pomp when he left for South Africa. He, possibly more than any other player, is the abiding image of rugby in the Seventies and of that great Welsh era. The flowing locks, the sideburns, the socks rolled down around the ankles – JPR was simply the best full-back around, and would still be considered by many to be the best ever in his position.

At over 6' and 14 stone, he was granite hard, happy to mix it with whoever came his way, and possessed of a confidence which by his own admission could be conceived as arrogance.

Williams not only brought a sense of security to proceedings but a willingness to counter-attack from deep. South Africa's bone hard grounds were expected to provide him with plenty of opportunities to do so. Clem Thomas described him on this tour as: 'Impregnable as ever. He had physical and mental toughness and courage, which at times seemed to border on dementia, because he was so brave and fearless.'

JPR hadn't played for three months prior to the tour, after being injured playing for London Welsh. So did he have to undergo any fitness tests to prove his readiness? 'No, the onus was on me – they said that I knew whether I was fit or not. It was that simple, and I wasn't going to miss the tour.'

If he departed with his reputation already assured, he came back with it enhanced. His coach Syd Millar would write later that JPR was: 'The best full-back ever to put on a pair of rugby boots. Any kicking the South Africans did – and they won many Tests this way – JPR Williams treated with contempt.'

The second full-back was Scotland's Andy Irvine, the man who had kicked 'Duckham's penalty' against England to win that crunch Calcutta Cup match a few months earlier.

In so doing he proved that he had the requisite nerve to go with his long-range boot. Both qualities would be needed in the months ahead. Irvine only had ten caps to his name at that stage, and at 5' 10" and just over 12 stone gave away inches and bulk to his fellow full-back, but he would emerge from the tour as one of British and Irish rugby's abiding stars, as well as a record scorer in South Africa, having amassed 156 points.

There was much more to Irvine's game than his kicking however. He was a handler, a runner and a thinker, although his thinking in the spring of 1974 didn't extend to the moral issues surrounding the tour: 'I was only twenty two years old. I was just thrilled to be selected. It was a burning desire really, and I was thrilled to be able to play with the likes of Willie John, Gareth Edwards, JPR, Mervyn. They were legends when

I was still in school. They were my heroes... So yes I was naive, I didn't understand as well as I should have perhaps. But I was a starry-eyed kid.'

Wing was one of the positions which seemingly looked much weaker than three years previously. Gerald Davies and David Duckham were huge losses for sure, but 1971 also had the unstoppable John Bevan, who'd rampaged against the All Blacks again for the 1973 Barbarians. His defection to rugby league left a considerable hole, but there was always someone waiting in the wings.

JJ Williams was another relative novice at international level going into the summer of 1974, with only six caps. But he'd scored tries against Ireland and France during the preceding Five Nations campaign, and in so doing had shown enough to convince that he could shine on the biggest stage of all.

In fact every Welsh rugby fan in 1974 would swear that JJ scored three not two tries for his country during that Five Nations campaign. In their final match against England at Twickenham, he was called back after scoring what he – and every Welshman in the ground – thought was a perfectly good try. Bobby Windsor, candid and blunt as ever – and with the broadest of grins on his face, recalled simply that 'JJ scored, Duckham told lies'. Irishman John West, refereeing his first international match, made a crucial decision which effectively cost Wales the match and at least a share of the Championship – ironically won by Ireland.

It also made West famous as the subject of a song titled 'Blind Irish Referees' by an up-and-coming Welsh comedian named Max Boyce.

Williams had already booked his place on the flight by the Twickenham match anyway, especially after his mentor at Llanelli had tipped him to flourish on the Highveld: 'I was confident of going, yes... Carwyn James told me afterwards that he'd made sure that I went.'

Williams was one of four Llanelli players to travel, making

the club the best represented in terms of that 1974 party. Clive Rees spiritually brought that number to five.

Singapore-born but Llanelli-bred, he still called the town home and would return there to recuperate after the tour ended. He'd also played for his hometown club before departing for London Welsh, where he honed his skills to an international standard. As with so many London Welshmen, and so many Lions tourists, he was a teacher by profession. In terms of caps he was the least experienced of the squad, having won his first, and so far only cap against Ireland in the drawn game in Dublin that season. He was also – at twenty-two years old – the youngest tourist. Often undervalued, though never by team-mates, he was rugby's original Billy Whizz (a cartoon character from the popular *Beano* comic) long before the same epithet was bestowed upon Jason Robinson.

Billy Steele of the RAF, Bedford and Scotland was a 'flying' winger of a different nature. Well-established for his country despite having missed that season's Five Nations, he would start the tour on fire and go on to start the first two Tests on the right wing. If Williams was an out and out sprinter, Steele lacked a touch of pace, but more than made up for it in other ways.

His Scottish compatriot Ian McLauchlan would describe him as 'The Dancer' – the kind of player who given the challenge of beating three opposing players within a five-yard area would happily do so, as in fact he demonstrated with one of the tour's best tries against Eastern Province. But given a clear run in from halfway, he would struggle.

As it turned out, Steele's lasting Lions legacy had nothing to do with his on-pitch exploits, but with a song that has since passed into rugby legend.

Irishman Tom Grace completed the tour's quartet of wingers. The Dublin accountant was something of a talisman, whichever team he played for. His first cap for Ireland was a rare win in Paris, and he scored the try that drew their match against New Zealand at Lansdowne Road in January 1973, the only time the All Blacks have failed to beat the men in green.

Good enough to captain his country in the years ahead – one of fifteen of the 1974 Lions party to do so – he missed out on the Test matches in South Africa, but came home as the tour's leading try scorer. That in itself was some achievement considering the illustrious company.

Centre, like wing, was another position where the Lions of '74 had to start from scratch. None of the '71 vintage returned, so places were up for grabs, and partnerships were there to be forged.

The Four Home Unions were perfectly evenly represented here – by an Englishman, an Irishman, a Scotsman, and a Welshman – and it was the Welshman, Roy Bergiers, who travelled with the biggest reputation. He'd already toured South Africa – alongside Phil Bennett – with his club side Llanelli in 1972. It had been a steep learning curve – three wins and three losses – but the Scarlets put the experience to good use. Less than four months later, Bergiers scored the try that helped Llanelli defeat the New Zealand All Blacks.

The centre had only made one appearance for Wales during the 1974 Five Nations campaign however – and that in their last match, the defeat at Twickenham: 'I'd had a poor national trial prior to the Five Nations campaign, and missed out on Welsh selection for the first few matches. But I was back in for England, and back on form by then too.' Bergiers was the kind of solid citizen who fitted Millar's requirements – a man of character, dependability and talent. Yet when the news broke, he was taken by surprise: 'I was taking gym club in school, and a good friend of mine had snuck out to his car to listen to the announcement on the radio. Of course he came in and it was as though he'd been selected himself. It didn't really register for a while... but then you see the other names on the list and you start thinking... wow.'

Englishman Geoff Evans (not to be confused with the

Welsh second row of the same name who travelled in 1971) was another who combined graft, guile and a dash of speed. He played for the same Coventry team as David Duckham – and it was a team that held its own among England's elite during that period, having just secured the John Player Cup for the second successive season in 1974.

Evans had dropped a goal – not his forte by his own admission – during England's battling draw in Paris a few months earlier, and was another who departed for South Africa with high hopes of securing a Test berth.

With one stellar Irishman unavailable, it fell to another to take his place. Stepping out of the all encompassing shadow of Mike Gibson was another Ulsterman, Dick Milliken, who had the unenviable task of filling some of the biggest boots in Irish and Lions history. But hard-running, hard-tackling and no-nonsense in his approach, he proved himself perfectly suited to the abrasive nature of what lay ahead. Only twenty-three at the time of the tour, he grew into one of its core characters. But for a career-ending injury, he might just have grown close to being comfortable in those unfillable boots over the years ahead.

The last, but in Lions terms by no means least of the centres who made it into the departure lounge was Scotland's Ian McGeechan. Yorkshire-born and based, but having made his Scotland debut in the same match as Andy Irvine two years previously, he was equally at home at centre or fly-half – and made for a valuable squad member on that basis alone. At 5' 9" and less than 12 stone, size was a concern. South Africa's centres were traditionally bullet hard and physically intimidating, while the Scot wasn't built for taking on that type of challenge. As it turned out, and not for the last time, McGeechan was a surprise package. He would, in fact, bring more value, pound for pound to the Lions cause over the coming years than anyone thought possible.

JPR Williams would be depending on those centres for cover and for good ball over the months ahead. Initially he had concerns: 'We looked pretty weak at centre. Dick Milliken was a shock call up; Roy, who went with a reputation, didn't really bring his form on tour, and neither did Geoff Evans. Ironically though, once Geech and Dick got together, they clicked. They both played so well in the end that not even [Mike] Gibson could get into the side. They were steady, could take and give a pass, and do the simple things well. It meant space outside, and it meant that JJ and I had a riot.'

At outside-half, The King had departed the scene, and the verdict on his replacement was well and truly in the balance. Was he an ace in the hole, or a knave? Phil Bennett had nothing of John's reputation and very little of his assuredness, despite having shone for both the Barbarians and his native Llanelli in defeating the All Blacks in preceding years. Bennett won his first international cap back in 1969, when he became Wales's first ever official injury replacement, taking to the field in place of the departing Gerald Davies. He played wing, he played centre, but failed initially to command the stage at number 10. The reason was simple; the outside-half spot was already occupied by an all-time great.

Rugby, like all sports, is a generation game. One generation's 'wow!' is the next generation's 'who?' Sides change, faces change, styles change – the game itself changes, which is one of the reasons why it's so difficult to compare and contrast the best throughout the ages. The generation that grew up venerating Barry John didn't necessarily venerate his successors, but from the distance of forty years, and from the perspective of a boy who stood on Stradey Park's Tanner Bank idolising Bennett, it is difficult to comprehend the fact that he was not always idolised thus. In reality the passing of the fabled red number ten jersey from one genius to another was anything but seamless. Barry John's sudden departure from the game left what amounted to a gaping chasm, one that many thought could not be filled.

For anyone growing up speaking Welsh and playing rugby in the Gwendraeth Valley, the natural inclination has always been to hold Barry John in awe. He is forever 'one of us', and yet not... His 'non-conformism' was played out on the rugby pitch, not in the chapel aisles. Add his imperious self-confidence, and the fact that he seemed to be without weakness on the field of play, and it was a pretty heady brew.

Even his off-field weaknesses, which came to the fore over the following years, have done little to dampen the myth. Anyone lucky enough to listen to him talk about the game, to sit with him as he recounts those long gone glory days, understands immediately why he remains such a magical, mesmerising figure. He reminisces as he played, words floating, hands wafting, a nonchalant shrug to sum up an impossible feat.

Of the other great Welsh outside-halves, Jonathan Davies was possibly the closest to him in terms of spark and attitude. Davies grew up in the village of Trimsaran, ten miles from John's Cefneithin. He too was a first language Welsh speaker. He even attended the same secondary school as John, Ysgol y Gwendraeth.

The Trimsaran boy, touched by tragedy as a youngster, became hard and fast, and played the game that way.

Ever the realist, and yet a dream of a player to watch, he carried the Welsh team on his shoulders through some of their darkest times, and managed to inspire them to a Triple Crown in 1988. Soon afterwards they went to New Zealand and were hammered. Davies had thoughts about how things could improve, but his thoughts were ignored. Disillusioned with the back-biting, shambolic, state of his own nation, he left for the north of England, and the challenge of rugby league. He forged a stellar career in that code too.

Davies certainly had a touch of Barry John's independent streak, and more than a touch of his cheek, yet it was Phil, not Barry, who inspired Jonathan the boy.

When I asked him recently to name his rugby hero, he didn't hesitate: 'Bennett. He was pure class... Actually, my first rugby hero was Gerald Davies, who was a complete magician, but he didn't play in my position. Then when I started going to Stradey as a boy, Bennett was the one, he was an amazing player. He was a catalyst for every side he played for – Llanelli, Baa-Baas, Wales, Lions – and he won everything, from Welsh Cups to Triple Crowns to Grand Slams to that tour to South Africa in '74. I don't really know what more you'd need to do to be classed as a great. You see it in Dan Carter today – different type of player – but just that touch of genius… I missed Barry's career really, knew about him, but didn't see very much, whereas Phil Bennett was a legend to me as a kid, and still is today.'

Where Barry John left his home town club Llanelli for the bright lights and the big city, Phil, the son of the steelworks, the boy from the shadow of the famous Felinfoel Brewery, never strayed. Bennett's move up to number 10 for the Scarlets wasn't that much of an issue after John left the club for Cardiff: 'I never felt any pressure in following Barry at Llanelli. We'd see each other out and about when I was younger and he'd chat to me about playing for the youth team, and ask how things were going, and it was a nice relationship. I was three years younger, and Barry would never be worried in terms of seeing me as a competitor or rival, he just wasn't that way at all…

'It was a bit strange though playing against him after he'd moved to Cardiff. I remember the first time at Stradey, their bus pulled up, and our captain Norman Gale hated Cardiff with a vengeance. "Look at those big-headed bastards" he'd be saying as they came off the coach… And of course half of them are west Walian boys themselves, boys we'd played with. Barry was wearing a Barbarians tie. Norman never played for the Barbarians, so it was: "Bloody Barbarians… who does he think he is?" And when Gerald got off, another who'd left Llanelli for Cardiff, and he had this cravat thing on, well… "Look at him" says Norman, "He's wearing a bloody cravat – he's from Llansaint, the bastard!" So we were all like lunatics before the game even kicked off. And Barry was being marked by his brothers – Alan and Clive – who both played for us – so it was bedlam. Anyway we beat them 9–0, so you see for me there was never really that element of not being good enough to step into his shoes at Stradey.'

But what about doing the same for Wales?

'That was much more difficult, because I respected him so much as a bloke, and admired what he'd done with Wales and the Lions over those years, and then he'd just gone, disappeared almost. And I didn't know the ins and outs, but I just thought he was crazy... And all of a sudden there I was at 10, following this legend, with everyone looking to me.'

During those early months, Barry John's name followed him like a creeping shadow. And Phil was not Barry – never could be. No wonder that famous red shirt was such an uneasy fit at first: 'Well, it was a huge task wasn't it? This wasn't Llanelli any more... Yes, I felt the pressure and I needed to figure out how to deal with that pressure. I just thought that if I could keep my head down, and we were winning for the most part I'd be OK. Then I think that one game, the Baa-Baas game against New Zealand in '73 helped me a great deal. It made people think "hang on, he's not so bad this boy if he can do that."'

Seeing Bennett out and about around Llanelli, or even being lucky enough to visit him at home for a chat, is to recapture your childhood. He is still that small, dark, intense, ridiculously modest figure, still the man you remember from your youth. If Felinfoel Rugby Club were struggling on a Saturday, he could surely lace up one more time, spiral some touch-finders and throw in a jink or two for good measure. He never left because he never felt the need. This was home.

His autobiography was titled *Everywhere for Wales* and yet everywhere he went, Bennett carried home with him, as though in a metaphorical knapsack slung over his shoulder. This sometimes worked to his own detriment – and that of his team – as during his captaincy of the ill-fated Lions tour to

New Zealand in 1977. That time the knapsack seemed to be weighed down with bricks. In Welsh he would be known as *'mab ei filltir sgwâr'*, the son of his square mile – a home-bird, prone to uncertainty, to insecurity, to a lack of confidence. A character who felt the *'hiraeth'*, that indefinable Welsh longing, whenever he ventured too far away from hearth and home, from the place that defined him. Someone, in fact, that any west Walian boy could relate to.

For his followers, his falibility was one of the reasons he was adored. He, unlike Barry, was human on the pitch. You could tell from the way he moved whether it was a good day or an off day, and sometimes he seemed to be consumed with the burden of expectation.

When things went well, which was most of the time, Phil almost had a touch of those beautiful, famous white horses, prancing and dancing their way across the dressage ring at the Spanish Riding School in Vienna. He would seemingly skip across the turf on tiptoes, as though on hot cinders – especially in the wake of a successful place-kick. But on the occasional off day he could look forlorn, lost. A Welsh mountain pony huddled against the wind – hunched, wary and nervous.

His blossoming on the world stage owed much to one man, the same man who'd been instrumental in some of Barry John's finest moments.

Whereas Barry's relationship with Carwyn James was one of shared heritage, familiar faces, places and language, Phil's bond with the coach was just as strong, forged by their shared devotion to Llanelli's cause: 'Carwyn was an idol of mine as a boy, because he was Llanelli's outside-half. Then I met him properly at the age of thirteen or fourteen. I was playing for a small secondary modern school, Coleshill, at the Llanelli Sevens, and it was one of the great moments of my life, because we won the thing. We beat Millfield, Llanelli Grammar School, Bradford Grammar in the final – they had six England internationals in their seven. So it was an incredible achievement... And Carwyn was there and saw me play. And he told me he wanted to take me to Llandovery College for the next few years, where he was a teacher. Now it was a prestigious private school, so the first thing I said was that we couldn't afford the fees, but he said not to worry, there'd be no fees... What he actually said was; "I won't make you a scholar, but I'll make you a damn good rugby player." Unfortunately my father had a serious injury in the steelworks soon afterwards, so I had to go into the steel industry at fifteen purely to help out with the family finances.'

But the coach didn't forget, and neither did the protégé. Years later, with their friendship firmly forged, James would be a regular visitor to the Bennett family home. Phil's wife Pat, as she's done for so many unexpected guests over the decades, would roll-out the welcome mat and willingly play the perfect hostess. Phil would sit and listen to the worries, the woes, the insights and the inspiration: 'He was a lonely man, and he'd stop on his way home and knock, with a bottle of wine, and we'd talk, and he'd eventually fall asleep in the chair. And I knew it mattered to him, I knew he appreciated it. I knew because he did one thing – incredibly kind really – we lost a little baby boy, four days old, which absolutely devastated Pat. I lost interest in rugby completely, and then Carwyn said; "Phil can you get a week off next week?" When I asked why, he said that he'd booked for us to go for a week's holiday in Spain, on the club. Now people didn't do that in those days. So I owed him a heck of a lot.'

And this was the man Syd Millar had to follow in 1974. It says much about the Ulsterman's influence that Bennett is glowing about him too: 'I thought he was a wonderful coach. He knew himself that he had limitations, but he'd played in three Lions tours, and knew exactly what was needed. He knew that we could look after things as backs, that he had to concentrate up front, but then he'd come over and have a chat, offer this and that, without ever presuming anything. He knew how to treat us as men as well as players.'

Bennett had made his mark on Millar too. Victory over the All Blacks in 1972 with Llanelli, followed by that famous win over the same opposition in early 1973 with the Barbarians, cemented his place at the forefront of the coach's thinking. After all, that Barbarians classic was deemed to be a continuation of the 1971 rivalry – a Fifth Test if you will.

And Bennett had truly shone – instigating what is still considered to be one of the best ever rugby tries. It helped too that McBride and Slattery, two Irish confidantes, had sampled the little man's genius first-hand.

Yet niggling concerns remained. Even though a certainty to tour in 1974, he was by no means a certainty to start the Test matches. England's Alan Old was the other outside-half in the party, and was seen as a real contender for the Test berth at number 10.

In Wales, the general rule of thumb was that a rugby playing teacher tended be a southerner, a 'Hwntw', like JJ Williams, Clive Rees, or Mervyn Davies. The honourable exception was Bangor's finest, two-time Lions tourist and all-round gentleman, Dewi Bebb. The winger tore swathes off southern hemisphere defences – in both South Africa and New Zealand – long before his north Walian or 'Gog' successor George North terrorised Australia's finest. In England the teaching generalisation applied in reverse – if you were a decent rugby player who made his living as a teacher, then you came from the north. Roger Uttley was one such on the 1974 tour, Yorkshire-raised Ian McGeechan was another, as was Fran Cotton, as was Alan Old.

The older brother of international cricket star Chris, Alan had been the cool, calm pivot when England claimed their historic win at Ellis Park in 1972. His next international match had been their equally momentous victory in Auckland the following year. He had also played in all England's Five Nations matches during the 1974 campaign, making an invaluable contribution to their first win over Wales in eleven long years. And yet he still had plenty to prove. Despite kicking seventeen points in England's defeat to Ireland, crucial mistakes in that match and during the previous one against Scotland counted against him when pre-tour evaluations were made. He, like Bennett, needed to make a positive impression as soon as possible.

The beneficiary of Old's misstep in England's defeat to Ireland was scrum-half John Moloney, who capitalised to score a crucial try in a close-run encounter. Ironically they would be half-back partners during Old's most famous contribution to the Lions cause a few months later, when he amassed a record breaking thirty-seven-point haul against South West Districts in Mossel Bay.

Such is the nature of a Lions tour. Sworn enemies need to become functioning, interdependent partners in the blink of an eye. Moloney made the trip very much as an understudy, which would have been a chore for most, except for the fact that he was understudying the undoubted star of world rugby at that time – Gareth Edwards. The Irishman had good hands and a good turn of pace. He'd made his international debut, along with both Tom Grace and Stewart McKinney, in that famous Paris victory in 1972, a match in which the scrum-half scored a debut try. That, incidentally, would be Ireland's last victory in Paris for twenty-eight years, until the coming of the new millennium, and Brian O'Driscoll. The luck of the Irish didn't hold for Moloney in South Africa however, and his injury very early in the tour put added pressure on both Edwards and the squad.

Edwards himself had, by his own admission, struggled for fitness during the 1971 tour of New Zealand, and was given a thorough run for his money by the All Blacks' own legend, Sid Going. By 1974 though, Edwards was master of all he surveyed, and more to the point – he was ready and raring to go in the Lions cause.

Capped at nineteen, his country's youngest captain at twenty, Edwards had played two Tests for the Lions in South Africa back in 1968. If McBride was captain and totem, then

Edwards was seen, even before departure, as very much the inspiration – the go to man. His only qualm was that the squad might be carrying too much baggage, not only in terms of political issues, but in terms of the weight of expectation: 'Our success in New Zealand in 1971 was totally unexpected, especially after that Queensland game. And yet after that win against the All Blacks, everyone at home expected '74 to be easy. There was no appreciation of the changes in personnel, the different challenges. We knew that South Africa was a completely different experience for a touring team, a completely different opposition, and every bit as difficult. You can argue the toss as to whether they were in transition, but there was simply never a poor Springbok side.'

The backs would always look to Edwards first, and in the months ahead they would combine to play some breathtaking rugby. In fact, despite subsequent criticism, they would uphold and build upon the fine tradition laid down by the legends of 1971.

But while the backs looked to Edwards, he with all his experience and knowledge looked to his front. Why? Because he knew exactly where the forthcoming battle would be won or lost.

CHAPTER 5

Grunt Up Front

*'We need men who can dream of things
that never were, and ask why not.'*
John Fitzgerald Kennedy, to the Irish Parliament, 1963

THE TOUR'S IRISH leaders, McBride and Millar, wanted their
own dreamers to have a distinctly hard edge. In fact they
wanted men who would invade the dreams of others and
make them nightmares. If the backs – barring Edwards and
Williams – were something of an unknown quantity going
into the tour, the forwards had a much more formidable and
experienced look about them. In terms of looking for the
Lions strengths in 1974, one needed to look no further than
the front row, and in particular the crucial position of prop.
The process of bullying the 'Boks would begin – or end – right
there.

The Lions coach was a prop who had toured South Africa
three times already – he knew exactly where the strength
of Springbok rugby lay, and exactly where they would
attempt to dominate. Attacking that principal strength, and
destroying the myth of the Springboks' almighty 'skrum',
became Syd Millar's first – some would say abiding – priority.
And he certainly had the tools to do the job, even without a
considerable quota of '71 veterans.

Ian McLauchlan was always destined to tour, and this
time there would be no doubt about his standing within the

squad. Woe betide anyone who made the mistake of referring to 'Mighty Mouse' as 'the replacement prop' in 1971. Calling him a replacement at any time, in any circumstance, is asking for trouble. The law of *omertá*, the 'what goes on tour' ethos is still very much a part of rugby's culture, and you'll very seldom find anyone prepared to break ranks and admit honestly that they might not have been bosom buddies with every last one of their fellow tourists.

McLauchlan is the exception. For *Behind the Lions*, a sumptuous book of players' recollections, he went on the record with this assessment of his Celtic rival Ray McLoughlin: 'I have to say that I didn't rate Ray McLoughlin as highly as everybody else seemed to. He never did anything outside the scrum. He was totally immobile. It pisses me off that after forty years people are still saying that he was the first choice loose-head [in 1971]. He wasn't even there. When we won the First Test match he was back in Ireland, and Sandy [Carmichael] was back in Scotland. The players who won the Test match, their names are there and anyone who wants to make a song and dance about the players who went home, well would we have won the Test match if they hadn't gone home? I don't think so.'

Brave words, especially when referring to a two-time Lions tourist and one of Carwyn James's trusted inner circle during early stages of the 1971 trip.

But McLauchlan had after all scored the winning try in that First Test back in '71; he had earned the right to speak his mind, and by 1974 he was indisputably in the front rank, as JBG Thomas called him: 'The most amazing forward in the side.'

At only 5' 9" and less than 15 stone, he was indeed a freak of nature in terms of his effect on the giants who opposed him. He was at that time also captain of Scotland, and became a crucial part of the Millar brains trust.

Today McLauchlan is one of the most vociferous 1974 Lions in terms of emphasising Millar's influence: 'You must remember that in 1971 Doug Smith and Carwyn were a team of equals. In '74 Syd was the man who was in control – total control. He was very much undervalued, when you see some of the guys who get knighthoods today, well Syd should definitely have had one for what he did, not just with the Lions but afterwards with the International Rugby Board. He didn't get the recognition then, and maybe still hasn't today. Syd led the tour, not Willie John, not Alun Thomas – that's a fact... I admire Syd hugely.'

McLauchlan's Scottish compatriot Sandy Carmichael also made it back for another tour. He, along with Ray McLoughlin had been invalided out in '71 after their 'makeover' by Canterbury, with Carmichael's battered visage one of the enduring – and least savoury – images of the tour. He might well have felt that there was unfinished business to attend to with the Lions, but he never got the chance to fulfill his dreams. One possible reason was his reluctance to initiate fisticuffs.

He and Fran Cotton exchanged a few pleasantries in training during the early days of the tour, but before the First Test match, in his own words: 'Syd Millar told me that I didn't have enough "knuckle", while Fran certainly did. In other words, I wasn't prepared to start flinging the punches. I accepted that fact and in some way I was quite proud of it.'

Despite the disappointment of his non-Test selection, Carmichael still contributed a great deal, and was in no doubt that: 'This must have been the strongest Lions squad that ever toured... just to be a part of it was astronomical.' That, from a veteran of '71, said a great deal.

And so to the two Englishmen who completed the propping contingent – Fran Cotton and Mike Burton. Both tough as teak, neither averse to a bit of a rumpus, and both physically imposing specimens. Cotton was from Wigan, in rugby league's heartland. His father Dave senior had been a stalwart performer for St Helens and Warrington, while his brother Dave junior also played for Warrington. Rather than follow family tradition, Fran chose to follow his own path – or – as he put it himself, the path laid down by his school: 'The difference was that I passed an 'Eleven Plus' exam, so I got into Grammar School. That meant that I played rugby union. If I hadn't have passed I would have gone to a school that played rugby league. It was as simple as that.'

And so Newton-le-Willows Grammar School unearthed a true union icon. Such was his formidable talent that he went on to play Test match rugby for the Lions on both the tight-head and the loose. His selection for the 1974 tour certainly owed something to that versatility – to the fact that he could cover either side of the scrum with ease.

During the early Seventies though, the jury was still out on the giant from the north, because there were other, equally formidable English giants who'd come out of the west. Cornishman Stack Stevens toured with the Lions in 1971, while Mike Burton of Gloucester was also leaving his mark on the rugby world, and on many an opponent too. He had already beaten the Springboks in South Africa, when England won so memorably at Ellis Park in 1972. At that stage he, not Cotton, was the legend in waiting.

The following year though saw Cotton come to the fore: 'In 1972, Mike Burton played in the Test against South Africa that England won, then really my career took off later that year when I played for the North West Counties against the All Blacks at Workington, and we beat them. That got me selected for England ahead of Mickey, and I kept that position right the way through from then on, apart from injuries. So that was a big turning point.'

By 1973 Cotton was starting every Five Nations match, and he started too on that famous afternoon in Auckland, when England beat the All Blacks in their own back yard.

Their rivalry was still a close run thing though – Cotton played the first two matches of the 1974 Five Nations campaign, defeats to Scotland and Ireland, but Burton stepped in for the last two, a draw in France and a win against Wales.

Burton was perceived by some to be the more combative of the two and revelled in his larger than life persona – of being the man for a difficult spot. According to his front row colleague Bobby Windsor: 'Burton was a great man to have in the party, not just on the pitch but for morale. If ever you were cheesed off, Mike was the man to sort you out.' On the flight out to South Africa, Burton had listened to his skipper's private pep talk. Holding up his fists ready for action, McBride had warned: 'You know it's going to be hard... it may come to a bit of this.' Burton nodded in agreement: 'I was trying to tell Willie that I would follow him through the thick of it and right out the other side.'

As it was, Burton was one of the tour's first casualties, along with Carmichael – which gave Cotton his chance at tight-head. Once in possession, it was a position he never relinquished.

The man who looked after Burton and the rest of the Lions invalids would prove to be one of the tour's busiest individuals – he was Dr KW Kennedy, who'd gained his experience at Guy's Hospital, London.

Luckily Dr Kenneth William Kennedy was also a pretty decent rugby player, plying his on-field trade with London Irish. He'd been good enough in fact to become a regular for Ireland at hooker, and to have been chosen for the 1966 Lions tour to New Zealand. He missed out on the next two tours, and was especially chagrined about being overlooked for '71. But by 1974, he was back in the fold.

His selection was made easier by John Pullin's absence, but Kennedy, the most experienced international player on the plane after McBride himself, brought more than just rugby talent and hooking nous to the table. His medical skills were also a factor.

It seems quite unbelievable today, but this was an amateur age, an age where touring teams travelled without any professional care. The Lions didn't actually take an official team doctor on tour until Dr Jack Matthews accompanied the 1980 tour to South Africa (and they could have done with a whole surgery's worth of medics on that tour). Thus, as Syd Millar himself explained later: 'I chose Ken not just for his skill on the field but because of his medical expertise... He really kept a lot of the guys going.'

So Kennedy played nine matches, and proved to be worth his weight in Witwatersrand gold as the team doctor. He also achieved something completely unique in terms of those Lions tourists. He somehow found the time to get engaged to Miss Shelley Latham, famed throughout the land as Miss South Africa 1973 and a finalist in the Miss World contest. Yes, it was tough being a Lion.

And when it came to the Lions of 1974, the toughest of the lot was undoubtedly 'The Duke' of Windsor. If Kennedy was the handsome hooker, Robert William, better known as Bobby, was the handful. A product of Cross Keys, Pontypool, and the steelworks, he had won his first cap the previous autumn against Australia – a match in which he scored a debut try, his one and only try in the red of Wales.

To this day, Windsor maintains that he was actually second choice hooker for the 1974 tour, with Kennedy boarding the plane in pole position.

But when Wales had played England at Twickenham a few months earlier, Windsor saw John Pullin as his main rival for the number 2 Lions jersey: 'At Twickenham, I had Glyn Shaw of Neath and Phil Llewellyn of Swansea either side of me, and John Pullin opposite. In those days the tight-head used to strike for the ball as well, an especially good tactic on the opposition's ball. And Phil Llewellyn, God bless him, took about five or six against the head that day. John took one or two off us mind, but even though we lost the game, we got the better of that battle. The irony is that Phil then went back home to Swansea, and I went out to South Africa... I thanked Phil years later, because when I asked Syd Millar "Why me?"

85

Syd said that anyone who could take six against the head off John Pullin was the kind of man they wanted on tour. I said "Thanks Syd", and left it at that!'

In reality, that match against England saw the Welsh scrum travel backwards so rapidly at times that they were, according to Windsor: 'Passing Phil Bennett on the way.' So there must have been more to Millar's decision – much more. In truth the coach saw something else in Windsor that made him a man, and a hooker, apart. He could take the rough stuff, and he could dish it out without any compunction. In South Africa, that was a priceless commodity.

JJ Williams summed it up this way: 'Bobby was there because he made a hard team a ruthless team – and he really was bloody ruthless. He was always number one. With Ken Kennedy they took what they knew best. He was Irish, they knew him very well and he was good as a medic. But Bobby was never number two in the pecking order.'

One of the tour's key moments according to Billy Steele was an early meeting at which Bobby made his feelings plain to his team-mates: 'When I'm down on the deck and these bastards start kicking me and stamping on my head, I don't want to look up and see the numbers on your backs. I want you right there with me.' They could easily have been the words of Ray Prosser, his equally uncompromising coach at Pontypool, and they were manna from heaven to both Lions coach and captain.

With Willie John McBride taking one second row berth, there were three more places up for grabs. And if Bobby Windsor's demeanour made him a perfect Valleys Bill Sykes, then Gordon Lamont Brown's demeanour made for the West of Scotland's answer to Oliver Twist. That being the case, first impressions would have been very much mistaken. Blond haired, softly spoken and angelic of face, he was the son a former Scotland international goalkeeper, and younger brother of Scotland number 8 and captain Peter Brown, himself a victor over the Springboks as far back as 1965.

Having made his name on the 1971 tour to New Zealand, and played in the final two Tests, Gordon Brown would prove a massive figure both physically and psychologically in 1974.

Quite simply he was a beast in a Lions shirt – not only among the first to the fray, but among the first to the try line – his eight tour tries left him trailing behind only the wingers Grace and Williams.

There are some legendary rugby smokers, whose names conjure indelible images. Take Serge Blanco's pre-match dressing room routine before dazzling for France, or Carwyn James illuminating a cigarette before illuminating one and all through the misty haze, or Willie John himself, puffing on his pipe whether deep in thought or celebration. They were just a few of a long and illustrious rugby lineage who liked to light one, two… or twenty. Christopher Ralston of Richmond and England was known to his fellow tourists as 'Lurch'. At 6' 6'' he was the tallest of all the touring party, and its most conspicuous smoker.

And if he enjoyed a good cigar, he'd had cause to light them in recent seasons – a veteran of the 1972 England win in Johannesburg and their 1973 triumph in Auckland, he was chosen along with his England team-mate Roger Uttley, another who'd tasted victory in New Zealand in 1973.

In South Africa, Ralston would play a role in one of a number of iconic Bobby Windsor stories.

Scrummaging sessions had become particularly intense at one point on tour, and when the Test match eight were given an almighty shove by the midweek pack, captain McBride demanded more from his own men. They promptly steam-rollered through and over the dirt-trackers, leaving Ralston heaped on the ground and gasping in agony. Responding to an inquiry after his health through gritted teeth, he admitted that the pain was 'excruciating'. He wasn't best pleased to hear Windsor mutter that: 'It can't be that bad if he's using big words like that.'

Roger Uttley wasn't one for big words, but he was a big man. Another of the party's northerners, he was honest enough with himself pre-tour to know he stood way down in the pecking order at fourth choice lock. But the selectors had seen something else in Uttley. He was 'Peter Dixon, but better' according to Clive Rowlands. The intimation being that Uttley was already being lined up as a number 6 long before he boarded the plane for South Africa – an intimation confirmed by Willie John McBride when we discussed the make-up of the party.

Uttley went on to play more matches than any other player in the weeks ahead – sixteen out of a possible twenty-two – and more impressively, he played all four Tests.

Another Englishman, and another veteran of their southern hemisphere successes, expected to be a Test match starter on the flank. Tony Neary had in fact been a try scorer on that famous occasion in Auckland in 1973, and had been ever present for his country over the course of twenty-two matches building up to the Lions tour. He was also a future England captain.

A solicitor by profession, and a very successful businessman before life took a darker turn, Neary missed out to Fergus Slattery in the Test match stakes in 1974. He would eventually get his reward three years later, when he became a Test match Lion on the 1977 tour to New Zealand.

Stewart McKinney was ostensibly the fourth pick at flanker and considering the big names left behind, John Reason intimated that the Ulsterman: 'Knew better than anyone that he was lucky to be on the tour at all.' He had plenty of plus points though, as Clive Rowlands was happy to explain: 'McKinney was hard... Just the hardest man. He wasn't going to take a backward step – that was a factor. As it turned out, one punch from him sparked the whole tour.'

He certainly made not one, but two invaluable contributions – one with his boot against Orange Free State, and another with his fist, against Eastern Province.

One would help win a desperately close run game, the other would help cement the Lions reputation as no pushovers.

Tommy David had only won two Welsh caps by the summer of 1974 and it would surprisingly stay like that for another two years.

Furthermore, he had played no part in the recently ended Five Nations campaign, being kept out of the side first by injury and subsequently by the excellent form of Dai Morris and Terry Cobner on the flanks. But he had already gained rugby immortality for his part in the 'try of the century' scored by Gareth Edwards for the Barbarians in 1973, and he seemed ready-made for the fast grounds and physical challenges of South Africa.

As JJ Williams put it: 'Tommy David was told by Syd Millar about a year before that he was going. They wanted him because they liked his style.' David himself refutes this: 'I was as surprised as anyone, especially because I wasn't in the Welsh side.'

But he did have one ace up his sleeve in terms of his credentials as a Lion. Carwyn James was a fan: 'Carwyn told me; "Tom, you'll be on the plane"... I was a guy from Rhydyfelin in Pontypridd, who'd never really achieved a great deal... And along he came and took me down to Llanelli a couple of months before the New Zealand game in 1972... He changed the whole way I played rugby, he made me think, anticipate things. He was a different class.'

Prior to the Lions tour, David and the rest of the Llanelli quartet were allowed to sit out the club's biggest game of the season, the Cup final against Aberavon in May. They still won, and David, Bergiers, Bennett and Williams toured, giving the Llanelli club the prestige of being the best represented of all among the 1974 Lions party.

And in terms of that party, David was another of those larger than life Lions, a man who enjoyed nothing more than rampaging, ball in (usually one) hand through the opposition's ranks. If not the Crimson Pirate of Hollywood legend, then he was certainly the Scarlet Buccaneer... eyes glinting with humour when in company, and wild with fury when in full flow. All he really needed was a pair of knee length boots, a gold earring, a bandana and a cutlass, and he would have been a worthy successor to the famous Welsh sea robbers of old – the likes of Barti Ddu and Harri Morgan.

The fiery, abrasive Fergus Slattery would complete the quartet of flank forwards, and along with Neary would be a front runner to start. Indefatigable, aggressive and fast over the ground, Slattery had been selected – along with Quinnell and Brown – for the Third Test in New Zealand in 1971, but had been forced to stand down due to injury. Having missed his opportunity three years earlier, he would not do so again. An independent and inquisitive mind, Slattery was determined not to pass up any opportunity on tour.

This prompted McBride to recall years later that his Irish colleague had participated in two separate tours in 1974, one with the rest of the squad, and one with himself.

Number 8 was felt to be one of the most intriguing positions in terms of Test selection. The Lions of '74 were blessed with two very different players – supremely talented and effective in their own way, and capable of producing their best against the 'Boks.

Andy Ripley had scored a try for England in their recent win over Wales, and created one for Tony Neary against Scotland. He boarded the plane as most people's pick for the Test berth at number 8. He was a man in form, a man of breathtaking athleticism and confidence, and a man seemingly born for the hard grounds and fast rugby of South Africa. Knowingly unconventional, and a rebel whatever the cause, he swiftly became a favourite among South African fans – especially the ladies. He was less popular – or at least his liberal interpretation of Lions official dress code was less popular – with tour manager Alun Thomas.

More comfortable in sandals and T-shirt than 'number ones', Ripley was at one point reprimanded for his lax effort at an official function and told that he must do better next time. The specification from Thomas was that he was expected to turn up in blazer, trousers and tie. He did just that – wearing trousers, tie and blazer as instructed, but no shirt, and no shoes.

Ripley had plenty of fans in South Africa before the Lions even arrived according to JJ Williams: 'Andy had already caused a stir when England went out there two years previously. They looked at him like a real hero.' And to be fair he looked the part. But as Williams went on to explain: 'He was a great athlete, but not necessarily a great rugby player... Mervyn always felt he'd be the one for the Tests, and I think Syd knew he would be as well.'

Mervyn Davies was in many ways the anti-Ripley. He'd scored his own try in the England vs Wales match a few months previously, he had Lions form and was the ultimate big game player. Instantly recognisable on the field for his white headband and Zapata moustache, he was instantly recognisable off it too – the headband replaced by a floppy hat and an almost permanent cigarette clamped in either hand or mouth. He may not have looked like an athlete, but Davies was a complete player.

Tight or loose, with ball in hand or on the back foot, he was dependable and unflustered. Geoff Evans, who played with him for London Welsh, Wales and the Lions, said simply that Davies was the best player he ever played with, bar none:

'He was the key player on both the '71 and '74 tours, as he was for Wales during those glory years – he was the heartbeat of the team.' Ian McLauchlan voiced similar sentiments when he called Davies the most influential player on that tour to South Africa – the perfect number 8.

Windsor may have given Davies a run for his money as the most vital component of that Lions pack, but he articulated his countryman's worth better than anybody: 'He was a hard bastard, an outstanding player, and a great captain too. Wales won in Paris under him in '75, and we won the Grand Slam in '76. Now I love Benny, but Benny would say himself that if Merve had captained the Lions in '77 in New Zealand, we would have won that series too. Easy.' By then Davies had been forced into retirement, after suffering a brain haemorrhage playing for Swansea in a Cup semi-final, ironically against Windsor's Pontypool.

So Davies at 8 completed the original Lions of '74. They would be joined by both Mike Gibson and Alan Morley along the way, and each would play a part in creating history.

They were certainly a mixed bunch, and not just in terms of nationality. None were professional sportsmen remember, and whereas every man jack of last year's touring party have made a handsome living from the game, forty years ago the Lions were drawn from all quarters in terms of employment.

McBride was by then a bank manager. Brown also worked in a bank. Ripley was a qualified chartered accountant – later a city banker. Prior to touring he had just finished a stint as a lecturer at the Sorbonne in Paris – no wonder so few of the squad got to grips with what exactly he did for a living. Irvine had given up an extra year at university in the hope of touring. There were solicitors, armed forces personnel, doctors, accountants, an auctioneer, a number of teachers and, of course, two legendary steelworkers. Windsor, in fact, needed shop floor representation when he asked for time off to tour. He also took on another job – as a bouncer in a Newport nightclub – to make some extra cash to cover his family while he was away.

Donations from local clubs helped too, although they were essentially illegal in those amateur days. Windsor left for London with £40 in his pocket, and his first chore on arrival at the team hotel was to gather as many Lions 'freebies' as he could send back home before departure. Anything that wasn't nailed down was fair game.

There was a willing market back in Gwent, and every penny helped: 'Luckily, when we got out there, the South

African Board said that their country was ours. I pretty much took that literally. They even said that they'd post anything we gave them back free of charge to Britain, air freight. I'd phone the wife and the first thing she'd say was; "What are all these brown boxes arriving all the time?"'

Gareth Edwards had a particularly understanding boss at his engineering firm, and an even more understanding wife at home. Maureen Edwards gave birth to their first son Owen on a Tuesday, only to see her husband jet off for three months on the Friday. In his own autobiography, he remembered the lure of the trip like this: 'The overall desire to play this game we loved was too powerful. We were young men in love with the sport... You felt you didn't want to be left out because you might never get back in.'

And that from the best player around. When I quizzed him recently about the decision to go, he appreciated just how much others sacrificed on his behalf: 'Maureen actually didn't want me to miss it either. It may well have been selfish from my point of view, but she was totally supportive, she understood. I was worried that the birth would be delayed, I was worried about my work too. If it hadn't have been for the backing of my employer Jack Hamer and my family, I would never have been able to do it.'

Others had tougher decisions to make, especially the teachers selected to tour. Many Labour-run council education boards were against a tour to apartheid South Africa. And while the likes of McGeechan, McLauchlan and Uttley found their paths smoothed, the likes of JJ Williams in Wales found it a lot harder.

In fact he decided that he would tour and be damned – changing his career path and leaving teaching altogether: 'I was a head of department in Maesteg, Mid Glam council was very Labour orientated, so they voted against me going. It didn't affect me at all – I wasn't going to get paid, so what? We'd manage somehow. I wanted to be a Lion no matter what the cost... Looking back now perhaps it was a bit selfish, but I was young and I had the chance to be a Lion. Decision made.'

The contrast with modern-day rugby players, and Lions of a more recent vintage, is stark. Phil Bennett was a son of the steelworks. Going on tour with the Lions brought practical concerns for him as it did for many others: 'I remember Felinfoel Cricket Club giving me something like a hundred quid – a huge amount of money. I remember being so touched by that gesture, it meant the world to Pat and I because I knew she'd be OK while I was gone… And when I came home, I went back to the cricket club for a celebration, and was told a great story. Felinfoel had been fielding in a league match when the Second Test was on, and when I scored my try, all the boys and the two umpires came sprinting into the pavilion to listen to the radio. And the batsmen were just standing there saying: "What's going on? This is a league match boys." That's what it meant in the village.'

Different times. Last year's Lions, who triumphed so thrillingly in Australia, didn't need handouts from friends. They were the best paid tourists yet. They set out with a tour salary approaching £50,000 – for a month's work – and that improved to well over £60,000 when winning bonuses were added. Now that in today's climate is a damn good annual salary for the vast majority of the population. Add in individual sponsors, endorsements, ghosted features, and you've got an exceptional amount of money for such a short timescale.

In 2013, each of the Home Unions were paid £50,000 per representative in compensation, and it cost almost half a million pounds just to kit out… yes to kit out… the party. In 1971, Sandy Carmichael recalled that after much debate the squad was given one red tracksuit each as their only tour freebie.

By 1974 they had graduated to having to pay a token few pence for a new pair of rugby boots… just so that they could maintain their amateur status.

In the same vein, the Australian rugby union made an estimated £40 million from the 2013 tour, wiping out their long accrued debt and then some. Now here's the kicker. In 1974, despite the fact that the SARB made around £2 million – which in today's money would equate to over £20 million and was an astronomical figure for the time, the Lions players themselves were on a basic out of pocket allowance of seventy-five pence per day. Despite the fact that it was a fifty per cent increase on fifteen years previously, it still equates to less than £9 in today's terms. Yes, times have most certainly changed.

And would the Lions of 1974 have swapped places with today's stars? Do they feel envious? Not according to Gareth Edwards: 'No, I wouldn't swap with them – and there's no envy for them – in fact I have a huge amount of respect for those boys, because I appreciate the demands that are required of them in a professional game... No-one achieves anything of note without sacrifice, so there's no envy, maybe just touch of regret in that we can't still do it at our age. I do miss that buzz and excitement when I watch them.'

Ian McLauchlan feels that maybe something has been lost over the years: 'I admire those boys in that they're carrying on a tradition. They don't have an easy time of it at all. We had a hell of a time back then, and I'm not sure these boys today can have the same enjoyment or fun out of a tour as we had.'

Rugby isn't the only thing that has changed beyond all comprehension, that is unrecognisable, forty years on. The same applies to South Africa, which now enjoys its status as one of the continent's main political and economic influences, one of its most powerful voices on the international stage, and one of its main tourist destinations.

In 1974 South Africa was a pariah.

Its white minority governed the country and enjoyed its vast riches while its non-white majority were left without rights, without a voice and without a future. The situation was intolerable to any individual of conscience, it couldn't – and didn't – go unopposed.

One British player did in fact speak out against apartheid publicly, making his stand when the opportunity presented itself. John Taylor, the Wales and London Welsh flanker, was a sole voice of integrity. He had toured South Africa with the Lions in 1968 and had been so chastened by the experience that he refused to play for Wales against them in 1970. Anecdotal evidence suggests that his international career suffered as a consequence, despite his brilliant tour of New Zealand with the 1971 Lions.

His exclusion by the Barbarians in 1973 seemingly confirmed his ostracism – a fact that still rankles to this day. He won his last Welsh cap during the 1973 Five Nations campaign, but was still considered a decent bet to make it onto the plane in 1974. It never got that far.

Back then he put it this way: 'I feel were I to play I would be helping to condone and perhaps perpetuate the Government that currently exists in South Africa.' Those sentiments were strong enough, but years later he put it more poetically, insisting that he differed from many of his colleagues in thinking that: 'The brotherhood of man is a much bigger thing than the brotherhood of rugby.'

In 1974, for thirty players faced with what they perceived to be the opportunity of a lifetime, the brotherhood of the Lions surpassed all else.

Regardless of misgivings, and despite opposition, they accepted the invitation to travel. The reaction to Taylor's stance differs from player to player. Gareth Edwards, who has given more consideration than most to the rights and wrongs of his decision, had this to say: 'I admire John Taylor a great deal for the reason that he never tried to influence us. He said that he wasn't going, and that he wasn't putting himself forward for selection, and I remember telling him: "I hope you don't expect us to do the same?" And he said that he didn't expect that at all. He was making his own decision, and we should do the same. He didn't pressure us at all.'

Others aren't quite as convinced. And as one '74 veteran put it: 'John Taylor wouldn't have made the tour anyway. He was a great player, but he was all done by that stage at the highest level. So when he said it was down to apartheid... Well he would say that wouldn't he?'

For the rest, the situation in South Africa was not something they understood, or chose to understand. JPR Williams remembers that: 'We were under a cloud, no doubt, and of course we talked about it. But I wanted to go because I'd never been before, and I thought going out there and beating them might be a good thing. I think subsequent events proved me right. If we'd gone and lost, then it might have been different, but doing what we did to their rugby team was surely a good thing. And to be honest, if put in that position again, I'd still make the same decision now.'

Bobby Windsor summed up the complicated nature of the argument in very simple terms in his life story. Working class and brutally honest in his opinions, he explained that: 'I worked on the motorways with all colours and creeds, and I played with and against black players. I was living in a council house in Bettws, Newport, with a family and I was flat broke. What the hell was happening or not happening in South Africa did not concern me. I didn't give a stuff.'

For Windsor there was no choice. He simply had to go, and who were politicians and campaigners to tell him otherwise. Many players felt the same.

In fact there were other matters which proved equally stressful to the likes of JJ Williams. He was so desperate to succeed in the alien environment of South Africa that he'd even trained in a wetsuit back home in those sodden south Wales valleys.

When he finally met up with his team-mates at their London hotel it took time to get acclimatised to this rarified atmosphere too: 'It was intimidating in London for obvious reasons, but it was intimidating meeting up with the players as well, mind. People like Willie John McBride – your heroes – and people like Andy Ripley, who was from a different world to me altogether.'

Williams, Ripley and the rest would go on to experience a whole new world together, a world which would give them common ground for decades to come. But first they would have to deal with an almighty storm, a storm that hit British shores, and British and Irish rugby with a thunderous crash.

CHAPTER 6

Weenen

Definition of apartheid – noun *[mass noun] historical*
(in South Africa) a policy or system of segregation or
discrimination on grounds of race. Adopted as a slogan
in the 1948 election by the successful Afrikaner National
Party, apartheid extended and institutionalized existing
racial segregation. Despite rioting and terrorism at
home and isolation abroad from the 1960s onwards, the
white regime maintained the apartheid system with only
minor relaxation until February 1991. Origin: 1940s:
from Afrikaans, literally 'separateness', from Dutch *apart*
'separate' + *-heid* (equivalent of -hood)
The Oxford English Dictionary

THE MONOLITHIC VOORTREKKER Monument is one of those
places which stays with you forever – once visited, never
forgotten. It stands erect, high on a hilltop overlooking South
Africa's capital city Pretoria, dominating all, imposing itself
on its surroundings and on those who come near. Its form
was apparently inspired by the pyramids of Egypt, but at
first sight it registers as part grand masonic hall, part Mayan
temple – though any sacrifice celebrated here is purely that
of Boer self-sacrifice. Built from granite the colour of earth
– in a certain light you could swear that its blood red earth – it
resonates, oozes almost, with ominous omnipotence.

It is quite simply designed to awe. Understanding the
Afrikaner mentality, and the seeds of South Africa's racial

catastrophe, involves understanding the country's history – and this is as good a place as any to start.

Work began on the monument before the outbreak of the Second World War, and it was completed more than a decade later. Inaugurated on 16 December 1949 – by then Prime Minister DF Malan, it stands to this day in memory of South Africa's founding fathers, the Afrikaners who set forth on the Great Trek in the 1830s, abandoning their homes in Cape Colony to escape the yoke of British colonial rule.

They were Dutch, German, and French by extraction, and Calvinist or Huguenot in terms of religion. Some came for commerce and stayed, others – particularly those French Protestants, fled religious persecution at home. They brought with them an independence of spirit, a will not to look back, and a determination to make a new life in this new land. They brought too a willingness to get stuck in – that famous Calvinist work ethic – and an equally strong belief that they had been chosen by God.

They created a home at the ends of the earth, and flourished despite the hardship. Flourished that is, until the British came. Of course the British would claim that they were there first. As the Dutch East India Company had initially set up shop having seen the potential of southern Africa, so the British East India Company spotted an equal opportunity. And the British backed up their claims with a well-armed fleet and force of arms.

The Cape's strategic importance, especially during the Napoleonic Wars at the beginning of the nineteenth century, meant that the area quickly became a base of some importance and activity – the British were there to stay.

So Empire took hold, more settlers arrived, and English customs and language started to supercede the hybrid Dutch vernacular.

If the Boers felt the threat immediately, they were soon left in no doubt that they were on a direct collision course with their colonial masters. In 1807 the British abolished slavery at home, and by the early 1830s the Bill was passed and enforced in southern Africa too. After decades of tension, perceived subjugation and ever growing imperial provocation, the Afrikaners decided that they needed to get away from British rule.

The first Trekkers set out into the hinterland in 1835, and in the decade that followed well over ten thousand travelled inland, suffering illness, depredation and death in the name of freedom. They eventually settled new lands, and formed new colonies – chiefly the Transvaal, and the Orange Free State.

The all-important date of 16 December – the date that the Voortrekker Monument was inaugurated – commemorates a red-letter day in Boer history. It is a day of huge significance.

On the morning of 16 December 1838, a Boer commando, or volunteer militia unit – self-supplied, saddled and armed – awoke from a fitful night's sleep on the banks of the Ncome River in Zululand. There were almost 500 men present, men who'd left their families and ridden out into the wilds under the command of one of the great Boer leaders, Andries Pretorius. His iconic status within Afrikaner society can best be judged by noting the name of the country's capital city.

The commando had camped the previous night – as they always did when in hostile territory – inside their laager of intertwined wagons, a moveable stockade that offered protection and security. It was protection they knew they would need if their plan came to fruition. As they struggled to their feet and gazed out through that misty South African summer dawn, they saw a sight that had horrified bigger forces to the extent that it had become legendary. Surrounding the laager were upwards of 12,000 Zulu warriors, the cream of a warlike nation, and in terms of battlefield expertise, nothing less than a killing machine.

The ferocious and disciplined Zulu impis had already carved out their empire and their terrifying reputation in the preceding years. Firstly under the all conquering Shaka, then under Dingane – the half-brother who murdered him. Yet on this December dawn the Zulus were encountering a different kind of foe. Far from being afraid, far from being cowed, this set-piece conflict was exactly what the commando had craved. The Boers had ventured into the heart of Zululand's unknown with the express intention of bringing King Dingane's forces to battle, and crushing them.

Why were they there? Vengeance – what the Afrikaners called 'wraak'.

Earlier that year, on 4 February 1838, Dingane had effectively ceded a significant part of his own empire to another Boer leader – Piet Retief. This the Zulu monarch had done by putting his mark on a piece of parchment paper.

Two days after what Retief saw as a hugely successful – and painless – negotiation, Dingane insisted that the party of whites – around seventy men including Retief's son – attend a celebratory dance at his Royal Kraal. Suspecting nothing despite repeated warnings that there was evil afoot, the Boers were confident – or naïve – enough to leave their guns at the kraal's entrance. They were taken completely by surprise when the Zulu king shouted his command: *'Bulalani Abathakathi… Kill the wizards.'* Retief's party were quickly overpowered and executed. Some had their skulls staved in by Zulu clubs, known as knobkerries, others were impaled – all died. Retief was saved for last, having been forced to watch the slaughter, including the death of his own son.

As though the massacre of the commando weren't bad enough, Dingane followed his treachery with a devastating strike against the Boer families left behind. He commanded his impis to search them out and: 'Eat them up.'

In his masterpiece of Zulu history, *The Washing of the Spears*, Donald R Morris describes the advancing Zulu impi rushing over its unsuspecting victims like a malevolent wave: 'What followed was seared into the Boer soul as no other event in their history. The impis fell on the defenseless clusters of wagons in the predawn blackness of a moonless night.'

Around 550 perished: forty-one men, fifty-six women, 185 children and around 250 Khoikhoi servants. The Khoikhoi, known to their European masters as 'hottentots', were Cape natives. Not that their colour spared them from the slaughter. The brutality extended far beyond the usual Zulu custom of hacking open a victim's belly – there was castration, extreme mutilation, limbs were hacked off and embryos ripped from the womb. The devastation was never forgiven nor forgotten.

So as Pretorius gazed out from the safety of his laager on the dawn of 16 December 1838, what he saw was a chance for revenge, and it would be meted out with extreme prejudice.

The battle lasted a couple of hours, but few of those thousands of onrushing Zulus made it anywhere near the Dutch laager. When it was all done, and the impi had retired – crushed and demoralised – the whites counted over 3,000 bodies in the surrounding scrub. Not one Boer had been killed. What became known as the Battle of Blood River would forever be a cause for national pride and celebration.

After their eventual defeat of Dingane, and after they had conveniently found his signed treaty among the rotting Boer corpses at the Royal Kraal, the Boers returned to the site of the massacre of the innocents months earlier. When they raised their first settlement on the spot where their men, women and children had died, they called the place Weenen, Dutch for Weeping.

All these elements are commemorated at the Voortrekker Monument. The wagon laager is there – one of the numerous symbolic features – as are the Zulu assegais which frame the gated entrance. Retief, Pretorius and others are represented there, and a carving of a strong, proud Trekker mother and children is given its own special place of honour.

On 16 December every year at midday, the sun shines through an opening in the monument's dome. Its rays find an inscription inside, which reads: 'Ons vir Jou, Suid-Afrika,

'We for thee South Africa', taken from the poem – and later anthem – 'Die Stem'.

If ever a site sums up the history, the travails, the character of Afrikaner South Africa, then this is it. In simplistic terms it is a celebration of the Calvinist crusader taming the wilderness.

Of course to non-Afrikaners, the Voortrekker Monument signifies something else entirely. For what were the original Trekkers fleeing from besides imperial, perfidious Albion, but the abolition of slavery, and the introduction of equal rights. Those covered wagons carrying civilization and Christianity into savage lands were in fact about to wreak havoc on hundreds of thousands – eventually millions – of indigenous people, perpetrating one of the biggest land grabs in history.

Apologists argue that the racial issue has been exaggerated when considering the Great Trek – many Trekkers did not in fact own slaves, and it is true that the Boer Republics when they were eventually recognised did away with slavery. But they constitutionalised racial separation, they implicitly believed in racial supremacy, they allowed suppression and they built a world where power was solely the white man's prerogative.

Incredibly, almost a quarter of a million people – a tenth of the country's white population – attended the Voortrekker Monument's opening in 1949. By then the official system of separation in South Africa had already been established. It was introduced by the newly elected National Party during the previous year. They would build their new, post-war South Africa on the foundation stone of 'Apartheid'.

* * *

Peter Hain was born in Nairobi on 16 February 1950 – exactly two months to the day after the Voortrekker Monument was officially consecrated.

Although he was Kenyan by birth, his parents were both

South African, his mother's family among the original British settlers to reach the Cape at the beginning of the nineteenth century.

Walter and Adelaine Hain took their family back to South Africa before Peter's first birthday, and Hain was raised in Pretoria, very much a South African. But his South Africa wasn't that of the Voortrekker or of apartheid. Having grown up in its shadow, Hain describes the monument today as: 'A bleak edifice of power and domination. It encapsulates the siege mentality intrinsic to the Afrikaner. It's up there on the skyline, saying we will not be beaten.'

Hain's family was at the other end of the political and cultural spectrum to the country's white Afrikaners. They became supporters of the Anti-Apartheid Movement and of a man who was regarded at that time by South African authorities as a terrorist – Nelson Mandela.

Peter was a sports-mad pupil at Pretoria Boys High School, an historic institution which produced South African cricket great Eddie Barlow, World Cup winning rugby captain John Smit, and South Africa's first ever black rugby captain, Chiliboy Ralepelle. None of them were ever observed playing rugby by security officers as Hain was, since his parents were followed everywhere – even to school to watch their son play.

Hain recalls that his family's support for the newly formed and quickly burgeoning Anti-Apartheid Movement made them targets, and made night-time raids a part of life. He awoke one night as a child to find Special Branch Officers busy searching his bedroom for anything which might incriminate his parents: 'One of my first memories is of being woken up in the middle of the night as a ten year old, to be told that my parents had been put in jail.'

Adelaine and Walter were imprisoned. They were banned from public places and gatherings: 'One of the clauses in the banning order was that you couldn't communicate with another banned person. It was designed to silence you.' His parents even needed special permission to be able to talk to each other.

When police opened fire on peaceful protestors in the township of Sharpeville in 1960, killing sixty-nine people, there was uproar both within South Africa and abroad. The authorities responded to the threat of international expulsion and armed conflict within its own borders by acting swiftly and decisively. The African National Congress was banned, leaders were jailed and exiled.

Nelson Mandela, the man put in charge of the ANC's recently formed military wing, Umkhonto we Sizwe (Spear of the Nation), was arrested and put on trial.

During that trial in 1962, Peter Hain remembers his mother being a conspicuous presence in the courtroom, simply by dint of often being Mandela's solitary supporter – the only figure in fact – in the whites-only section of the public gallery. As Hain later wrote: 'He would always acknowledge her with a clenched fist, which she would return.'

In 1963, Mandela, along with nine others, was charged with further offences of sabotage and treason – the defendants faced with the real possibility of being sentenced to death. In April 1964, Mandela made a courtroom speech that would resonate down the decades. It concluded with these words: 'During my lifetime I have dedicated myself to this struggle of the African people. I have fought against white domination, and I have fought against black domination. I have cherished the ideal of a democratic and free society in which all persons live together in harmony and with equal opportunities. It is an ideal which I hope to live for and to achieve. But if needs be, it is an ideal for which I am prepared to die.'

Instead of the death penalty, he was sentenced to life imprisonment, a term to be spent at the maximum security prison on Robben Island, off the coast of Cape Town.

Mandela's capture, trial and sentence were indicative of the extremes to which the apartheid regime was prepared to go. According to Hain, the Sixties and early Seventies were a time when: 'They simply crushed any political opposition. The Anti-Apartheid Movement within South Africa was almost completely oppressed. It didn't explode again until Soweto in 1976.'

By the time of the Soweto Uprising, precipitated by student protests and this time marked by the slaughter of hundreds of young innocents by white police officers, the Hains had gone into exile.

When Hain senior's work as an architect dried up: 'Firms were simply told not to employ him,' according to his son, the family decided that they had to leave their own country for England. They did so in 1966, the journey by ocean liner from Cape Town Docks taking them past Robben Island, where Nelson Mandela had already been incarcerated for two years.

He would stay there for another sixteen.

The family continued their support for the anti-apartheid cause on arrival in Britain. Peter was sixteen when they arrived, and was soon an active campaigner. More than that, he had vision. He saw an opportunity for the movement to be far more effective: 'I followed sport very closely, and that was unusual for the Anti-Apartheid Movement... The political struggle went on, we tried to stop trade, we continued to support political prisoners, all of that. It was very difficult to do anything about the economy; we had mixed success on British arms sales to South Africa, that was hard too. But with sport you could actually do something about it yourself. You could stop matches, you could stop tours.'

If political successes for the anti-apartheid cause were limited and hard won, its targeting of sport – one of the true bastions of Afrikanerdom – proved to be an inspired strategy. It would soon have stunning and long-lasting effects.

CHAPTER 7

The Voyage of the Damned

'Quis custodiet ipsos custodes?' 'Who will guard the guardians?'
Nelson Mandela, *The Long Walk To Freedom*

IT'S AN AGE-OLD question, and the great man wasn't the first or the last to ask it. It's applicable to prefects, teachers, policemen, priests, judges and parents – anyone who wields any power in fact, and anyone who preaches morality. But it's particularly relevant to politicians. And it was especially relevant to the tour of 1974, where the political double standards were on show for all to see.

Not that the Anti-Apartheid Movement was guilty of anything other than sticking firmly to its principles and pursuing its unstinting campaign for justice. Although the battle against apartheid had been raging in the political arena for many years, the efforts of Peter Hain and others had recently started to bear fruit on the sporting stage in particular – South Africa's sporting isolation was already under way.

The country was ostracised by the Olympics as far back as Tokyo 1964, and cricket had taken its own stand too. To this day The Rt Revd David Sheppard is the only ordained clergyman ever to play Test cricket. Later to become Bishop of Liverpool, in 1960 he was an experienced Test batsman, good enough to be chosen for England's tour to South Africa. He felt compelled to turn down the opportunity, choosing to do what he felt was right as opposed to what was right for the team. His reasons: 'I do not consider cricket in South Africa as a non-political game. South Africa has never played against the West Indies, or against India or Pakistan.'

That same year Basil D'Oliveira left his native South Africa, where he stood no chance of playing for his own country, and came to the UK. Having captained a non-white team on tour to Kenya, and having made an impression on a number of British observers, he was given invaluable support by some influential figures. That most mellifluous of cricket commentators, John Arlott, for example, helped D'Oliveira secure a contract in the Lancashire League.

By 1966 – the year the Hain family arrived at Southampton Docks – D'Oliveira was playing for England, and by 1968 he was facing Australia in an Ashes series. Dropped after the First Test despite top scoring with eighty-seven, he was picked again for the Fifth and scored 158 in England's first innings. That should in most observers' minds have booked his place on the plane to South Africa that winter. There was only one problem – D'Oliveira's colour.

South Africa's Government had already made it quite clear that D'Oliveira – as a Cape Coloured – would not be allowed to play for England in his homeland. The MCC's response was not to pick D'Oliveira for the touring party.

There was uproar in Britain, and not only from the Anti-Apartheid Movement. There were meetings with the ruling Labour Government's Minister for Sport, Denis Howell; *The News of the World* newspaper even wanted to send D'Oliveira to South Africa to cover the tour as their correspondent. Then, incredibly, three weeks later D'Oliveira was back in the squad – but the tour was off!

He was called up as a replacement for Warwickshire's Tom Cartwright, who had withdrawn with a shoulder injury. Fair enough one might think, except that Cartwright was a bowler, not a batsman. In South Africa, Prime Minister Jon Vorster issued this statement: 'The MCC [England] team is not the team of the MCC, but of the Anti-Apartheid

Movement.' South Africa would not welcome them as things stood. Having backed themselves into a corner, the MCC had no choice – they called off the tour.

The repercussions were huge. The proposed South Africa tour to England in 1970 was also cancelled, and although the Rest of the World team that took its place still included the cream of South African cricket, Barlow, Proctor, Richards and the Pollock brothers, a political statement had at least been made.

Australia then followed suite, under the leadership of its very own cricketing legend, Sir Donald Bradman. In his guise as chairman of the Australian Cricket Board, Bradman felt compelled to visit South Africa himself before the proposed 1971/72 tour.

Although a true conservative, and sympathetic to the cause of South African cricket, his meeting with Prime Minister Vorster went badly. An indignant Bradman, apparently incensed by the insinuation that black players didn't have the mental capacity for cricket, asked Vorster whether he had ever heard of Garry Sobers.

Since the West Indies all-rounder is still considered an all-time great to this day, it was as provocative a question as the Australian could muster. In the aftermath of that ill-fated meeting, Bradman and his Board made a resounding statement: 'We will not play them until they choose a team on a non-racist basis.' The tour was off, and South Africa's cricketing isolation had well and truly begun.

* * *

And yet rugby was different. John Taylor was an honourable exception – but those exceptions were few and far between. Or as Peter Hain put it succinctly: 'John Taylor was a colossus, and to be perfectly honest, in moral terms, the rest were pygmies.'

Now Test match results are completely irrelevant to an

argument of principle, but I'll include them here because they may well come in handy for another – later – argument.

So here goes; the Springboks toured France in 1968, winning the Test series two-nil. Australia toured South Africa in 1969, losing friends at home and suffering a four-Test whitewash for their troubles.

In the same vein, and despite plenty of opposition at home, New Zealand toured South Africa in 1970, losing the Test series three-one in the process.

The Springboks tour to Great Britain and Ireland during 1969/70 went ahead too. And it was a disaster. Venues had to be switched amid security fears, police encircled pitches to protect players and keep protesters at bay, and there were demonstrations aplenty. There were violent clashes too – especially outside the St Helen's ground in Swansea – ironically the very ground where Garry Sobers had hit a miraculous six sixes in one over during a cricket match the previous year.

Peter Hain and his tireless supporters certainly made their mark this time around, and the Springboks suffered. Their Test record was testament to that – they lost two, against Scotland and England, and drew two, against Ireland and Wales. Anglophile number 8 Tommy Bedford was one of the undoubted stars of South African rugby at that time. He had been a student at Oxford, was liberal in his views and was aware of the bigger picture. Years later he would play an integral part in promoting black rugby, taking a leading role in the clandestine process of reconciling black and white, of bringing the ANC and the country's rugby authorities together so that South Africa could eventually be re-admitted into the international fold.

In many ways the winter of 1969/70 was a personal awakening for Bedford. He later admitted to being shocked by the strength of the opposition to the tour: 'I'd seen the anti-Vietnam demonstrations outside the American Embassy but never imagined we would face comparable opposition.

We spent all our time surrounded by police cordons and barbed wire... 1969 was a watershed in many ways. It was the beginning of the end.'

Bedford captained the Springboks to their defeat at Murrayfield, but there was worse to follow, both on and off the pitch. Two weeks later, on the Saturday before Christmas 1969, South Africa was due to play England at Twickenham. Bedford and a number of team-mates had already boarded the team bus outside their hotel when it was hijacked and driven away by an anti-apartheid protester. With half the team left behind, it soon became apparent that the driver wasn't heading for Twickenham. He was eventually overpowered by a group of players and the bus crashed. It was surreal and it was frightening – South Africa lost to England four hours later.

Peter Hain remembers the tour this way: 'The idea was to run onto pitches, to besiege hotels, all in a non-violent fashion. The '69/70 tour was the first time this had ever been done, and it had a massive impact. Nelson Mandela told me years later that they'd heard about it despite the news blackout at Robben Island, because the wardens – fanatical rugby fans – blamed Mandela and started shouting and screaming at him. What they didn't realise was that they were communicating something huge from the outside world.'

The protestors' success came at a price however. As Hain recalls: 'We were non-violent. We weren't going to attack anybody. We invaded pitches to stop matches, and if the police came to take us away we didn't fight that. It was the principle of non-violent action. But St Helen's, Swansea was different. They were rugby vigilantes. The police dragged people off, and took them to the stewards who then beat them up... very badly. There were broken jaws, one almost lost an eye.' The rugby fraternity was closing ranks.

Around twelve miles down the road at Llanelli, another figure described by Hain as a hero, another principled rugby man, took his own stand. When his club played the Springboks in January 1970, Carwyn James prepared the side, and gave the pre-match team talk. He then sat in the changing room for the duration of the afternoon, making his own feelings about apartheid abundantly clear. James would never judge his own players when they toured in 1974, but this was his personal stance.

Gareth Edwards played against South Africa for Cardiff, Wales and the Barbarians on that tour. He later remembered the complexity of the whole period: 'The anti-apartheid demonstrations prior to and during the tour... brought to the forefront matters concerning South Africa. Yet they really only added to the confusion of what was happening there.'

Put simply, young rugby players wanted to play against the best, whoever they were and wherever they came from.

So on the big stage, the circus went on. France went to South Africa in 1971, drawing the Second Test after losing the First. The Springboks travelled to Australia that summer too, in what proved to be another incendiary tour. The rugby was easy enough – three wins out of three against the Wallabies, but off the field things went completely haywire. Queensland Premier Joh Bjelke-Petersen, himself an arch-conservative, felt that the situation had reached crisis point and called a state of emergency.

Protestors in Sydney attempted to cut down the goal posts pre-match, whilst thousands of demonstrators in Melbourne faced off against mounted and baton wielding police. Yes, it was some trip, and it made a lasting impression on one new cap. Morné du Plessis was a rising Springbok star on his first tour, but what he saw in Australia started him on his own journey of discovery: 'As a young guy my eyes were opened. Now the world was a much bigger place in those days, and distances were far longer, yet you found yourself thousands of miles from home, asking how people in Australia could be so angry about what was going on in your own country. It made me realise that we had to be doing something wrong.'

And still the madness went on. England toured South

Africa – and won – in 1972, the Lions toured – and won – in 1974. That November, South Africa travelled to France and beat their hosts two-nil, the French reciprocated the following summer, 1975 – and lost again.

New Zealand did in fact take a stand of sorts. They cancelled a tour to take on the Springboks in 1967 after South Africa's refusal to compromise on 'the Maori question'. That is, South Africa's point-blank refusal to countenance the inclusion of Maori players in the travelling All Black party.

By the time New Zealand were due to tour again in 1970, the term 'honourary whites' had been introduced by South Africa so that Maoris like Sid Going, and Samoans like Bryan Williams could be included in the squad. That tour went ahead – but the All Blacks lost again.

The contradictory nature of the South Africa/New Zealand relationship continued over the coming years. The Springboks proposed tour in 1973 was called off due to huge pressure from agitated New Zealanders – the risk of the tour being a magnet for protests was deemed to be too great by both the New Zealand Rugby Union and the Government.

That said, they were the two global giants, their rivalry was the bedrock of the game, and they quite simply needed each other. The All Blacks themselves were back in South Africa by 1976, when again they lost the all-important (to them) Test series three-one.

Yes, rugby was different. It may have been the bastion of the Afrikaner, but the Afrikaner was a very important player on the world stage. So the scene was set for outright conflict before the British and Irish Lions of 1974 even kicked a ball, or threw a pass, or landed a punch in anger.

* * *

Pressure in the UK and Ireland had been mounting. When the tour of '74 was announced, and the squad chosen, the UK Government felt compelled to act.

The Labour Party had come back to power in the election of February that year by the skin of its teeth – Harold Wilson ousting Ted Heath's beleaguered Conservatives in the midst of huge economic problems and in the wake of the three-day week crisis. Yet Labour failed to secure a working majority, and would have to call another election later that same year to consolidate its hold on Government.

In the interim period it did its level best to get the Lions tour called off.

The official request from Minister for Sport Denis Howell to the Four Home Unions committee was that the Lions should not travel, due to: 'The strong feelings we have about this tour... Our advice to them would be that it's rather unwise for them to go.'

Albert Agar, Secretary of the Four Home Unions responded that: 'We are determined to go to South Africa... There are two views on this subject, but we believe that by maintaining sporting contact with South Africa, more progress will be achieved than by abolishing that contact.'

His argument was seemingly strengthened by the fact that the Lions would be breaking new ground in 1974. For the first time they would play a 'Coloured' and a 'Black' team in South Africa. The Proteas represented the South African Rugby Football Federation, a union which played under the banner of the SARB. There were plenty more coloured players who refused to be governed by their oppressors, so the Proteas were by no means supported by all. But their presence on the fixture list, as when England toured South Africa two years previously, was seen as a step in the right direction.

The Leopards were the team of the SAARB, the South African African Rugby Board, formerly the Bantu Rugby Board.

That is to say, the official team of black South Africans – though again not necessarily the one which represented the majority of black players or supporters.

Peter Hain dismissed these sides as: 'Representing the

Uncle Tom rugby organisations in South Africa. The terms coloured and black were classified in law. And you want to know how absurd these racial restrictions were? The Proteas were coloured, the Leopards were black. So not only were there no blacks in the Springbok team, there were no blacks in the coloured team!'

And yet there were non-white South Africans who did support the Proteas and the Leopards. There were others who supported neither, and yet they could still find some good in the Lions tour. And there were some who both backed Peter Hain's campaign to stop the tour, and yet saw no anomaly in supporting the tourists once they'd arrived. Such was the contradictory and complicated nature of the battle.

In South Africa, as elsewhere, so-called experts vie for the spotlight, and the opportunity to express their opinions. Credibility is sometimes difficult to come by. Mthobi Tyamzashe has credibility in abundance, but cares little for hogging centre stage. Most recently he was Group Executive of Corporate Affairs at Vodacom South Africa, but it's his sporting rather than business background that marks him out.

He was raised in the Eastern Cape and grew up to be a rugby man. As both a player, a fan, and later an administrator at club, provincial and national level, he came to know the intricacies of South Africa's sporting allegiances. Understanding the political complications involved in following a particular team and a particular sport stood him in good stead as his reputation grew.

He was one of the founding members of South Africa's influential National Sports Congress, and when the country's political landscape was remapped in the mid-Nineties, he became director general of the Department of Sport and Recreation. He subsequently went on to become chairman of Boxing SA and of South Africa's Commonwealth Games Association, before heading up South Africa's bid to host the 2011 Rugby World Cup.

Tyamzashe was a twenty-year-old student when the Lions toured his homeland in 1974. His thoughts on the tour and its effect are fascinating:

'It may seem strange to say that a tour that worked against the sports boycott could be viewed as a positive influence but I do not feel conflicted by my fond memories of those Lions... We were obviously on his [Peter Hain's] side. The whites were saying; "You guys can't play with us, but we'll help create your own league". That happened in all sports, the black league, the coloured league, the Indian league... So we did believe that South Africa should be isolated, that teams should not come here.

But if they did come, then they must beat the South Africans. So a team like the Lions, who beat the hell out of them, we were like; "Yes... Now you know. You see that you need us." They were playing with just twenty per cent of their resources – wouldn't they be better off using a hundred per cent and being inclusive? It was almost like the tour showed me what I must strive for in my later involvement in rugby. So in that sense, I don't see any conflict between my stance then and my stance now. That's who we were, and that's what we were dealing with.'

And what if the campaign to stop the tour had been successful?

'If I talk about that tour, it's more than just a rugby tour. It sustained us in terms of our hope. If they didn't come... If they'd gone to Argentina or somewhere like that instead, we'd have lost out. We'd have lost that little bit of extra pressure that the Lions brought with them. The defeat of the South Africans was seen by many of us as poetic justice. If they hadn't come we wouldn't have had that. So you must look for the positives always.'

The British Government did not ban the tour, but it made absolutely sure that the world knew it objected. It essentially washed its hands of the Lions. As JBG Thomas wrote later, it made manager Alun Thomas the first ever British sports official to lead a group of players abroad having been 'virtually disowned' by his own Government.

Wilson's Government also expressly forbade its Embassies in South Africa, or any of their staff, to have anything at all to do with the touring party. In official speak, as trumpeted by Under Secretary of State for Foreign and Commonwealth Affairs Joan Lestor, staff: 'Should not extend hospitality or attend matches or receptions for the team. This applies to all matches and social functions during the tour.'

So, in political terms, except for the dubious support of the right-wing National Front, the Lions were pretty much friendless – ostracised by their own people. It was a lonely place to be.

Today, few of those players who did travel in 1974 would quibble with the need to ask questions of themselves. Did they do the right thing? Were they fully aware of what was at stake? Yet they can also point to the fact that many politicians weren't necessarily practicing what they preached. Edward Heath, Conservative Prime Minister between 1970 and 1974, was at least open enough during a speech at a Lord Mayor's banquet in London in 1970 to put it this way: 'Abhorrence of apartheid is a moral attitude, not a policy.'

Even Labour politicians when they came to power struggled to reconcile ideals with the practicalities of government. When a motion was tabled to expel South Africa from the United Nations in 1974, it failed because of stern opposition from three countries in particular – Great Britain, France and the USA.

Their lucrative trade links, as well as South Africa's strategic importance in terms of the Cold War and the threat of communism, proved to be a stronger motivation than their opposition to apartheid. In this particular case, it seemed that morality was selective.

So the Lions were an easy target in terms of staking a claim to the moral high ground, and the Labour Government was more than happy to make an expedient example of them.

Nowhere was this better summed up than on their triumphant return, when Minister for Sport, Denis Howell, the man who'd told them in no uncertain terms not to go, turned up to welcome them back with open arms at Heathrow Airport.

Their achievement, he said, deserved to be recognised. For the players themselves, his presence summed up the political game perfectly. Fran Cotton speaks for most with this assessment: 'The politicians showed themselves to be total hypocrites. The Wilson Government banned any contact with the Embassies and the Consulate out there, and then when we came home off the back of a fantastic winning tour, there was Denis Howell, the Minister for Sport, waiting for us. You've got to understand the hypocrisy of it all. At the end of the day sport was an easy target. If they'd really wanted to make a difference then severing trade links would have been a far more aggressive and worthwhile direction for them to take.'

JJ Williams is more succinct in his summation: 'Pathetic. Just pathetic.'

Howell's hypocrisy – and that of his Government – seemingly knew no bounds, and appalled even those who opposed the tour.

Peter Hain was there at Heathrow too – still protesting, and still an inconvenient conscience. He would go on to become a long serving Labour MP for Neath, and eventually Secretary of State for Wales. He found Howell's volte-face 'utterly disgusting'.

All that was in the future, but during the last days of April 1974 there was still a chance of stopping the tour. If the Unions couldn't be dissuaded, then what about the players themselves?

When the team gathered at the Britannia Hotel in London, they were greeted by Hain and over a hundred protestors: 'We organised a sit-down in the lobby, and Willie John McBride was asked to come down and talk to me. I tried to persuade him not to go [to South Africa], but it was rather a ritualistic conversation frankly, they were set on going.'

Did Hain feel that his actions prompted any hesitation in any players? 'No, I'm not sure it did, really. McBride was courteous, but not interested at all.'

McBride himself remembers being asked to talk to his players – and agreeing to do so. But he feels absolutely no need to apologise, to feel guilt-ridden forty years down the line: 'Regrets? No, none at all. Who the hell was I to start sorting out the politics or the struggles of another country? If I started thinking like that I wouldn't play against anybody would I? Apartheid was a fact of life in South Africa at that time. No-one could justify it, but there it was. I had been there, I could feel it changing, and I knew that the day would come eventually when they had to do away with it, when apartheid would disappear. The biggest irony is that the Cold War was the most important factor of all – the fear of communism helped apartheid. Once the Berlin Wall came down, apartheid was gone. No-one's ever pointed that out, but it's true... So us deciding to go or not to go and play a game of rugby in South Africa wasn't going to stop apartheid was it?'

The Ulsterman admits that his own mind at least was made up long before he talked to Peter Hain at the Britannia Hotel: 'I don't know where he was coming from. He was outside the Britannia, and we were trapped inside. So I agreed to meet him, as long as there was no publicity about it. And we met, and he gave me this petition that he had, and I listened to what he had to say. Then I went straight upstairs and talked to the team – as he'd asked.'

McBride's speech to the players was to become the first legend of the 1974 tour: 'I gathered them all in the team room, and told them what Peter Hain had told me. I told them I was going, and that I was going out there to win. I told them that if anyone had any doubts, any at all, now was the time – the door was open. There'd be no point in coming to me the following day, or following week, or month. If they had any qualms about what they were doing I said; "You're no good to me and no good to the team." Well, you could have heard a pin drop... Nobody moved. And after a fair old while I said; "I gather you're with me?" And they applauded.'

It was McBride's line in the sand moment. Just as Travis at the Alamo offered his besieged Texans the chance to cross that line, and take their last opportunity of surviving the oncoming Mexican onslaught, so the Ulsterman offered his squad the chance of a change of heart. Travis and his men stayed and died at the Alamo. As it was, every Lion stayed too – and lived with his conscience.

After the air had been well and truly cleared, they could get down to the nitty-gritty, and McBride told his team what they could expect in the weeks ahead.

As well as the off-field political pressure there would be on-field intimidation, thuggery, downright cheating. They would have to fight fire with fire, and they would have to stick together like no side they'd ever played in before. The players sat in silence, taking it all in. Then a voice from the east Wales valleys piped up from the back of the room: 'I'm bloody well going to enjoy this!' Bobby Windsor had made his first contribution to team morale. They were going to South Africa – and they were going to South Africa to win.

It was the first instance where they'd stood together, united. For McBride, it was an excellent omen: 'It's a remarkable thing – from that day forward the loyalty within that team was unbelievable. It still is to this day.'

Their virtual house arrest would soon be at an end. It had been arranged for the Lions to leave early for South Africa rather than head for their traditional base in Eastbourne, so that they could acclimatise to the very different playing conditions. In truth they couldn't get away soon enough.

Peter Hain was left bitterly disappointed, and by his own admission forty years later, just plain bitter: 'Whatever they say, they were a part of the problem not the solution... I could understand young rugby players, selected for the Lions – the pinnacle of their career – thinking about it in just those terms. But not everybody was like that. John Taylor wouldn't go, but there were no other John Taylors unfortunately, and there was no Carwyn James on the coaching side either. So I can understand it but I also remain very angry about it. Some of them remain unrepentant to this day.'

If they would never be forgiven by some, others could empathise with their nerves and their excitement. Ahead of them lay twenty-two matches, some nothing more than exhibitions, some a matter of rugby life and death. They would break new ground by playing non-white teams, the first ever Lions team to do so.

They would play some of the most uncompromising provincial rugby that the southern hemisphere had to offer – not Canterbury, Auckland, Hawke's Bay and Wellington maybe – but Western Province, Northern Transvaal, Orange Free State and Natal.

And they would play four defining Test matches against the mighty Springboks – matches that would mark them out forever. The Lions were finally on their way, on their voyage of the damned.

CHAPTER 8

The Rooineks are Coming

'One of the most rugged, virile, unconquerable races ever seen
upon the earth… the modern Boer – the most formidable
antagonist who ever crossed the path of Imperial Britain.'
Sir Arthur Conan Doyle, *The Great Boer War*

EVERYTHING DECIDED, THE Lions could now focus on what
lay ahead. As always there had been a certain amount of
wrangling about the tour itinerary, and the South Africans
had included a number of intriguing fixtures in addition
to the Proteas and the Leopards. As well as the traditional
strongholds, Western Province and Eastern Province in the
south, Transvaal, Northern Transvaal and Orange Free State
on the Highveld, and Natal lurking on the east coast, the
Lions would have to contend with the likes of the Quaggas,
a Barbarian type team guaranteed to test, and the Southern
Universities, at a time when university sides were considered
worthy and challenging opponents. The tour would have its
share of 'gimmes' for sure, but less so than previous tours.

If South Africa's provinces didn't quite terrify in the
same vein as their equivalents in New Zealand, they were
a formidable proposition for any touring team. They were
certain to test British and Irish mettle, to contribute to the
softening up process so beloved by southern hemisphere
hosts, and to exploit any weaknesses to the full. Each one
craved the Lions scalp above all else.

The Lions arrived at Johannesburg's Jan Smuts airport

on the morning of Tuesday, 7 May 1974, to be greeted by hundreds of fans, including a fair share of Welsh expats. The delighted Dr Danie Craven, rugby legend and president of the South African Rugby Board was there to greet them too. But no sooner had they cleared customs and negotiated their first delicate piece of political protocol than tour manager Alun Thomas was running into trouble. In an off the record conversation with a group of familiar and trusted journalists, Thomas admitted his disappointment at the British Government's very public lack of support. These comments were picked up by a local 'hack' – not one of the trusted circle – who got a major scoop. The sympathetic JBG Thomas, as a friend of the manager, felt compelled to come to his defence in his post-tour analysis: 'The obvious and justifiable comment made privately by Thomas, that it was a "stab in the back", was cabled round the world from Jo'burg.'

If manager Thomas had been defensive before departure, he now became extra wary. His sense of mistrust rose to the extent that it affected his, and to a lesser extent the squad's, relationship with the press in general.

Meanwhile, the Lions themselves had decamped to their first South African base, Stilfontein, around ninety miles from Johannesburg.

It had been chosen specifically because it was near enough to the location of their first match – in Potchefstroom – but secluded enough for them to get on with their training. Vitally important too in terms of preparation, it was at altitude.

Stilfontein was a town established at the end of the Forties around the local mines – it was quiet, private and very much out of the way. To those who were looking forward to sampling South Africa's legendary hospitality, it was a grave disappointment. But that was the whole point, there were no distractions and they had the better part of a week and a half to get to know each other as players and as men.

Roy Bergiers, having heard about Lions tours past, was nonplussed by his new surroundings, a one-horse town which even the horse had apparently chosen to leave: 'My great mate Delme Thomas won't thank me for saying this, but it was like his home village, Bancyfelin. You'd walk down the main street, and realise that actually, that was it. There was a post office and a pub and nothing else. But of course it was superb in terms of training.'

It was the first indication of just how much homework Alun Thomas and Syd Millar had done – nothing, seemingly, had been left to chance. They would be equally thorough in ascertaining where they stood in terms of local interpretations of the laws of the game, especially at the line-out, and in terms of getting the referees they wanted for big matches in the weeks ahead.

So if their first few days on South African soil proved an uneventful sojourn in terms of tour tales, they proved invaluable in terms of everything else, as they acclimatised under the watchful eye of not just Millar, but Ken Kennedy, on hand with salt tablets, medicine, and even breathing exercises. He was aided by JPR Williams, who felt that those early days were significant in terms of laying the ground work: 'The training at altitude was revolutionary for the Lions – it reflected well on Syd for sure. And yes, Ken and I looked after the party from the off, including blood samples, iron tablets – all that kind of stuff.'

Tom David remembers Syd Millar's influence being a key to their success from the start: 'There are more coaches nowadays than players. Back in 1974 there was one coach. No fitness guru, no defensive coach, no specialists at all, just Syd. I've got total respect for him for what he did. Plain spoken, what you saw was what you got – typical prop forward in some ways. In fact I remember Syd saying to me at the bar one night; "Tom after this tour, when you go back, it's my opinion that you should concentrate on being a tight-head prop." He then explained why he thought so. And I just looked at him and said outright "No." And he said "Why won't you consider it?" And I said "Look how ugly you are Syd." He laughed because he could take that kind of thing, another strength of his. But he was dead serious about the propping idea, mind.'

JJ Williams came from an athletics background. He too was impressed with the way the new Lions coach went about his business: 'I don't think Syd Millar had the praise he deserved for his preparation. What we were doing was way ahead of its time – not just the scrummaging stuff. He was ahead of his time in a number of ways – even I found his running sessions hard for example. So it was professional for its time, despite the fact that we only had a manager and a coach looking after us.'

Williams and his fellow backs were spared the really tough stuff. That was reserved for the forwards. And if the physical build-up was gradual for the most part, that certainly didn't apply to scrummaging practice, which was intense from the very off.

In fact the scrum, and scrummaging practice, has continued to be the focal point for touring Lions teams in South Africa ever since. The only other Lions to win a series against the Springboks since 1974 were the illustrious tourists of 1997, coached by Ian McGeechan and managed by Fran Cotton. The forwards coach was Jim Telfer, whose 'beasting' scrummaging sessions became legendary.

The Lions tour of 1974 set the template for all who followed. According to Bobby Windsor: 'You're talking fifty, sixty scrums per session, all "live", no machines. Both front rows were desperate to get into the Tests, and to be fair both sets of three could have. The toughest opposition we faced all tour was probably what we came up against every day in training. So there were dust-ups, and there was a bit of blood left on the training pitch now and again, but it was accepted. We knew we couldn't back down at all, even with our mates.'

Fran Cotton was talented enough to challenge for both the tight-head and loose-head berth at the highest level. That made him a dangerous team-mate as well as formidable opponent. Initially, there was a sense that he was taken on tour as a loose-head. His experienced rival for that spot soon made his feelings plain: 'After the very first training session in South Africa, Ian McLauchlan, who was a very competitive kind of bloke, came up to me and said; "Look, I'm out here to play all twenty-two games," in other words, I'd have to knock him off his perch in order to get in. It was absolutely the right attitude. And as it happened Mickey Burton's injury early on meant that I got a run at tight-head instead.'

McBride himself revelled in the competition for places. In his own autobiography he recalled going on the 1962 Lions tour as a raw twenty-one year old and having the front to tell the incumbent second row, Wales's Keith Rowlands, that he'd come on tour: 'To get your place in the Test side.' It was a good thing therefore to want to knock the other fellow off his perch, and an even better thing that there were plenty capable of doing just that. As Fran Cotton recalls: 'One of the real strengths of the '74 Lions was that we had two sets of forwards of pretty much equal ability. You accepted the odd flare up because it was that competitive. There was never any ill feeling about it though, because we all wanted to play – and Willie John encouraged that.'

As training intensified, so did the list of casualties. Windsor hadn't initially made it to Stilfontein with the rest of the party – a bout of food poisoning left him needing hospital treatment on arrival in Johannesburg. Fran Cotton felt that the 'food poisoning' might have had something to do with Windsor's attempts to drink with Mervyn Davies and JPR Williams over the course of the flight. Either way, he soon made his presence felt when he rejoined the squad. While one hooker was a late arrival, the other was dealing with all comers – Mike Burton's freshly wounded knee, as well as niggles affecting Uttley, Old, Grace and McKinney kept Kennedy busy. At least it made choosing the team for the opening match a somewhat easier task.

That opener, against Western Transvaal, would take place

on Saturday, 15 May, in Potchefstroom, a venue rich in history. Even today, *The Lonely Planet* guidebook calls it a 'staunchly conservative town', back then it was a stark welcome to the world of Afrikanerdom. Not only was the settlement the second oldest in the region, but it had once been the Transvaal's capital. More than that, it had played a significant role in not one but two Boer Wars. That's the British title for those historic conflicts by the way. To the Afrikaners they will forever be Wars of Independence.

The opening shots of the first conflict in 1880, were fired once again on that most symbolic of dates, 16 December, in Potchefstroom. During the Second Boer War two decades later, the place became infamous as the site of a British prison camp.

When modern readers see the words concentration camp, thoughts immediately turn to the Second World War, but in fact the British vied with the Spanish in Cuba for the dubious honour of being the first to introduce these internment centres at the turn of the century. Boer women and children were corralled within barbed wire fences in their thousands while their menfolk fought on and their farms burned. Tens of thousands died of disease, starvation, and neglect causing uproar not only within the Boer republics but among British liberals at home.

The facts are as stark as they are frightening, and although these hellish places can never be compared to the extermination camps of the Nazis, they were horrific enough to leave scars which lasted for generations. The fact that almost as many black Africans died under similarly barbaric conditions during the conflict was largely ignored for the best part of a century afterwards. Despite plenty of evidence to the contrary, this was seen as very much a white man's war.

The Boers won almost every major battle from 1899 to 1902, but somehow contrived to lose the war. There were some alive who still remembered the conflict, and there were many for whom the British would always be the enemy. Different from the Zulus perhaps, but never to be trusted, and always to be fought without surrender. These were the Afrikaners – the white tribe of Africa – and rugby was their way of national expression, of exacting revenge, and of asserting superiority.

Academic and author John Nauright once summed up the Boer approach to rugby this way in a study of sport and culture in South Africa: 'Thus Afrikaner nationalists viewed rugby as part of the overall project of instilling bodily control and discipline, coupled with moral and religious righteousness in the public presentation of Afrikaner nationalism.' Yes, the game was that fundamental to the psyche of the unreconstructed Boer.

With all this in mind, but mainly with the express intention of asserting their own domination as early in the tour as possible, the Lions picked a particularly strong XV for what on paper promised to be one of the easiest outings, against Western Transvaal.

Five of the squad's previous Lions were included. The side would take to the field safe in the knowledge that JPR Williams was there as an immovable object behind them, their very own version of that famous Virginian, Thomas 'Stonewall' Jackson. Jackson too had fought, and died, in the service of a debatable cause – becoming one of the most famous Confederate casualties during the American Civil War, but his unyielding reputation had terrified the enemy.

At the other end of the Lions battle-line, the front row would be anchored by Messrs McLauchlan and Carmichael, with the recently restored Windsor in between. McBride and Brown would pick up where they left off in New Zealand at second row, while the back row of David, Ripley and Neary might well have been nominated as prospective First Test starters – they certainly fancied themselves in that guise.

Among the backs, all bar Williams were Lions newcomers – Edwards was kept back, giving Irishman Moloney an early chance to shine. Bennett though was to start at 10, along with his Llanelli colleague Bergiers in the centre. The other midfield berth went to McGeechan, while the wings would be Scotland's Steele and Wales's Rees.

On Wednesday, 15 May, McBride, on his fifth Lions tour, led his men out carrying the team's mascot one handed, high above his head. Conditions were good, the ground was hard, and there were 25,000 raucous locals awaiting them. This is what they'd come for. The chase was afoot.

Fate decreed that the captain didn't score the first try of the tour, but at least it settled for next best. After only five minutes, Bergiers launched into one of those bone-shaking tackles that had helped make his name. The turnover ball was shipped to David, who ate up yards with that familiar, almost simian gait. Cradling the ball protectively in one palm – like King Kong cradling Faye Wray – he fended off tacklers as though they were stop-motion T-Rexes.

Up in support and ready to take his pass was Gordon Brown – who plunged over the line with both arms outstretched and a look on his face which transformed from concentration to jubilation in the blink of an eye. It was the first of nine tries that afternoon. The next by Billy Steele – again courtesy of a crunching tackle and turn-over by Bergiers – came less than five minutes later, and meant that the Lions were breathing easy where they'd worried about struggling for air.

Moloney added a third try before half-time, while Ripley, David, Edwards and Rees all got their names on the score sheet that day too. In fact David and Edwards claimed a brace each, with the Lions feeling confident enough to tap quick penalties and take some risks.

The fact that Edwards was on the field at all was one of the few negative aspects of the whole experience. Moloney dislocated his shoulder early in the second half, meaning that the Lions had to expose their prized asset to the rigours of rugby in those parts a touch sooner than expected. More worrying though was the fact that Edwards would have to be continually exposed to those rigours for the forseeable future. With Moloney out for the next few weeks, there was no alternative unless they called up a replacement from home. The management gambled, and decided it was Edwards or bust – he would have to carry the tourists at some point anyway – he might as well get an early start.

In his match report for *The Western Mail*, JBG Thomas described the performance as: 'A sensational start', and singled out Roy Bergiers in particular as 'a tower of strength'. Post-match though, the centre acknowledged that he had a major problem. He, like John Moloney, had taken a serious knock. Unlike Moloney, Bergiers had serious aspirations of becoming a Test match Lion. He had been caught late by one of Western Transvaal's hard men, and the encounter would have long-lasting repercussions: 'I'll never forget the guy's name, because it affected my whole tour after that. They had this guy called Jan Tromp. They called him 'The Leopard Man', the legend was that he'd killed a leopard with his bare hands. But he was a dirty bastard. So my flank was open and he came around with his knee and caught me in the ribs. I displaced a rib cartilage and was out for a while afterwards, too long as it happened. I remember Syd trying to cheer me up afterwards by saying that he'd had plenty of those injuries over the years as a prop, and that I'd be fine. I just said; "But Syd, I'm not a prop."'

From then on, Bergiers was playing catch up.

His Llanelli colleague Phil Bennett had a more encouraging afternoon. Seven conversions and three penalties got his tour off to an ideal start, and meant that with twenty-three points he equalled Bob Hiller's record from the South African tour six years earlier. The fifty-nine points to thirteen win (tries earned four points in those days – they were only worth three back in 1971) also meant that the Lions had registered a record win on South African soil. The next few weeks would prove that all records were there to be broken – and broken again.

* * *

131

With the wait over, and the nerves settled by a confidence boosting opener, they would now have to settle into the unique rhythm of a rugby tour. Wednesday to Saturday to Wednesday, from plane to bus to hotel, from training paddock to pitch. Other routines started to take shape too.

When the focus was on the pack, which was often, Gareth Edwards was given responsibility for the backs. His second in command, JPR Williams, still couldn't resist the odd excursion into the realms of forward training, being especially keen to show his scrummaging prowess. He'd done this in New Zealand in 1971 and lived to tell the tale, but in South Africa he learned quickly that some things were better left alone. Millar and McBride, McLauchlan, Burton, Windsor and Cotton in fully confrontational mode being foremost among them.

He retreated to the comfort of the backs, and for the most part he and they were left to their own devices in terms of training drills. They did just fine. In fact Edwards feels compelled to point out that the backs were more than happy with the way things were developing, both on and off the pitch: 'Look, Syd knew that to beat the South Africans we had to take them on and dominate them up front. We knew conditions were different to New Zealand, we knew that our opponents were different, so you factor in every equation and come up with your best answer. Don't be fooled into thinking we were disappointed as backs. It gave us huge confidence, because we knew we had the right boys in the right places to damage the Springboks. They gave us a great feeling of being up to the task.'

Up front, Bobby Windsor had taken on the mantle of tour entertainer, his deadly serious response when asked what kind of omelette he'd like for breakfast: 'One of those egg ones of course,' became one of the most oft-repeated lines of the tour – as it did at after-dinner speeches over the decades to come. But Windsor had also made an early impression on one very influential individual. Not the coach, or the captain, but Ian 'Mighty Mouse' McLauchlan. Windsor recalls that the Scotsman was always pencilled in as the Test match prop, and had the ear of the 'top brass': 'I played the very first game with him, and there was a bit of niggle, which suited me. I could almost see The Mouse thinking; "Och aye, this bloke's a bit of a nut case". And I think that's what got me into the Test side. They felt they needed nutters out there, and Ken Kennedy, good player though he was, well he just wasn't vicious. I was.'

Andy Ripley was anything but vicious, but he was another of the tour's prime characters. Every player who shared a room with Ripley has his own unique story. Roy Bergiers came back to his room in Stilfontein to find an unexpected guest on his bed: 'I walked in, and there was this kitten. It had an infection in its eyes; it was a mess, blind basically. And he'd put his towel on my bed... my bed, mind... and it was perfectly at home there. Of course you couldn't be cross with him because he was just this lovely guy, and completely eccentric. So the kitten was there for the duration. Before we left he managed to find a home for it locally, he just had that way about him, they loved him out there.'

It wouldn't be the first stray to latch on to the Pied Piper of the party over the months ahead, and many of those followers would turn out to be female. Whenever the Englishman worked up a head of steam on the pitch, which was often, the cheers from male supporters in the stands would be drowned out by higher-pitched squeals of delight. Ripley took all the attention in his stride – his favourite T-shirt after all read 'I'm So Perfect It Even Scares Me'.

At the opposite end of the scale, Commonwealth sprinter JJ Williams found it difficult to shake off some unwanted attention from one of his own team-mates. As training intensified, Williams expected to reign supreme in the sprinting sessions. Yet the challenge to his status didn't come from his fellow three-quarters Rees or Grace or Irvine – but from flank forward Fergus Slattery.

Ignoring his fellow grunts, the Irishman would place himself among the backs, singling out Williams and staying as tight to him as possible. In real terms that often meant that he would be within a foot or two from beginning to end of any given sprint. If Williams relaxed he would be faced with the ultimate humiliation, not only being beaten in a foot race, but being beaten by a forward.

It said much about both their characters that one continued to lay down the challenge, and that the other thrived on it. Of the flattery from Slattery, Williams had this to say: 'He could beat me if I didn't take it seriously. He was an animal. Even if he went out and drank himself rotten, he would still come and stand next to me the next morning. He would be running, and he'd be sick... he'd be spewing, but still going – vomit all over him. But bloody hell he was quick.'

So the flyers were flying in every sense. Their next stop was Windhoek.

CHAPTER 9

Cape of Good Hope?

*'This cape is the most stately and the fairest cape
in the whole circumference of the earth.'*
Journal of Francis Drake, on seeing
the Cape for the first time in 1580

BEFORE THE CAPE came the Kalahari. The land to the west
was vast and empty until you hit the forbidding Skeleton
coast. It is known today as Namibia, and has been since
officially gaining independence in 1990. Before that it was
known to whites as South West Africa, and before that as
German South West Africa.

That was in no small part thanks to the empire building
efforts of Otto Von Bismarck at the end of the nineteenth
century. Determined to rival British and French expansionist
policies, Germany too grabbed more than its fair share of
African soil, massacring indigenous tribes at a rate of knots
– this was especially true of Namibia, where over seventy-five
per cent of the Herero people were exterminated.

During the great Boer uprising at the turn of the twentieth
century, their westerly colonial neighbours naturally
supported them. They were after all tied by blood, language,
and most importantly anti-British sentiment. The Boers lost,
the British never forgot.

In 1910, South Africa itself was granted dominion status,
forming a United South Africa and incorporating four
provinces: The Cape, Natal, Transvaal and the former Orange

Free State. Boer War heroes became statesmen, none more so than Louis Botha, the Union's first prime minister, and his powerful deputy, the Cambridge educated Jan Smuts. They were both genuine Afrikaner legends, commanders who had gained respect from friend and foe – and none had fought harder against the British Empire. Yet on the outbreak of the First World War in 1914, they stood firm against plenty of internal opposition and professed their loyalty to the British cause.

German South West Africa was now the enemy, and would need to be dealt with. First though, Botha and Smuts would need to deal with enemies closer to home. Many Afrikaners were naturally sympathetic to the German cause. Another war hero, General Christiaan Beyers, had actually visited Kaiser Wilhelm in Germany, and at the outbreak of hostilities in 1914 he resigned his post as Military Commandant General in disgust. Beyers cited the fact that his countrymen had forgotten: 'The barbarities committed in our country during the South African War.'

Another high ranking officer joined the anti-British cause, in fact the very man who commanded South African forces on the border with South West Africa – Lieut Col. Manie Maritz. He declared an independent South Africa, and a new republic, with the backing of Beyers and other high profile 'bittereinders'. They gathered their forces, around 12,000 strong, and prepared for the impossible – a war which pitted former diehard Afrikaner allies against each other.

Botha and Smuts didn't hesitate. They took personal charge of the loyalist campaign and soon restored order.

By the end of 1914, the Maritz Rebellion had been smashed, and some of the vanquished had joined the Germans across the border. By May 1915, Botha had not only invaded South West Africa, but had entered Windhoek from the east. With Smuts leading another force inland from the south-west coast, the Germans were thoroughly beaten by July. If the South African campaign of conquest had been brief, it had also been overwhelming, and would have long-lasting repercussions.

For South West Africa now in effect became an extension of South Africa itself. Though never officially annexed, it was the de facto fifth state of the Union. In 1919 it was decreed to be a 'mandate territory' by the newly formed League of Nations, and so it stayed for the next seventy years, experiencing many of the ills that afflicted its big brother, including of course – post 1948 – apartheid.

The seeds of revolution had already been sown by the Seventies with the foundation of SWAPO, the South West Africa People's Organisation, but it would take another two decades to fulfill the rebels' long held ambition of gaining independence.

So in 1974, for the Lions, South West Africa was just another traditional stop off on the grandest of rugby odysseys.

* * *

There were a number of elements that made Windhoek different. The German influence was still strong, and its lager was among the best in the world. Its location on a highland plateau meant that its rugby stadium was among the highest in the world. And if South Australian Charles Hawker had once been honest enough to describe Australia's capital city Canberra as 'a good sheep station spoilt', then Windhoek in 1974 may well have been termed 'a worthy watering hole wasted'.

It was still very much a frontier town.

But the Lions were there to play not to party, and that meant taking on one of South West Africa's favourite sons, Springbok stalwart, Jan Ellis.

Aged thirty-one, and a veteran of thirty-one Tests, he was getting a bit long in the tooth according to some observers. In fact he would still be starring for the Springboks two years later when they defeated the mighty All Blacks. Ellis was an almost mythical figure in the south west, and he had already left one series-changing mark on Lions history. In the First Test of the 1968 tour, it was the tear-away flanker who had upended Barry John, breaking his collarbone and ending his tour in the process. That act also put paid to any chance the Lions had of upsetting their illustrious hosts.

Six years on, Ellis might have lost a little of his lustre, and a yard or two, but he was still a formidable figure. In front of 12,000 of his own personal fan club, as well as a couple of Springbok selectors there especially to watch him play, he would prove an inspirational leader to his team.

Gareth Edwards had played for the Lions of 1968, and had played in the corresponding fixture at Windhoek during that tour. If his memories of Ellis might not have been fond, at least he had left his own mark on Windhoek, scoring two tries in a 23–0 win against South West Africa.

He had also toured there with the Cardiff club as a young man in 1967. Little did he imagine then that he would be returning as a Lion over the years ahead, let alone a Lions captain. But this time around, that's exactly what Edwards was – he would lead the side into battle for the first time: 'Those boys were very physical, and we were 6,000 feet up. I felt privileged to be captain of course, but I remember we struggled that day. They were simply big, rough, tough Afrikaners. Now I'd been before and kind of knew what to expect. A lot of the boys were new to it – this was their baptism. So I suppose I felt a sense of responsibility.'

As though leadership didn't bring enough pressure, Edwards had more on his mind that day. If anything should happen to the captain, the playmaker, the only fit number 9 during the next eighty minutes, the Lions could be down to Tony Neary, Alan Old or Ian McGeechan as acting scrum-half. If needed, it would be Old's turn in Windhoek, but later in the tour, when Moloney was sidelined again, the Lions resorted to even more desperate measures. Prior to the match against the Leopards in East London, they approached former England scrum-half Nigel Starmer-Smith, who was in South

Africa commentating for the BBC, as to his availability. At this early stage in proceedings though, Edwards wasn't too perturbed: 'I was aware of the issue, but really we felt that we could fly someone out overnight if need be, so we didn't feel there was that much pressure for back-up. To be honest maybe I thrived on that. I knew that every team wanted to take my head off, but I felt I just wanted to be in the middle of it, to make my statement on behalf of the Lions.' And he did that day.

Clive Rees, Ian McLauchlan and Tommy David started their second match in succession, Rees switching from the left wing to the right. Edwards and Cotton had already stretched their legs in the first match too. Having come on at tight-head for Carmichael in Potchefstroom, and with Burton still crocked, Cotton started the second match in that same position.

But the rest of the side were all first time starters. Irvine at full-back, JJ Williams on the wing, the combination of Evans and Milliken in midfield and Old at outside-half would all be feeling those 'first night' nerves. The pack once again looked formidable enough on paper – Kennedy in between McLauchlan and Cotton was a Lions veteran, Ralston and Uttley at lock were familiar partners, and two experienced Lions – Davies and Slattery, joined David in the back row.

Windhoek was the highest venue at which the Lions would have to play, even higher than Johannesburg, so altitude and heat were bound to play their part and take their toll this time around. What the Lions weren't expecting was the onslaught from the fired up home side, who had the temerity to take an early lead through a penalty from outside-half Karg.

Old responded with his first points of the tour, before Edwards himself scored the opening try. The home side felt aggrieved, insisting that Edwards had come down short – it wasn't irresistible force but illegal movement that had taken the Welshman over the line. If they were wound up pre-match, they were even more so now, and in response to one skipper's inspirational leadership, the other responded in kind. Ellis picked and drove from the back of a five-yard scrum, and this time there was no doubt that the try was valid.

Old was nervously finding his feet and struggling with the boot. When he took a fist to the face, it was Irvine who slotted the shot at goal. The Lions reached half-time a point ahead at 10–9, but Old, Irvine and the rest were finding life hard on their first Lions outing. They were in a real game this time around.

Nerves were settled somewhat at the beginning of the second half. Clive Rees had an inimitable running style, but it was effective enough. With legs seemingly going one way and body going in another direction entirely, he made it two tries from two matches after latching on to a deft chip from Milliken.

But any breathing space was soon closed down, and the score remained tight. South West African winger Willem Prinsloo scored the try of the game, breaking into midfield and then sprinting for the corner. Despite the attentions of the covering Irvine, he somehow managed to make it to the try line.

By his own admission this match wasn't the Lions full-back's finest. Added to the fumbles and the miss-kicks, the concession of a vital try made for a miserable afternoon: 'I was particularly pumped up for that one, but so were their team. Conditions were totally alien, rock hard ground, so high up, and we struggled. I struggled... I think it was a higher level of rugby than I had been used to. It was an incredibly fast game. And because of the altitude it was incredibly difficult to gauge the high ball and the bounce of the ball. It took a while, so it was a real baptism of fire. In the end Gareth Edwards galvanised us, he inspired us in fact, and we pulled away.'

But not before another penalty from Karg put the home side into a 16–14 lead with ten minutes to go.

The Lions responded with a show of character which would become their trademark over the next twenty matches.

In the heat of the afternoon, in the heat of battle, and in that most rarified of atmospheres, they managed to find a way. A Davies palm from the tail of a line-out found Cotton on a well-rehearsed peel. Irvine, doing what he did best, came bursting into midfield at pace and found Milliken who crossed for the try. At least the Irishman had made a positive impression during the course of the afternoon – and with Irvine adding the conversion and a subsequent penalty the Lions finally found daylight. It ended 23–16 to the tourists, any breath they had left could be exhaled deeply.

JJ Williams was among a number who were left counting bruises and worse that day: 'I took a knock from Jan Ellis on my knee, but I didn't want to tell anyone because I was scared it would affect my chances. So I kept on training afterwards, and basically sorted myself out. Because we were there on our own, just thirty-two of us, it made us mentally tough.'

Watching from the stands, Phil Bennett felt a sense of relief, and a sense of just how important Gareth Edwards was to the tour: 'It was so hot, it was revolting in the shade you know. And looking at those poor bastards playing, I really felt for them. And to be fair Edwards carried them that day, almost single-handed. But they won a game that they could have lost, and the tour took off from there.'

'Moving forward' is one of those dreadful modern-day phrases beloved by those who have something to hide or those who have nothing to say. It's a favourite of politicians, a perfect example of the former, and of sportsmen – all too often a good example of the latter. Back in 1974 it would have been a case of 'onwards and upwards'. There really was little else anyone could say about the Windhoek experience.

Except for Syd Millar that is. He found the Windhoek experience both invaluable and disconcerting. Today, it's the different interpretations of the laws in the northern and southern hemisphere that cause consternation, as evidenced by the 2013 series in Australia. But in previous decades it was blatant bias that upset the tourists.

A list of four prospective Test match officials would be presented to the Lions by the South Africans prior to the First Test, and the tourists would then choose the most acceptable. The candidates would all be South Africans of course, so by no means neutral, but at least the Lions had a say. Cas de Bruyn had refereed poorly during that South West Africa match, and had apologised in person to Millar afterwards. That had been noted.

The coach was also concerned enough about Andy Irvine's form to try a drastic measure. He took JPR Williams aside and asked him to intervene: 'I got asked early in the tour by Syd whether I'd mind taking Andy out and teaching him how to catch a high ball. Well you can't do that – not with a fellow international. And I'm not sure I wanted to teach him anyway, not at that stage, because he was still a rival too.'

So Irvine escaped embarrassment, and the Lions escaped South West Africa. They'd kept their unbeaten record, they'd blooded more raw recruits and most importantly they'd come through unscathed in terms of injuries. Their talisman Edwards had shown the way, and ended the match as he'd begun it – on fine form.

The best news of all though, was that after two weeks in the backwaters of southern Africa the Lions were finally heading for one of its main attractions, Cape Town.

Few Lions would disagree with their esteemed fellow tourist Sir Francis Drake's opinion of the Cape, even if the welcome wouldn't be quite as hospitable as usual.

Reports of Joan Lestor's Commons speech regarding British Embassy staff were filtered through to the Lions on arrival, but in truth it was water off a duck's back by then. Fewer official functions, fewer speeches, less small talk equalled no hardship. They were essentially in their own rugby bubble, immune to the political storm at home, cosseted away from the political tragedy nearby.

At that time, Nelson Mandela was imprisoned five miles off-shore on Robben Island. The place has become a must visit – a pilgrimage almost – to visitors over recent decades. When Barack Obama visited this barren, rocky outcrop, and saw Mandela's cell in 2013, he declared himself 'humbled'. When England's football players were offered a tour of the prison while based in Cape Town during the 2010 World Cup, none took up the offer.

The 1974 Lions weren't afforded the opportunity for a visit. And ignorance was bliss according to JJ Williams: 'We were staying in the Arthur's Seat Hotel. Most likely from my room I could have seen Robben Island. It was never mentioned, I didn't even know it was there.'

And yet for all their lack of interest in, or knowledge of, the political and social battlefield, Williams and his team-mates felt that they were doing some good at least. Cape Town was the place where the Lions would later make history by playing a non-white team for the first time: 'We went into the townships, we had dinner with the black players, we saw the other side of things. And because the Afrikaners were the vainest rugby people in the world, by beating them the way we did, it must have left them questioning their position on everything.'

Andy Irvine, one of the squad's youngest members, was in fact affected by what he saw: 'Once I was out there I could understand more in terms of what was upsetting the anti-apartheid demonstrators so much. It wasn't a nice environment. They weren't allowed to get onto the same buses or trains, to go to the same beaches. Schools and restaurants were segregated. I genuinely didn't realise until I was there how bad things were.'

But the Lions were shielded from the worst of it. JJ Williams credits Alun Thomas for this: 'The boys were protected from all the political stuff by Alun. Even though we criticised him, and made fun of him, he did a good job in lots of ways. He handled all the shit that came our way without much support.'

For the first time since setting foot on South African soil, the Lions could unwind a little, and even brave the cable car journey to the top of Table Mountain. The Cape at the end of May can be a contrary place to say the least in terms of weather, but for the Lions' first visit, even the elements rolled out the red carpet. And even though the British Embassy had refused to do just that, plenty of locals lined up to offer hospitality.

While the players got to be tourists for a couple of days, the management were planning for their next challenge, and Boland were traditionally seen as just that. Based in Wellington, and representing the winelands and west coast, Boland – Afrikaans for the land on top – incorporated a number of South Africa's premier wine growing centres – towns such as Stellenbosch, Paarl and Franschhoek. If the area was an easy and enjoyable day trip from the city, then in rugby terms it was considered a hard day at the office for touring teams.

The match took place on Wednesday, 22 May 1974, the day before Syd Millar celebrated his fortieth birthday. If Millar had a case of sour grapes in terms of the winelands, it was a hangover from his last visit – as a Lions player in 1968 – when he'd been given a stern test by local prop David van der Merwe. He was still playing, and now lay in wait for another unsuspecting tourist.

The Lion dealt the 'dead man's hand' this time around was Fran Cotton: 'I was on the loose-head that day in Wellington as I recall. And I still remember the fella's name too, David van der Merwe. Well we won convincingly, and I didn't really have any issue with him at all if I'm honest. Sometimes different props cause different problems, but he didn't for me that day.' Millar took note.

Cotton was just one of a formidable front eight chosen for the match. Windsor and the fit again Carmichael joined him in the front row. What was already being seen as 'The Old Firm' – McBride and Brown – were in tandem behind them, and David, Ripley and Neary reconvened to replicate the back three from the opening match. David was in fact making his third start in three matches – a necessity due to the continuing fitness concerns over McKinney in particular. The Welsh Williamses were at full-back and wing – along with Tom Grace, making his first appearance of the tour. Milliken and McGeechan partnered up at centre for the first time, while Edwards and Old continued at half-back.

Over 20,000 locals turned out in the sunshine and the heat, but at least this time they were at sea level, and the Lions proceeded to get into their groove soon enough. An early Old penalty was followed by an eye-catching charge from David, providing the impetus for Tom Grace's first try of the tour, with pretty much his first decent touch.

David had a knack for wowing crowds and the odd selector, although he and Wales coach Clive Rowlands never saw eye to eye. Rowlands could appreciate the player's talent nonetheless: 'Tom was a super player when the game was dead, great for getting his team going. The game could be going nowhere, the team could be struggling, and Tom would have done nothing. Then he'd have ten minutes of absolute brilliance and get everyone else going again. Now ten minutes doesn't make you a Test player, but it makes you an important man on a Tuesday or Wednesday, against guys who are kicking shit out of you and making life hard. He was a very good footballer.'

David himself was fully aware of the coach's ambivalence. Considering that Rowlands was on the Lions selection panel too, the flanker was therefore a touch surprised to be selected to tour at all. When he asked Millar about it over a beer one evening, he was told that he owed his selection to Fergus Slattery, who'd returned to the Ireland camp after playing with David for the Barbarians in 1973, and informed Millar that he would be an ideal pick for the hard grounds of South Africa.

And now that he'd made it on tour, the Welshman was determined to make it into the Test side: 'I'd scored two tries in the opener, I'd played the first three, we'd won each one and I was in the form of my life. I was very confident at that point that I'd be a Test player, especially since we were winning.'

Alan Old might not have been quite so confident of grabbing a Test spot, but he was at least settling into his groove, with two kicks either side of half-time extending the Lions' lead. He then set up a try with a huge up and under. JJ Williams had followed up more in hope than expectation, but when the punt was dropped by the covering winger, he picked up and found Milliken in support for his second try in two matches. Old's conversion put the Lions out of sight, and despite a couple of penalties to the home side, it was now a case of each man in red staking his claim.

None did so with more conviction than Milliken. One of the few successes against South West Africa, the Irishman continued to show good form with another forceful display, and his second try of the match again highlighted his knack for being in the right place at the right time.

That prince of outside-halves, Cliff Morgan, once explained that one of his natural attributes, and an advantage he had over his lean, silky Welsh fly-half rival Carwyn James, was the fact that he had 'big buttocks', enabling him to ride tackles. There was much more to Morgan's game than a wide load of course, as there was to Milliken's, but the Irishman shared that particular gift, making him difficult to contain and giving him a sound base in terms of offensive tackling.

With twenty minutes to go, Tom David's tour took a turn down a blind alley. A pulled hamstring meant that he was off, and out of action for the foreseeable future. Uttley came on in his stead, and the rest is history. The Lions meanwhile closed the match out in style. Brown rampaged, McBride supported and crossed for his first try of the tour – not bad for a soon to be thirty-four year old. Then Edwards added one more, his fourth in three games, with an unstoppable burst.

Thirty-three points to six was as convincing a win as anyone could have wished for. Cotton and his cohorts had done their job well, Old and his backs were sharper than in the first two outings, and Cape Town and its environs had proved a fruitful stop off.

Good thing too – next up was a flight to Port Elizabeth on the Eastern Cape, where things were about to take a decidedly nasty turn.

CHAPTER 10

Taking Sides

'If you are neutral in situations of injustice, you have chosen the side of the oppressor. If an elephant has its foot on the tail of a mouse and you say that you are neutral, the mouse will not appreciate your neutrality.'
Archbishop Desmond Tutu

'Dyfal donc a dyrr y garreg'
Welsh Proverb

WHEN IT CAME to apartheid and South Africa, neutrality was indeed a difficult stance to maintain. Everyone had to make their own stand, everyone had to find – and justify – their personal perspectives. This was especially true of the 1974 British and Irish Lions players, and to some extent the same holds true even forty years later.

Gareth Edwards has written extensively about his relationship with South Africa over the years. He clearly loves the country, and always loved the touring experience there. Yet the friendships made and the welcome extended were always balanced by his nagging doubts. He understood that the white Government's policies were abhorrent, he knew that they had to be demolished. How best to do so? He used the old Welsh proverb *'Dyfal donc a dyrr y garreg'* as a part of his reasoning. Its literal translation is 'persistent tapping will eventually break the stone'. If you consistently chip away at something, no matter how big, your efforts will eventually bear fruit.

Even today, Edwards is ambivalent about his decision to tour back in 1974, but he genuinely feels that the Lions' presence, and what they achieved during their visit, may just have been one small chip at the base of the stone.

Of course there were many within South Africa who spent decades chipping away and there were others who broke themselves against the rock.

Port Elizabeth itself saw both the best and the worst of the anti-apartheid struggle during the Seventies. The Eastern Cape likes to think of itself as one of the more progressive, liberal parts of South Africa, both in terms of politics and sport. It is after all the birthplace – and burial ground – of Nelson Mandela. But its claim to progressivism would be truly tested in 1977, by one of the most tragic episodes of the apartheid era.

Local anti-apartheid activist Steve Biko was arrested in the August of that year and taken to a Port Elizabeth police station, where he was interrogated to within an inch of his life. The day-long ordeal in the infamous Room 619 left him with severe brain damage.

He never left police custody, and would die less than a month later.

The details are horrific, and Biko's name has come to symbolise both the terrible oppression of the white regime and the sacrifices made in the name of equality and freedom.

Biko's death inspired others to take up the fight, or in the case of another young man from the Eastern Cape, to escalate his own efforts. Daniel 'Cheeky' Watson was a white rugby player – and a damn good one. Good enough to play on the wing for Eastern Province against the New Zealand All Blacks as a precocious young talent in 1976. Good enough to make his mark in that match, and to be selected for the junior Springboks – the Gazelle XV – to take on the All Blacks once again a few weeks later. One of Watson's team-mates for that match was future South Africa coach Nick Mallett.

In fact Watson was so good he was invited to a full national trial in 1976. He refused the offer. Instead he decided to turn his back on white South African rugby, and with it any chance of fulfilling his childhood dream.

Watson joined a club in the black township of KwaZakhele in Port Elizabeth, and from then on he, along with his older brother Valence, played their rugby among black players and in front of black crowds. They were ostracised by the white community and by the white rugby playing fraternity. Arrested, threatened, shot at, Watson's family also became targets, his home was burned to the ground. He described living a life where he was constantly 'checking the rear view mirror'.

According to Peter Hain, 'Cheeky' Watson is: 'A true hero – a man of immense courage.' Like Biko he came to symbolise the struggle not just in the Eastern Cape, but throughout South Africa and the world.

By 2013, Daniel 'Cheeky' Watson was president of the Eastern Province Rugby Union. His son Luke was captain of their franchise team, The Southern Kings, during their first season of Super 15 rugby.

Unlike his father, Luke Watson did become a Springbok, but he caused huge rifts within South African rugby by doing so. He had been pressing for selection for a couple of seasons before his inclusion in 2007. Many felt his form made him a certainty for the Springboks, but he was continually ignored by national coach, Jake White.

There were claims and counterclaims. Some said that Watson simply wasn't good enough, that there were better players. White himself was quoted as calling Watson: 'A most overrated player.' Others said that his non-selection was down to the coach's bias, to the player's outspoken attitude, and to the fact that Watson carried too much political baggage for White.

When he was eventually selected for the Springboks squad, it wasn't Jake White's decision at all, but a move instigated by SARU President, Oregan Hoskins. The positive discrimination in favour of Watson didn't sit well with White or his Springbok players.

So when Luke Watson did finally play for the full national side he felt like an outsider in the dressing room, even going so far as to claim later that he had to 'struggle to keep myself from vomiting' on the famous Springbok jersey. For his part, Springbok skipper John Smit claimed that Watson's presence was 'cancerous'.

Watson was good enough to win ten caps for South Africa – and held his own on the international stage. He will always feel that he should have been selected purely on merit, and that the political machinations ruined his Springbok career before it ever began.

He continues to be an outspoken critic of the old values, the perceived Afrikaner hypocrisy within South African rugby, and he continues to divide opinion within his own country. Ironically enough, as 2013 came to a close and Jake White took up a new coaching post with the Durban-based Sharks, one of the first phone calls he made was to Luke Watson. The approach, or rapprochement, was to find out whether Watson was fit and might be interested in joining his former national coach in Durban for the 2014 season. White's opinion these days: 'The past belongs in the past.'

In terms of the British and Irish Lions, the Watsons had varying experiences. Luke actually captained the Cape Town-based Western Province side to a narrow defeat against the tourists during the 2009 tour, before essentially fleeing South Africa for the more welcoming rugby climes of Bath.

'Cheeky' Watson was just a nineteen-year-old prospect back in 1974, so missed out on the chance to challenge the unbeaten Lions. By the time they toured again, in 1980, Watson was well on the way to becoming the white rugby fraternity's public enemy number one, and the black rugby fraternity's champion.

He talked about that tour during an interview for *The Independent* newspaper in 2009, and didn't remember it with any fondness: 'I think of the 1980 British & Irish Lions who came here, none of whom, the captain Bill Beaumont included, ever showed any interest in the reality of what was going on in this country. Beaumont's attitude was, he didn't want anything to do with us... Only one player wanted to find out the truth and that was Tony Ward of Ireland. His actions gave us a lot of hope. He said; "Show me what's happening" and we took him to the Townships... The other Lions who just weren't interested? I believe they have a lot of blood on their hands. They are just as guilty as the people that oppressed this country.'

He'd come a long way. Four years before the Lions tour of 1980, Watson himself had been playing against the touring New Zealanders.

Two years before that, as a young up-and-comer, as a local talent and most importantly as a white, he would at least have been allowed to watch the 1974 Lions vintage from the comfort of the stands at Boet Erasmus if he so chose.

At the same time, non-whites were still watching matches at the stadium from their 'cage' in the corner of the ground. Mthobi Tyamzashe was a part of the Eastern Cape's black rugby fraternity: 'The Eastern Cape was rugby country for us too, not football like the rest of South Africa. We were exposed to the game from an early age... It was even our street game, you know, street against street and so forth... But ours was also a highly politicised area. If you look now at people in positions of leadership across the country, you'll find that many of them are originally from the Eastern Cape.'

Tyamzashe lived 'just a stone's throw away' from the spot where Steve Biko was taken away for detention three years later. He was politically aware, but also young and enthusiastic. And so, in 1974, he adopted the British and Irish Lions as his team: 'The visiting team was the team black South Africans tended to support, on the basis that the Afrikaners must be beaten. Someone must take up the fight and help us win.'

The Lions certainly took up the fight. In the match against Eastern Province, there would be fighting, lots of fighting.

CHAPTER 11

The Summer of '99'

'When the legend becomes fact, print the legend.'
The Man Who Shot Liberty Valance, 1962

FILM DIRECTOR JOHN Ford would have appreciated the '99' call. If his own legend is to be believed he enjoyed a good ruck, and he engineered one of the great screen punch-ups between John Wayne and Victor McLaglen in *The Quiet Man*.

And so in 1974, rugby's own Irish pugilist, the Lions' 'Quiet Man' was said to have originated a special call to arms, a rallying cry that would immediately bring all fifteen British and Irish players into confrontation with their nearest opposing player on the pitch. That call was '99'.

If history deals in myth and reality then the '99' call is a prime example of how boundaries can blur over the passing of the years. Ian McLauchlan says it never existed at all, Fergus Slattery called it a 'load of old crap', and a number of other players insisted they never heard it called once throughout the tour. Even McBride himself has started to play down the significance of the '99' in recent years, arguing that the whole thing has been overdone.

So did the actual call exist at all, or is it a tall tale told so often around rugby's camp fires that it has become accepted as fact?

Sitting in the back garden of his family home in Newport, Bobby Windsor responds with a shake of the head when I put this to him. 'Myth... Absolute myth. It all came from a press conference after a dirty match – and there were plenty. A South African journalist asked Willie John if he'd given his boys any command to retaliate to provocation. Willie for some reason came up with this "99" line. And that was it then, the papers were full of it. Of course, over the years it takes on a life of its own, and it's too late to change the story.'

So did they discuss the idea of concerted retaliation? 'Oh yeah, of course. We knew that if one of our boys took a shoeing, everyone should pile in. Not the backs, well except for JPR, but all of us up front. So it was an accepted part of our approach, but we didn't need a call, never.'

Roy Bergiers answers almost word for word along similar lines: 'I didn't hear a call ever. It was a frame of mind. Heck it went all the way back to the Britannia Hotel, we were on our own, and we had to stand up for ourselves. And the Boers, or the Dutch, well they had this pioneer mentality, this hard, uncompromising outlook. They had their own view of us, so we had to change it.'

'It didn't exist' says Fran Cotton: 'There was so much togetherness, so much unity, that if anyone was even touched, there was just a reaction. There was no need for any call.'

JJ Williams adds to the demolition job: 'There was no "99" call... I don't want to spoil the story, but there just wasn't a call. The reason you didn't need one was because it was always the same boys fighting anyway. Gordon, Bobby, Burto, Franny, Mouse, JPR, who'd just come running in like a bloody idiot, Stewart McKinney, who'd happily fight the world. It was the same boys every time. Then you'd have one or two like Merve who'd try and calm things down, and the rest of us, who kept well out of it.'

There are some Lions who still insist to this day that they heard the shout of '99', but when I put the question to the man who supposedly invented the call, adding that I have already spoken to a number of his fellow forwards beforehand, even the great man himself finally admits defeat: 'Yes, it's a myth,' says Willie John McBride: 'We talked about the situation, because I'd been on so many tours where our key players had been roughed up and dumped out of the tour. I was determined that this time we wouldn't take it, but I was also determined that we wouldn't go trying to get our own back individually either. Now before the Eastern Province game, we had an idea of what was coming – they would be targeting Gareth and Benny before the First Test. So it was simple, I said; "In an emergency, it's 999 and we're all in, together. Do you understand?" And boy did they. But there was never a call – ever. It wasn't needed, it was just a natural reaction from anyone near the incident. So there you have the myth of "99".'

Even if the call itself was pure invention, then the policy was fact. And it was borne out of necessity. If ever proof were needed that the Lions should prepare a strategy to combat intimidation, it came on Saturday, 25 May, at the Boet Erasmus Stadium in Port Elizabeth. This was when the tour began in earnest, and the legend of the Lions of '74 started to take shape.

* * *

The Eastern Province side had its own internal controversies, its own dressing room divisions, as the players prepared for the arrival of the Lions. The team would be skippered by prop Hannes Marais, the man earmarked to lead the Springboks in the all-important Test series. Marais was already a rugby legend in his homeland, but he was thirty-two years old by that stage, and had been lured out of retirement for the coming challenge.

Many within the Eastern Province camp felt they were a better team without him, and under the leadership of George Barnard, their number 8. But their coach, Ian Kirkpatrick, was also an assistant with the national side, so Marais was in, and he would lead. Having played against the 1968 Lions,

Marais could have been forgiven for being confident this time around.

In his own words the '68 tourists: 'Were a pretty useless lot, just on tour for the party.' If he was under any misconception that these Lions were cut from the same cloth, he was in for a rude awakening.

It was a record crowd for a provincial match at Boet Erasmus – 30,000 people and more. As they awaited their heroes, Springbok head coach and selector Johan Claassen paid a pre-match visit to the home dressing room. He was intent on giving the players a pep talk.

Willie John McBride and Syd Millar had come across Claassen in his playing days. He was a lock and a Springbok hard man, who'd played against Millar when South Africa beat Ireland at Lansdowne Road in December 1960, and when they did so again in Cape Town the following May. A young, uncapped Willie John McBride had been in the Ulster side, playing the biggest game of his career so far, when South Africa – and Claassen – came to Ravenhill in January 1961. By 1970 Claassen was South Africa's coach, and he was a particularly tough-minded one. Anything less would have been a betrayal of his Afrikaner rugby heritage. In true Corporal Jones fashion, he intimated to the Eastern Province players that the Brits 'didn't like it up 'em', and that they should rough up the 'rooineks'.

Eastern Province played in red and black hoops, the same colours as other famous clubs like Moseley in England and Aberavon in Wales. But as the Lions ran out onto the Boet Erasmus pitch, they were reminded of the last time they played a team in red and black hoops. That was in Christchurch, back in 1971. The team was Canterbury. This was to be Canterbury re-incarnate.

The Lions had juggled as best they could in terms of selection. Almost none of the backs who started against Boland started in Port Elizabeth. Irvine, Steele, Bergiers, Evans, Rees and Bennett all came in. But one constant remained – Edwards at scrum-half. For Bergiers, it was a comeback that brought mixed emotions: 'Yes, very much so. I came back for the Eastern Province game, and I did something I never thought I would. I had injections beforehand. I was pumped with pain killers in order to play. I got through, but Syd and Alun told me afterwards that I wouldn't be considered for the First Test. So I knew from then on really.'

Up front, Windsor also had to start his second match in succession after a training ground injury to Ken Kennedy, while Brown was asked to put in another shift in the second row, partnering Uttley for the first time. Mike Burton was finally ready to get into the action, and was desperate to make his mark alongside Windsor and McLauchlan. The other first time starter was Stewart McKinney on the flank, with Slattery and Davies to keep him company.

With the First Test approaching, it wasn't just the players hoping to make an impression. Each referee during the early matches was hoping that a decent showing would put him in the frame for the big one. Fonnie van der Vyver ruled himself out of the running by completely losing control in Port Elizabeth, and he did so from the very beginning.

Edwards was the natural target, and the Lions looseness at line-out handed the home side plenty of opportunity to pour through on their quarry. Going after Edwards made sense in tactical terms, and some of the hits were perfectly legitimate. Plenty more were late and loose, thuggery was the word that sprang to mind in the stands.

Sandy Carmichael, who had been on the receiving end in Christchurch three years previously, sat on the sidelines thinking it was just like old times: 'There was the biggest punch up you've ever seen in your life... We stood up to them, probably for the first time.' Roger Uttley recalls that everywhere he looked there was a fight: 'They were a thuggish side who tried to work us over... There was fighting left, right and centre, with McKinney and Burton in the middle of it – the boys weren't going to be messed about.'

Edwards as skipper asked the referee to take a harder line, then he asked his opposite number to talk to his players and calm them down. Since Marais was one of the chief culprits, Edwards may as well have tried asking him in Welsh. Finally, he decided that if no-one else was going sort things out, the Lions would have to do so themselves: 'I'd taken a bit of a pummeling early on in that game. They'd been waiting a long time for the chance to get at us. But it actually did us good as a team in one way, because it cemented our unity, and our mental toughness too. It made the new Lions, the boys who were on their first tour, stand up and be counted.'

Terry O'Connor of *The Daily Mail* remembered that fists weren't the only thing flying. An empty whisky bottle landed at the feet of Clive Rees, other projectiles were thrown too. Post-match, O'Connor stirred up a hornet's nest by expressing his opinion in print that there were some South Africans who were still unable to forget the Boer War.

Under the circumstances though, he could be forgiven that sentiment. Especially when one considers that in the weeks that followed, as his Springbok side was humiliated by the Lions, South Africa's coach Claassen would become more and more extreme in his Afrikanerdom.

The Broederbond was at that stage a secret and particularly powerful association. In simplistic terms, a Calvinistic equivalent of the Freemasons, it was dedicated to the advancement of white, Afrikaner interests. And white Afrikaner interests during the South African winter of 1974 consisted of asserting their rugby dominance over the British and Irish Lions, the oldest enemy, in any which way they could.

Despite the fact that it endorsed Dr Danie Craven's nomination for the Presidency of South Africa's Rugby Board, even Doc Craven himself was said to be mistrustful of the organisation's motives and influence. But both Johan Claassen and Hannes Marais were viewed as prominent

159

Broederbonders, men who saw themselves as rugby warriors, defending the honour of the Afrikaner people.

In their examination of the Springboks' sporting psyche, *Rugby and the South African Nation*, David Black and John Nauright recounted how anti-apartheid campaigner and journalist Donald Woods remembered Claassen's deepening entrenchment in 1974: 'As the losses mounted', team meetings became increasingly 'Afrikanerised... The national coach, Johan Claassen, a leading Broederbonder, eventually spoke no English at all in his team talk.'

As the Test series progressed, English speaking players from the Cape would become more marginalised, as Claassen brought in increasing numbers of Transvaalers and Free Staters. Speaking in Afrikaans was practical therefore, but speaking solely in Afrikaans could be construed as particularly pointed.

This wasn't anything new. There was a famous story about the selection of Western Province's Stephen Fry to captain the Springboks in their series against the Lions back in 1955. That particular choice had caused uproar among the Highveld Afrikaners, to such an extent that one leading rugby man was heard to exclaim that: 'You don't play an Englishman against an Englishman, you play a Boer against an Englishman.'

And Johan Claassen, who'd played all four Tests in 1955, was most definitely a Boer. Whatever language he used in the Eastern Province dressing room in Port Elizabeth, its effect was incendiary. The players had been charged with sending out a message at Boet Erasmus, and they did so with their fists. The Lions, as instructed by McBride, answered in kind.

As well as the ever eager Brown, who gave as good as he got for the full eighty minutes, the new boys were particularly enthusiastic about the prospect of venting their frustrations. Burton saw this as a chance to make up for lost time, and he started to deliberately leave space so as to invite Eastern Province forwards through on Edwards. Once they'd taken the bait he would fill the breech with his flailing fists. Windsor, the team enforcer, was glad to see the rest of his pack doing what he'd asked of them pre-tour, backing up their own.

McKinney, another pugnacious pugilist, was also a strict adherent to the new law of the jungle. He took aim first at an opponent who'd done the unthinkable and clobbered Brown, but he saved his coup de grâce for the second half, and for the cameras.

There was no national television in South Africa until 1976, which makes the scant surviving footage of the 1974 tour a rare treat for rugby fans. One of the few enduring images is of McKinney laying out Eastern Province flanker Kerrie van Eyck.

It had been a long time coming. When a line-out fracas spilled over into midfield, and Eastern Province number 8 Barnard stamped all over Chris Ralston, Gordon Brown took exception and took out the culprit.

As play swept back towards the touchline, a cluster of bodies grappled on the floor, oblivious to all around them. Mervyn Davies threw the entangled van Eyck clear of the scuffle by his collar, just as McKinney arrived and landed a knockout left hook.

He had obviously picked his target, convinced that van Eyck had kicked him more than once earlier in the match. As the home flanker toppled to the ground, Roy Bergiers had to jump out of the way – time seemed to stand still, as though no-one could quite believe they were taking part in such a surreal and unedifying event:

'It was like watching dominos fall, one after the other – one of ours, one of theirs, up and down the field' remembers Bergiers: 'I had experienced it before, but not since I was at college. It was like going as a student up to places like Fleur de Lys. And you'd have these grizzled old valley boys looking forward to it all year. They'd be thinking they were going to sort these pups out and have some fun. The difference at Boet Erasmus was that we weren't students, we weren't pups. We had a couple of old heads who just would not be intimidated.'

Luckily for McKinney and the rest, the referee was nowhere in sight, and no-one was sent off. The safety in numbers philosophy was proved to be right – both in terms of sorting out the intimidation and in terms of getting away with their own acts of violence. A referee simply couldn't send everybody off.

According to Windsor: 'You could have gone onto that pitch with a pickaxe and no-one would have done anything about it. It was open warfare, and the ref was just saying that he was following the ball. It was a license for carnage.' It was also a refereeing response that the Lions would get used to – an official with his eyes on the ball was bound to miss certain offences. In terms of expecting any protection, the Lions were on their own.

There was a rugby match played in Port Elizabeth too, and the Lions won that as well. Tries by Slattery, Davies and Steele and a plentiful supply of penalties for Phil Bennett ensured that they were always comfortable, leading by twenty-eight points to four at one stage in the second half. They let Eastern Province back into things late on, and it ended 28–14, but once again the forwards had dominated, significantly so against a side containing the Springbok captain.

Meanwhile the backs had played rugby, none more so than the weaving, darting Irvine, recovering his confidence after an uncertain start to the tour, and his fellow Scotsman Steele on the right wing. He scored one of the tries of the tour in Port Elizabeth, rounding off a move instigated by Bennett.

The outside-half was starting to show his razzle-dazzle with ball in hand by this stage, and after taking a pass moving blind, he jinked once, jinked twice and was suddenly moving in completely the opposite direction, out into open play. Irvine was up from full-back, and the ball swiftly found its way through the hands of Milliken and Bergiers to Steele out on the touchline.

There were three Eastern Province backs flying across to head him off, but Steele casually stepped inside off his right foot and, as all three defenders kept on going full pelt over the touchline, he sauntered over for the try behind their backs.

The Lions could be pleased with their day's work. Besides the pugilistic pilgrims Burton and McKinney, McLauchlan could also take a bow, having given Marais a particularly hard time. And Edwards had come through his trial by combat, both as captain and player. The only cause for concern was a late injury to Windsor and the Lions line-out. Both would get some extra attention over the next few days and both would come back stronger.

They'd made their statement. They would not be bullied. And so the legend of '99' was born.

They now proceeded to make another, equally impressive statement, by posting a record score in their next match.

CHAPTER 12

Record Breakers, History Makers

'They inspired us, and I decided to come to Wales
[to coach] because I adored the style they were playing.
I drew energy from what they did.'
Peter de Villiers, Springbok coach, 2008–11

SOUTH WEST DISTRICTS was a definite 'gimme', a term that was given a fair old airing recently in terms of the Lions 2013 tour to Australia. There were complaints then that the Australians had devalued the tour by fielding weakened teams in the pre-Test provincial matches. The accusation was that the locals were holding their best players back, preparing them for the Test series. This not only denied the Lions a look at them, but meant that they weren't given a decent challenge before the Tests.

There is an alternative argument that having been pushed hard by Queensland, having lost to Australian Capital Territory, and having lost ten key players to injury at various stages of the tour, the Lions had plenty of challenges to deal with as things stood.

They were flying replacements in from the four corners of the globe, and any tougher an itinerary could have derailed the tour completely. Balance is difficult, but it is also the key in so many ways on a Lions tour. Easier matches early on help build confidence and mould partnerships, but touring sides also need a taste of Test match intensity before the Tests themselves. That balance was far easier to get right on a twenty-two match tour than on its modern-day ten-match equivalent.

But what price someone in the next few years suggesting that the way forward for the Lions is to revert to the traditional four-match Test series, while curtailing the number of provincial matches? Some influential figures have already thought such things out loud. One such is Andy Irvine, at the very heart of modern-day Lions rugby and therefore perfectly placed to judge its future.

On the Fourth Test scenario he has this to say: 'It has to be a possibility, yes. But I still think it's unlikely... I am concerned about the makeup of future tours in regard to the Wednesday games though, because it is now becoming very apparent that both South Africa [in 2009] and Australia pulled their top players out of the Wednesday matches, and I wouldn't be surprised if New Zealand do likewise [in 2017], because the prize of the Test series is so great... From our point of view it means that we can be undercooked by the time the Test series comes around, and I'd say that the fans get a wee bit short-changed too... But if that's the price we have to pay for the continuation of Lions tours, then it's certainly a price I'd be willing to pay.'

So the 'gimme' is still there – for now – and still serves its purpose. After the trials of Port Elizabeth, the 1974 tourists were actually ready for an easier run out anyway.

Mossel Bay, home of the South West Districts, was situated around halfway between Cape Town to the west and Port Elizabeth to the east, and for one Lion, Alan Old, it was exactly halfway to paradise.

A week and a half before the First Test, everyone was looking for pointers. Old started at half-back with the fully fit John Moloney, and no-one was more thrilled than Gareth Edwards. Outside them were Milliken and Evans at centre, with Grace, JJ Williams and Irvine making up the back three.

Burton and Cotton flanked Kennedy in the front row, captain McBride was joined by Ralston at lock, while McKinney, Slattery and Davies, the back row trio who'd fought their way through the Battle of Boet Erasmus, were kept en masse. They were hoping for an easier afternoon's work this time around – but couldn't have imagined just how easy it would be.

The Lions notched up a record ninety-seven points without reply, scoring sixty of them in a second-half exhibition. JJ Williams, getting twitchy after scoring no tries in two outings so far, finally got his tour off the mark in some style. His six-try haul equalled the record set by David Duckham against West Coast/Buller in 1971. Alan Old topped even that. His total of thirty-seven points was an outright record for a Lion, eclipsing both Bob Hiller's twenty-three-point effort against Border back in 1968 and Phil Bennett's twenty-three points versus Western Transvaal a few weeks earlier. It's a record which still stands to this day.

There were sixteen tries all in all. Added to Williams's six, there was one each for Slattery, Moloney, Old, Grace and Davies, a brace for JPR Williams, and a hat-trick for Geoff Evans. JPR had come on as a replacement for Grace, with Irvine moving across to wing. It was a move that would pay huge dividends for the Scotsman as the tour progressed.

* * *

Having completed their missionary work, and indulged in an extra bit of well-earned rest and relaxation, the Lions headed back to Cape Town, and prepared to face one of their long established and traditionally difficult foes, Western Province.

The Saturday before the First Test is usually the time for a Lions coach to parade his prospective first XV. Eleven of Warren Gatland's starting fifteen for the First Test in Brisbane in 2013 played the preceding Saturday against New South Wales – but for Jamie Roberts's injury it might well have been twelve.

In 1974, the figure was nine, an indication that things didn't quite go as well as intended against Western Province. There is another theory – and an equally valid one – that there was absolutely no intention of going into the First Test with the same line-up as played that provincial match at Newlands anyway.

It later emerged that Syd Millar deliberately fielded a mixed side so as not to give the game away. The theory that he wanted to keep the Springboks guessing is confirmed by Roy Bergiers, who was selected for the Western Province game despite being told that he would not be considered for the First Test. Did that knowledge hurt?

'Yes it did. You felt, hang on, you'd trained hard before the tour, prepared well, found form, then the first game, that injury happened. Initially I was terrified they'd send me home. At least that didn't happen, but getting that far and then not being able to go all the way hurt... Of course, they won the First Test in Cape Town, and then just kept on winning.'

The full Lions side for this their sixth match was Williams at full-back, Rees and Steele at wing, McGeechan and Bergiers in the middle, with Bennett and Edwards at half-back. Seven of the forward eight had started the very first match of the tour. McLauchlan, Windsor, and Carmichael reconvened for the first time since Western Transvaal, McBride and Brown were in tandem, while Neary and Ripley were joined by McKinney, playing his third game on the trot thanks to David's tight hamstring.

The fixture took place at the famous Newlands Stadium, venue for the First Test, prompting some South Africans to voice their concern about the fact that the Lions would be getting a far better feel for the ground than the home side prior to the big match. Since Cape Town is the most English of South Africa's cities, Western Province were in many ways deemed the most similar of opponents. The team sheet would have a large proportion of British names, there was seldom the fervent antagonism experienced elsewhere from either the players or the crowd, and even the style of play was familiar. Yet Western Province were expected to push the Lions hard. They did.

In front of a packed house of 45,000, a bigger crowd than for the Springboks' international the following week according to some figures, the famous blue and white hoops kept it fast and loose, too loose at the start in fact.

It was the Lions who scored first, after just four minutes, and from the very first scrum of the game. A huge shove pushed the Western Province eight off their own ball, Edwards threw out a reverse pass and Bennett pumped the ball skywards. Bergiers took full-back Brink man and ball, but somehow the home team managed to scramble the ball clear on their own try line. What followed was comedic if you weren't wearing a blue and white hooped shirt. The relieving kick out of defence was anything but – travelling horizontally across the face of the posts towards the far corner. There, waiting gratefully was Clive Rees, who simply had to catch and fall in order to score the try.

Bennett kept the scoreboard ticking over before Brown pitched up in an ever more familiar supporting role to capitalise on a JPR Williams charge.

It was one of the tries of the tour, the full-back taking the ball on halfway and sidestepping his way once, twice, three times past on-rushing defenders and into space. Finally stopped on the twenty-five, he threw out a basketball pass to the supporting lock. An outrageous dummy – to nobody in particular – took Brown past one man, and then he simply aimed straight at the next and charged over him to score.

Williams on a counter-attacking burst was a common sight by 1974, but Brown's knack of timing a run, and building up a head of steam was a surprise. His new found fitness gave him another dimension. With ball in hand, momentum on his side and the line in sight, the Scotsman was a formidable proposition.

With an eleven-point lead, the Lions should have taken

the game away, but instead it was the Capetonians who came back fighting. And playing... For the first time the Lions were faced with a side which was not only winning the breakdown battle, but knew how to use the ball they won. Winger Read scored a try, the Western Province back row, with skipper Morné du Plessis and Jan 'Boland' Coetzee leading the way, targeted Bennett and profited, and as they went into the second half it was the Lions who looked ragged.

Despite another well-worked try from Read, the Lions just about kept their noses in front, some stern talking and even sterner tackling from Edwards and Williams in particular vital to the cause. They carried their side to the finish, and came out ahead by seventeen points to eight. That match, played on 1 June, was the last time a try would be scored against the Lions 'Saturday' team until the Fourth Test, the last match of the tour, on 27 July.

It was a match which would have a huge bearing on the tour in a number of ways. The home side's showing influenced the Springbok selectors as they looked ahead to the following Saturday. It also influenced Lions selection – if no-one had played themselves into a Test berth, one or two had definitely played themselves out.

It was also a match that had a huge bearing on one young South African fan. Peter de Villiers was a schoolboy in Paarl when the Lions of '74 toured his homeland, and when he went to watch matches in Newlands he watched, like all non-whites, from behind the wire.

He was there as a fifteen year old on 1 June 1974, and the experience left an indelible mark. The fact that the Lions played all comers off the park during the rest of the tour left another. And when John Moloney and Mike Burton visited his school, he became a Lions convert forever more.

Thirty-five years later, Peter de Villiers would coach South Africa to a two-one series win over the 2009 Lions tourists. He would do so proudly, as the first black coach of the mighty Springboks.

De Villiers wasn't the only fan at Newlands who came to regard the Lions with awe. They became heroes to any number of non-whites.

On the pitch, Western Province's captain Morné du Plessis took note: 'Things were different when touring sides came to Cape Town. The All Blacks in 1970 had come over and been supported by the non-white community too, so I understood the anomaly. I could play for Western Province one week and we'd have absolutely fanatical support, and the next week – in the same ground – those same supporters would be cheering the opposition. We lived with that. It's difficult for the new South Africa to even understand, or comprehend. But that was the way it worked, it was life at that time.'

The next match for the 1974 vintage would divide even non-white opinion. They would play against the Proteas, the South African Rugby Board's officially sanctioned 'coloured' team, on the following Tuesday. Some observers would view the fixture as a propaganda exercise, others as a step in the right direction. Some Lions would see it simply as a chance to stake a claim for a Test spot, others would value the opportunity of building bridges. A number of English players felt that the match was simply going to be dangerous. One of that number was about to have his tour ended in the cruellest fashion.

CHAPTER 13

Blood, Sweat, Tears and Fears

'This is a city whose people tasted non-racialism long before the rest of South Africa. As early as the nineteenth century, black and coloured people had the vote in the Cape.'

Helen Zille, Western Cape Premier,
Leader Democratic Alliance Party

So CAPE TOWN would be the setting for a new and controversial chapter in Lions history. In practical terms, it simply had to be the Cape, just as it had been for England two years previously. Here the Lions would play the 'coloured' Proteas, the SAR Federation XV, and claim forever more that they'd done some good.

In some ways maybe they did.

The match took place at the Goodwood Stadium, the Cape Town sun kept up its unseasonably good work, and there were 20,000 mostly coloured supporters there to watch. However unpopular the fixture was in some quarters, there were obviously plenty who felt it worthy of attention. To the Proteas team, the fixture meant everything, Captain Dougie Dyers explaining that: 'It was another chip away at the old apartheid block... We were showing the whites that this is the way the world is. You must adapt or you die.'

Even today, talk of the Proteas and what they stood for causes division among non-white South Africans. Dougie

Dyers has taken his fair share of flak over the years, and been called more than his fair share of names. Yet he is still happy to explain his thinking, still patient enough to answer questions, in order to present the Proteas case. And he still believes that the side played a role in changing attitudes within South Africa: 'I am of the opinion that for our community to get recognition in our own country, the opportunity to play against the Lions was a real step forward. Yes, there was opposition, but there was also support from the non-white community – just look at the crowd that day. I felt it wasn't good to hate everything that was white, so we made use of the system to push for integration.'

Roy Bergiers expressed a similar sentiment from a Lions' perspective. Was it a positive in political terms? 'Yes very much so, we felt we were breaking down barriers. We were visiting townships, meeting people from the black community. And we were also conscious that they were our supporters. They knew we were different. So it was a big game in a number of ways.'

Willie John McBride didn't play in the match itself, but feels even now that the fixture, followed by the one against the Leopards, is vindication of the tour going ahead: 'If we hadn't have gone, what good would that have done? And it's not just turning out for the games. We sat down with their players and administrators. Little things, but little things mean a hell of a lot, don't they, in the bigger picture.'

When the Proteas had played England in 1972, they had run the tourists uncomfortably close, eventually losing by just eleven points to six. But a few of the England team felt that the physicality of the match went way beyond the normal bounds. The political and emotional importance invested in the occasion meant that they felt duty-bound not to retaliate. The Lions would face a very similar conundrum.

With both McBride and Edwards rested before the First Test, the side was led by Fergus Slattery. The back line comprised Irvine, Grace, Evans, Milliken, Williams, Old and Moloney. Irvine and Moloney knew that they wouldn't be starting the following match, but all the others still felt they were in with a shout. Up front Cotton, Kennedy and Burton were backed up by the experience of Brown and the athleticism of Ralston. The back row was possibly the most interesting selection, especially considering that the fancied three of McKinney, Neary and Ripley had underperformed against Western Province. Davies was flanked by Roger Uttley, starting for the first time at 6 and Slattery himself at 7.

It was carnage from the off, as Slattery later recalled: 'They were tackling us before we had the ball, when we had the ball, and after we got rid of the ball.' The watching JBG Thomas wrote diplomatically that there was: 'Uncontrolled enthusiasm on the part of the Proteas, and remarkable restraint on the part of the Lions.'

Cotton was among those who could only restrain himself so long. He is captured in one photograph as he is just about to land a right cross on the chin of an opponent, and there is already another Protea prone at his feet clutching his face. Yes, Cotton was happy to demonstrate that he had 'knuckle' aplenty when it was needed: 'I'd played against the Proteas in '72, so I'd warned the boys that there would be a total lack of discipline throughout the game... And we just had to take the law into our own hands. Of course, we were aware of the political sensitivities, but we found some of their play totally unacceptable.'

It was one of those games where Roy Bergiers felt you needed eyes in the back of your head: 'These players were putting their bodies on the line, tackling with whatever part of their body they could, even if that meant the head. They were physically hard and they'd just bounce back up from a tackle and off they'd go again. Dirtyness? No, probably not. Enthusiasm? Yes – they would have died for their cause out there.'

Having watched the England encounter two years previously from the touchline, Alan Old had admitted that the only match he didn't want to play in on the 1974 tour was against the Proteas.

His dread would be well-founded. A player is physically at his most vulnerable in open play just before or just after he has the ball in hand. After twenty minutes Old threw a pass, and was caught late and low by centre Christian Cupido.

Cupido's arrow struck hard, but there was no love involved. Old's body position was so exposed that he was spun skywards. His left knee was shattered on impact. The initial sound, followed by the scream, was enough to send shudders through all present. He managed to hobble off the field eventually, and, after an inordinately long wait for an ambulance, was accompanied to hospital by his fellow outside-half, Phil Bennett.

The Welshman called it: 'The worst tackle I'd ever seen.'

Ken Kennedy was playing, the management felt they had to stay, so Bennett took responsibility for Old over the next two hours. It is not an episode he looks back on with any fondness: 'I took him to hospital because the management needed to stay with the team I suppose. But it was the one time I think there was a misstep on tour, it was amateur – amateur that there was no official doctor to look after him, amateur in every way. It was wrong really, I shouldn't have been the one there holding his hand. I could see his leg all over the place, he's literally screaming, and there's nothing to give him. Then we get to the hospital and it's the wrong bloody hospital... Being honest, looking back now, that wasn't the right way to treat a man who'd been so badly injured playing for the British Lions.'

In practical terms Old's injury would guarantee Bennett's place in the starting line-up for the First Test, but in emotional terms Old was his friend, and: 'You wouldn't wish that kind in injury on your worst enemy.'

The journey to hospital involved the ambulance crashing into other vehicles and losing its way – it would have made for great comedy value if not for the fact that Old was in such dreadful pain. His knee ligaments were shot, there followed an operation, and a stint in plaster. Old's tour was over. For Bennett, that day, and the ones immediately afterwards, were an emotional rollercoaster: 'You can't help but think if you're in my shoes; "That's Alan out of the tour, so I've got to be in haven't I?" But then you're thinking; "There but for the grace of God go I." And then of course you start feeling the guilt, the worry that he wouldn't ever walk again, let alone play again. So all those emotions are running through your head. I wouldn't want any man alive to go through what I saw Alan go through. It was horrible.'

* * *

As Old – and Bennett – were heading for hospital, the Goodwood show went on. Milliken moved to fly-half, Bergiers came on at centre. Uttley made a charge for the line and flipped a wonderful pass from behind his back towards the on-rushing Kennedy. Slattery was on his shoulder to take the next pass, and backed by his whole pack, the captain was driven over. If Uttley needed to score marks in order to get into Test match contention on the flank, he had done just that.

Gordon Brown added the second – his third in five matches, and although they led by only 13–6 at half-time, their fitness and class prevailed during the last quarter.

Tries from Bergiers, JJ Williams and Milliken exposed the Proteas' deficiencies in technique and experience. Quick thinking and hard running saw the Lions home.

The final score of thirty-seven points to six was comfortable, but the on-field experience had been anything but. Despite Old's injury, the Lions players found the time to mix with their counterparts afterwards. Edwards remembers: 'Talking to those boys afterwards, having a beer, it was the most important thing they'd done in their rugby lives.'

Captain Dyers remembered years later that: 'It made our people believe that they were good enough. We tried to be positive, and won support that way. When we played against England in 1972, we only lost by eleven points to six. The Lions were tougher, but actually I think that the likes of Willie John McBride and his squad did their bit. The whole thing paid off in the end... It eventually paved the way for multiracial trials, multiracial teams, and it paved the way for my people... We showed that we weren't a sub-species of anybody... Given the opportunity, anyone was good enough.'

One Protea certainly was. Outside-half Errol Tobias had dropped a goal, kicked a penalty and generally looked a class apart. He was twenty-four then, and coming into his prime. Seven years later, and a touch slower at thirty-one, he won the first of six Springbok caps against Ireland at Newlands. He was at centre that day, alongside Springbok great Danie Gerber. He went on to win five more caps, including four at outside-half, and toured New Zealand with South Africa in 1981.

When I mentioned Tobias to Roy Bergiers, he hadn't been aware of the connection. In fact he was taken aback, and then genuinely moved: 'Good God. I really wasn't aware, and I have a tingling feeling all over just hearing that name. Errol Tobias, crikey yes... When you say that name now, I feel a sense of pride. He was able to play against us and go on to something more. It makes you feel that something good came out of it.'

When pressed on the subject, Bergiers admitted to it being an emotional realisation: 'I just hadn't thought... But to know that I played against him, well... I just feel honoured. I want to go back through the old scrapbook now to find out more.'

When I asked Dougie Dyers about the impact of that match in relation to Errol Tobias, he had this to say: 'Yes, of course, it gave Errol a platform, it gave us all a platform, absolutely. Remember we had no facilities, very few opportunities, but at least it gave us a chance to show what we were capable of... Errol, and then Avril Williams, became Springboks despite the apartheid regime being in power. In fact long before the apartheid regime lost its grip on the country. To us that was a victory, and it is a vindication. Rugby was integrated long before we had democracy.'

After accepting the invitation to play for South Africa, Tobias was the target of unrelenting abuse from both sides of the apartheid divide.

He took extras on that unhappy, bitterly controversial tour of New Zealand in 1981. Branded a collaborator and an 'Uncle Tom' by anti-apartheid campaigners, he was seen as a 'token black' by many Afrikaners, a number of them his own Springbok team-mates. But the fact remains that Errol Tobias was the first non-white rugby player to play for South Africa, and that a full eleven years before the country rid itself of apartheid and held its first democratic elections. He played fifteen matches in the Springbok jersey, and scored twenty-two points in those six Test matches, including two demolitions of England in 1984.

Tobias was a supremely brave as well a supremely talented individual. Others, like Avril Williams and his nephew Chester, like Breyton Paulse and Chiliboy Ralepelle came afterwards. They excelled in the Springbok jersey too, as a part of the new multiracial South Africa.

From recent superstars like Bryan Habana, JP Pietersen and Tendai Mtawarira to budding stars like Siya Kolisi in 2013 – all owe something, however small, to the first.

And possibly – just possibly, to the Proteas too.

Yet even Tobias's story isn't enough to convince opponents that the Proteas and their like were anything other than traitors to the anti-apartheid cause. Peter Hain insists that: 'They called the Proteas and Leopards groundbreaking. Well they weren't, to me that's a total smokescreen. Black players needed passes to go and play games outside their own areas. They couldn't use the same facilities, the same changing rooms... I think it made the Lions team even more reprehensible that they went along with that charade.'

Those Lions have had a long time to ponder their actions.

Some simply don't feel the need to defend themselves, others maintain that whatever their motives for going, by doing so they did something positive. Bobby Windsor speaks for most: 'Don't tell me we didn't do any good. We did something – we played those sides, for the first time ever – and it was tremendous. Having a pint with them afterwards, it meant something – to them and to us. We were playing with and mixing with black people in South Africa, wasn't that something? I think we did more than we get credit for.'

According to former South African sports administrator Mthobi Tyamzashe, that Lions tour did have an impact both on and off the pitch, as did those controversial matches: 'It helped unearth talent that might otherwise have gone unnoticed, including Errol Tobias... So in a strange sort of a way, yes, it could be seen as a turning point. I don't want to overstate it, to say that it was anything bigger than it was. But having them here was one small cog, or one spoke, in the giant wheel that would then move progressively forward. That's how I see the tour.'

The final word in terms of the Proteas really should belong to Errol Tobias. He was fully aware of the schism, and the hostility from both sides, when he finally got his international call-up, yet he took his chance: 'Some people reacted furiously to my selection' he said years later: 'They felt that the apartheid laws should be removed before I played for South Africa... I was no politician... My goal was to show the country and the rest of the world that we had black players who were equally as good, if not better, than the whites, and that if you were good enough you should play.'

He was good enough, and he did play.

CHAPTER 14

'Ngadla' — I Have Eaten

'They do not respect us here. They do not rate us... You now have an awesome responsibility. This is your Everest boys. Very few have the chance in rugby terms to get to the top of Everest. You have the chance today. Being picked is the easy bit. To win for the Lions in a Test match is the ultimate.'

Jim Telfer, Assistant Coach, pre-match speech,
Lions vs South Africa, First Test, Cape Town, 1997

So THIS WAS it, Test match week in Cape Town. Thursday, 6 June, was Willie John McBride's thirty-fourth birthday and he spent it in cahoots with his coach, mulling over some of the biggest calls of the tour: 'The decision on Benny was taken out of our hands anyway, thankfully. But there were others. The props were so close, Ripley and Mervyn, Neary or Slattery in the back row. How do you say to Tony Neary that he's not in? That could have been the breaking point of the tour. If we didn't get that right, if we didn't win, then we'd have been in trouble. When you win nobody can question anything can they?'

While McBride and Millar deliberated, the South African selectors announced their side for the First Test. Much is made of the fact that the Springboks hadn't played a Test match for two years. Less is made of the fact that the Lions hadn't played one in three. But at least the tourists were battle hardened by the Five Nations, and had spent the past month in each other's company, playing, partying, and bonding.

South Africa would to a certain extent come together as strangers. This begins to explain why the selectors chose to base their XV around a core from one particular team.

Their last match, the 1972 defeat by England, had been under the captaincy of Piet Greyling, who had taken over after the retirement of Hannes Marais. It was his only game as skipper, and he didn't play for the Springboks again. Yes, the embarrassment was that acute. So much so that Marais himself had been persuaded to put away pipe and slippers in order to take charge again this time around.

Were they undercooked? Possibly. If so, Peter Hain's policy of isolating the Springboks was working. Take that supposition one step further and you might argue that he in fact helped the Lions secure their historic triumph. Hain himself is circumspect on this count: 'Yes, maybe it did. That wasn't the intention I can assure you.'

As it was, the Springbok selectors chose six of the side that had lost in its previous international against England. Dawie Snyman from Western Province had won his first cap at outside-half in that match, Gert Muller of the Transvaal had played on the wing.

Up front, Jan Ellis at flanker, John Williams of Northern Transvaal at lock, Piston Van Wyk, another Northen Transvaaler at hooker and the Transvaal's Sakkie Sauermann at prop were all selected again.

In terms of experience, Hannes Marais had been a Springbok as far back as 1963, Ellis was in his ninth season as an international, and Muller had donned his first South Africa jersey in 1969. Ian McCallum at full-back and Piston Van Wyk had been blooded successfully against the All Blacks in 1970. Sauermann was a veteran of both winning series' against France and Australia in 1971, as was John Williams, while Morné du Plessis had joined them in Australia to win his first cap at number 8. So that left six new caps, Kevin de Klerk of the Transvaal at lock, as well as centres Peter Whipp and Kol Oosthuizen, winger Chris Pope, scrum-half Roy

McCallum and flanker Boland Coetzee. Those five were all from Western Province.

Even though they played for different provinces, the two McCallums for South Africa were brothers. Ian at full-back had starred for the Springboks in their defeat of the All Blacks in 1970. He played for Natal, though not often enough – his profession as a doctor, and the form of rival Malcolm Swanby limiting his game time. When the selectors held their trial on the same day as the Lions played the Proteas, Ian's brother Roy hadn't even made it onto the pitch. Yet some underwhelming performances from other contenders added to his own showing against the Lions for Western Province, helped his cause. The fact that his provincial team-mate Dawie Snyman was to start at number 10 also worked in his favour, so the younger McCallum also got the nod. They would be the first brothers to take to the field for the 'Boks in over two decades, but they would find the experience anything but enjoyable.

In a series where they made mistake after mistake, where a lack of vision quickly descended into panic, the Springbok selectors had started early. Western Province had put up the best showing so far against the Lions, but they were the only major team to have played their fixture so far. They had also played their open, attacking brand of rugby in the sunshine. Just as the Springbok selectors were announcing that they'd picked seven Western Province players to run the Lions off their feet, it started to rain. Then it rained some more.

For the Lions, everything revolved around the front row. The unluckiest player in the party was quite possibly Sandy Carmichael. Having missed out in New Zealand through thuggery, he missed out again now. His injury early in the tour, as well as that to Mike Burton, had given Fran Cotton a chance to impress at tight-head. He had never looked back.

And yet Cotton wasn't expecting his own inclusion: 'Yes, I was surprised, because I hadn't played against Western Province. Sandy and Ian had started that game and went pretty well too. But I think they'd asked Bobby's advice in terms of who he felt was more suited, and I think he said that he'd prefer me.'

The man who could actually have influenced front row selection was Ian McLauchlan, invited, along with Gareth Edwards to air his views before the team was finally committed to paper.

Did 'The Mouse' have a hand in Cotton's elevation therefore? 'I hope so, I certainly knew how I felt about it, and who I wanted. Fran was like an immoveable object. He was a very tough man. Bobby was also a very tough man – and then some. South Africa had to be subdued. Bobby was the one to do it.'

With Ian McLauchlan and Windsor shoe-ins for the other two places, the front row had the lopsided look of a rickety set of steps. 'Packing down with The Mouse was like putting your arm around your missus' recalled Windsor, who had the difficult job of finding a modicum of comfort in between the 6' 2" Cotton on one side, and McLauchlan at 5' 8" on the other. Windsor, a sharpened stud length taller than the Scotsman in the middle, was more than happy with the players on either side of him.

Brown to accompany McBride in the second row was also a racing certainty. Athletic, abrasive, and already a winning Lion, he was a man for the big occasion. McBride, who hadn't won once in the six Tests he'd played for the Lions on South African soil, was confident that this time he would break his duck.

For all their strengths, the relative vulnerability of McBride and Brown in the line-out may well have influenced the thinking in terms of back row selection, where decisions would prove difficult and contentious. Tommy David had made giant strides early in the tour only to be hamstrung, while McKinney's late start meant he didn't have enough time to press his case fully. He, along with Ripley and Neary, had been comprehensively outplayed in their previous outing against Western Province.

Whereas their opponents Coetzee, Du Plessis and Dugald Macdonald had played themselves very much into their selectors thinking, Ripley and Neary now missed out. Mervyn Davies was chosen at 8, Slattery at 7 and Uttley, who had done enough against the Proteas to show his potential at 6, was the third of the trio.

In fact, if it was to be a battle first and an exhibition second, then the choices were perfectly sensible. McBride was among a number of team-mates who put Mervyn Davies at the top of the pile: 'The difference between Mervyn and Andy Ripley was control of the ball. He'd never let you down Merve, never lose anything. You only really noticed it when you played with him. But he was a truly great player.'

Both Davies and Slattery were men for all seasons, whilst Uttley would provide extra height, options and know-how at the tail of the line-out as well as extra set-piece bulk. What Peter Dixon and Derek Quinnell had done three years previously in New Zealand, he was to do this time.

Ripley was hugely disappointed, admitting to Uttley years later that he: 'Wasn't embittered, but hurt, angry.' McBride saw the hurt, recognised the disillusion and looked after his young Lion. 'Willie John cared for me' said Ripley, and that one all-embracing act summed up why the Irishman inspired such fierce devotion and loyalty among his players. Ripley, as ever, played up and played the game, contributing a huge amount to the tour, to morale and to the undefeated record. Neary took his rejection equally badly, and showed his disaffection more publicly.

As Phil Bennett put it: 'Tony Neary will go to his grave thinking he should have been in that Test side instead of Slatts, that he was the better player. He'll say to this day; "I was as good as Slattery on that tour." And to be fair he probably was. But we all kind of knew that it was Fergus they wanted, that it had to be Fergus really for the First Test.'

Even McBride himself concedes that there were some calls that just came down to pure gut instinct: 'Neary was upset and quite rightly so, because there was very little between them. But Slattery's form was outstanding, and we just felt we had to start with him. He had the best all-round game in defence and attack, so we went with him in the knowledge that we had Neary waiting in the wings. And it worked didn't it? It came off.'

Tony Neary would effectively become a bit-part player from then on, and yet managed to contribute some big performances in some very important matches throughout the tour. It was testament to his own, and to the squad's resolve according to the captain: 'The guys who weren't in the Test side kept on working like hell to get into that Test side. It created a really healthy environment, and it was one of the reasons why that tour will never be equalled.'

At half-back, Edwards was the second name on the team-sheet after McBride – although few would have quibbled if his had been the first. He was joined by his international partner for Wales, Phil Bennett. It beggars belief today, when he is rightly celebrated among the all-time greats, that Bennett could have been anything other than a shoe-in at 10.

Yet it was only Old's injury that guaranteed his starting spot, and he was conscious of that fact: 'Oldie will admit himself that he wasn't the quickest runner, but bloody hell he could kick a ball. And at altitude he'd be putting it about seventy metres to my fifty. He then scored a record number of points against the South West Districts, so to this day I don't really know which one it would have been. And I've never asked Syd or Willie either. I was just grateful for the chance.'

Yet the man from Felinfoel had that touch of genius, that ability to do things on a rugby pitch that no-one else on earth could. He might very well have started anyway, but now he had to prove – as he had done before for Llanelli, the Barbarians and Wales – that he was a big time player in search of the biggest stage. Gareth Edwards, JJ Williams and others insist that it was always going to be Bennett for that reason alone.

Willie John McBride feels that Bennett's genius was always there plain to see. It was the Welshman's attitude that surprised his captain: 'I remember going to Benny after Alan Old's injury and telling him that he may well have to play a fair number of games on the trot now, that it might be hard on him. And this sums him up, it tells you everything about this wonderful little man. He said; "Bill I'll play every day if you want me to." That's all you can ask. He was just phenomenal.'

Bennett's Llanelli colleague Roy Bergiers missed out at centre, to the burgeoning combination of Milliken and McGeechan. They had struck up a profitable partnership both on and off the field. It was forged in the heat of battle and would last the test of time as well as rugby.

McGeechan brought that little extra bit of footballing nous and an extra kicking option in midfield, whilst Milliken brought thrust, impetus and defensive solidity. As Bergiers's friend, Bennett could be forgiven for feeling a touch uncertain about the decision, but he appreciated Milliken's hard edge, and in particular McGeechan's brain: 'Geech is a lovely man, and he was a really underrated player. He'd suggest things in training, and you could tell that he had a wonderful rugby mind. He went on to be a great Lions leader over the years of course, but in 1974 he was just a great Lions player. And he and Dick were just right together.'

In terms of solidity, JPR Williams at full-back was head and shoulders above all else, not just on the tour but on the planet. Billy Steele got the nod on the right wing and JJ Williams, having shown of late that he hadn't lost his uncanny knack for finding the try line, was given the left wing berth: 'I'd been frustrated early on in the tour, but I still think I'd have made the Test side even without those six tries at Mossel Bay. I just think they knew who they wanted from the off. Think of Roger Uttley – there's another one that must have been planned all along. But anyway, what we did for those first ten matches or so was really just go around South Africa beating people up.

So by the time we got to the First Test word had got around that we weren't to be messed with.'

Williams and the Test players got down to their final preparation, and just to prove that everything changes while nothing changes they did so while avoiding eagle-eyed Springbok spies. Meanwhile a number of the non-Test players consoled themselves with a charity match against the female students of Cape Town University. The students won a contest that was at times literally too close, and a number of rogue Lions won new admirers. It was certainly one way to take their minds off the disappointment of missing out on the biggest match of their lives.

* * *

Saturday, 8 June, dawned murky, windy and wet. The Newlands pitch was bound to cut up, was bound to play slow and boggy, was bound to suit a team looking to dominate the forward battle.

And that was before the preliminaries started. Two matches were played in the preamble to kick off, meaning that any chance of starting the Test match with decent conditions underfoot were well and truly blown by mid-afternoon.

The Newlands pitch had the look and feel of Passchendaele even before the protagonists emerged from their trenches.

Max Baise was the Lions preferred choice as referee. He had officiated two Tests on the 1968 tour, and had taken charge of their recent rugby massacre of South West Districts. He shouldn't really have been on the Lions' shortlist of four at all this time around, the match in Mossel Bay taking place too late for him to be considered. But Fonnie van der Vyver's disastrous showing in Port Elizabeth opened the door, and the Lions had an easy choice to make. They felt as though they had the lesser of all potential evils in terms of their match referee – it was more than they could have hoped for. And so, with a sweep of his right boot, Phil Bennett of Wales became a Test match Lion and got the 1974 series under way.

Against the wind, the Lions found the first quarter hard going, with the pumped up 'Boks into their stride and onto the scoreboard first, thanks to a drop goal by outside-half Snyman. JJ Williams had a hand in those opening points: 'Memories of the First Test? A nightmare start. The first points were my fault. It was my first Test match, muddy, wet. JPR caught the ball almost on our line, ran across, and I was expecting him to hoof it safe. But he fucking gave it to me – with all of them charging up on me. So I ran across field, got caught behind my own try line. Scrum five, drop goal, three-nil to them. And I'm thinking Christ Almighty, I've just given three points away with my first touch in Test match rugby for the Lions.'

Despite Williams's travails, the Lions pack had, crucially, begun to exert themselves at the set-piece. As Springbok fans punched the air to celebrate their side taking the lead, discerning spectators, among them the Lions hierarchy, focused more on the near total disintegration of the Springbok scrum prior to the drop goal. South African rugby's totem and leader Hannes Marais had been airborne and travelling backwards almost as quickly as the ball. As the half progressed the Lions became more and more certain that they had the measure of their illustrious opponents. Mervyn Davies recalled it rather more colourfully years later: 'It was mud up to our ankles in places and that suited us just fine. We annihilated them up front and they were screaming and hollering in the scrums.'

Those screams and hollers from Sauermann and Marais carried like a triumphal fanfare to Windsor, McLauchlan and Cotton. By the end of the match those sounds weren't pleas for support but squeals of pain. Windsor puts this physical domination down to the collective will of all eight forwards: 'Sauermann was screaming his head off. We hurt him, and we meant to of course. But that was because we all put in the hit. Today when you see back row forwards hanging off the scrum... it's hopeless. You're fucking your front row up doing that. It's got to be eight, and that's what we had, from Merve forward to me.'

So they knew they had the match there for the taking?

'I knew, yes. I loved scrummaging. It was what I did. They were out to hurt me and I was out to hurt them, no mistake. And I knew we had them, no matter what was going on in terms of the scoreboard, and I knew what it would do to them mentally. I'll be honest with you, it was a fucking great feeling.'

Fran Cotton shared that feeling, if not so graphically: 'They'd historically dominated everyone at the scrum. When they realised that the reverse was the case in this instance, it completely drained their confidence. They were complaining to each other, and yes, there were plenty of loud noises, call them squeals or screams, which Bobby obviously loved.'

From his position of safety a few yards away, Phil Bennett took heart from watching the South African scrums go down, then back: 'I was close enough to the action to see them squirming, bending in, and then "Aggghhh" you'd hear the noises. And then Mouse would be like; "Hey, you've got seventy minutes more of that coming boys." From where I was standing it gave me huge confidence.'

JJ Williams had one of the best views possible of the damage inflicted by the Lions pack: 'Not just the front row mind you, all eight. People like Gordon Brown, immense scrummager. But the Springbok props were like Franny – big boys – whereas Bobby and Mouse would take them down so low that they couldn't cope. There was one scrum near my touchline. I was standing on the blind-side wing, looking down the tunnel – and there he was, Bobby, literally knocking the ball back with his head. He seriously did that – he was that low.'

For the skipper, in the boiler room along with Brown,

the sense of release gained from those opening exchanges of the match was almost beyond words. For McBride it was an awakening – a clear sign of what lay ahead: 'I knew after that first scrum, that very first scrum. We won the Test series in that first scrum. They never recovered from it.'

The skipper's conviction in his pack's superiority was passed along to his fellow players. Confidence grew in all quarters. When the 'Boks were caught offside after half an hour, Bennett lined up a shot at goal from just inside the twenty-five-yard line, on his favoured side – the ideal nerve settler.

Two downward prods of his heel, no sand, no tee, five steps back, one to the left, a quick glance and away. It took less than eight seconds between the placing of the ball and the actual kick. Eight seconds – try it sometime. It was the biggest kick of his life. He scuffed it: 'There were all sorts of emotions going through my mind beforehand, and none of them helpful. I remember thinking about being a kid myself, listening to Lions tours on the radio back home. Can you imagine, a boy from Felinfoel, or Trimsaran, or Cefneithin, listening from the other end of the world. Following your heroes – Terry Davies in New Zealand, RH Williams in South Africa – and now there'd be people listening to me, family, friends, it was a massive responsibility.'

As he looked up, Bennett's left hand rose to his face in an involuntary reaction of anguish. But as he watched, the ball wobbled, veered... and scraped its way over the bar. Bennett first scratched his head, then shook it – and with a rueful smile headed back towards his own half. But the skip was unmistakable – he – and the Lions, were on their way: 'If I'd have missed my confidence would have been shot, because really I should have kicked it. Despite conditions being poor, you've got to kick those goals. So heading back to the halfway line I was just thinking thank God I hadn't let anybody down.'

As the half progressed Edwards's kicking out of hand

mirrored that of Barry John in the First Test three years previously. Pushing, probing, unnerving, unsettling, teasing and torturing. Those much vaunted South African backs saw little of the ball, and their forwards were losing the physical and by now the psychological battle. Even their most solid citizen was taking a pounding – one perfectly timed hit from Mervyn Davies rattling Boland Coetzee to his boot laces.

There were great white sharks off the coast of the Cape that could have learnt lessons from Davies that day. As Coetzee brought a high pass down to his shoulder and started to work up a head of steam, Davies had enough time to line him up. From ten yards out, like 'Old Whitey' honing in on a seal or a surfer, Davies slammed his man upwards and backwards. The whole stadium shuddered. Springbok scrum-half Roy McCallum was close to the action: 'My heart just sank. My Man of Steel had dropped' he remembered years later.

With the wind in the second half, the Lions knew that they had the match – and first blood – within their grasp. Bennett landed two more penalties to establish and stretch their lead, before Davies again played a decisive role, ripping away possession and setting up a ruck inside Springbok territory. Having emulated one illustrious Welsh colleague with the boot already, Edwards now evoked memories of another, JPR Williams in that final Test in New Zealand, by booming out a huge drop goal attempt from the acutest of angles. It wasn't quite as far as the 'drop from the ends of the earth', being nearer the ten-yard line than halfway, nor was the reaction quite as extravagant. But the outcome was the same, three points. It finished the Springboks then and there. The sense of euphoria was palpable.

When Zulu warriors killed their foes in battle, they would let out a cry to celebrate the washing of their spears, '*Ngadla*... I have eaten'. The 1974 Lions had gorged themselves for the first time, and what's more they had feasted at the top table of world rugby.

It ended 12–3. There were no tries, there were few scoring

chances, but it was a hugely significant blow nonetheless. The Lions hadn't won a Test match in South Africa in their last nine attempts. They'd only won the First Test of a series in the country once before in the twentieth century, and they hadn't beaten the Springboks in Cape Town since 1938.

For those Lions who had been to New Zealand three years earlier, that First Test brought back the fondest of memories. JPR Williams for instance felt that: 'After New Zealand, I was aware of just how crucial a win in the opener was. Psychologically, Cape Town set us on our way, and we never looked back.'

Bennett concurs: 'I knew we'd achieved something special, because you just didn't win Test matches in South Africa. I'd talked to All Blacks before going and they'd said; "You won't win out there", and I talked to them years later and they'd say; "How the hell did you do that, we could never win out there". So it was a massive game and a huge boost.'

Springbok number 8 Morné du Plessis was a real athlete, a genuine star, as well as being a poster boy for South African rugby. He went on to captain South Africa over the following years in successful campaigns against both France and New Zealand. In fact he created history in 1976 by following in the footsteps of his father Felix, the man who'd skippered the Springboks to victory over the All Blacks in 1949.

In 1995, du Plessis was manager of the re-invented and integrated Springbok rugby team as they won the World Cup on their own soil. He is an influential, much cherished figure not just within South African rugby, but in terms of the global game. Of that Lions side in 1974 he had this to say: 'This was a truly great team we were up against. I don't think we felt confident at any stage as players, because they came with such a reputation in the first place. In one sense they were almost heroes of ours... In fact that First Test was probably our best showing, except for the very last one, but we were simply up against what would be a world-class team in any era.'

For du Plessis, his team-mates and the entire South African rugby playing fraternity, this experience was something new and overwhelming: 'It was the first time in the history of Springbok rugby that we were confronted by a more powerful, physical pack.' It was a terrifying, emasculating realisation.

Springbok centre Johan Oosthuizen had fractured a cheek, and would miss the rest of the series, but if he and his team-mates were hurting, their humiliation was only just beginning.

Post-match tradition dictated that Dr Danie Craven should present six new Springbok players with their caps and blazers. It should have been a proud moment.

Instead Craven made all who heard him cringe with embarrassment: 'It hurts me to be giving you these,' he scolded, 'because you have not earned them.'

He went through each of the six in turn, and none escaped the old man's scorn.

If the approach was scattergun, then plenty of buckshot hit home, some of it completely unmerited. Chris Pope on the wing had created a record 'by becoming the first Springbok ever to play for his country without touching the ball'. Peter Whipp had done better at centre because 'he did touch the ball once'. Lock Kevin de Klerk was described as looking 'like a big man here, but he wasn't a big man out there'. And the dogged Coetzee, aged twenty-nine and four years younger than his captain, was branded 'the old man of the team, and he played like one'.

Coetzee was hugely respected by his opponents – he didn't play again for the rest of the series, much to the Lions' relief. With friends like Craven... Marais too found out who his friends were in the following days, when he was unceremoniously dumped as Eastern Province captain for local favourite George Barnard. In personal terms and in terms of his leadership, Marais was facing the worst crisis – maybe the only one – of his career.

The original touring party. Back row (left to right): Clive Rees, John Moloney, Stewart McKinney, Roy Bergiers, Fran Cotton, Tom David, Geoff Evans, Billy Steele, Ian McGeechan. Middle row: Bobby Windsor, JJ Williams, Alan Old, Tony Neary, Roger Uttley, Chris Ralston, Andy Ripley, Tom Grace, Mike Burton, Dick Milliken, Andy Irvine, Phil Bennett. Front row: JPR Williams, Mervyn Davies, Ian McLauchlan, Gareth Edwards, Alun Thomas (manager), Willie John McBride (captain), Syd Millar (coach), Gordon Brown, Ken Kennedy, Fergus Slattery, Sandy Carmichael. (Mike Gibson and Alan Morley would join the squad in South Africa.)

37 Mayals Avenue.
Swansea
SA3 5DB

5th April, 1974

Dear Roy,

A quick note of much congratulations on your selection. It is a great honour, and I know you will take full advantage of it. You will be hearing soon from my Assistant Manager, Syd Millar and from our Captain, 'Willie John' on what we require from you between now and the day of departure. Please read, mark, and digest what they will be asking of you, as the success of our Tour will depend on it. Their suggestions and instructions are the most important priority for the moment. In the meantime I am enclosing copies of:-

1. An interview with Syd, the message of which, it is vital we all understand and appreciate that South Africa is a harder Tour than New Zealand.

2. An article of the laws sent over from South Africa which gives you an idea of their interpretation and what sticklers they are for the letter of the law.

The prime object of our Tour is to win the Test Series, and we start now thinking and planning for this to happen. May I also remind you of two other vital facts underlined in the Memorandum you have received from Mr. Albert Agar.

1. To treat as highly confidential our Assembly Hotel and departure details.

2. Cessation of playing prior to commencement of Tour. What we expect is spelt out quite clearly, and is in your own interests. Be firm, definite and lay down clearly that you do not wish to play more than once a week and not at all after April 20th.

Finally would you please let me have per return - I repeat per return:-

a) Name of wife or intended with date of birth if between May 6th and August 1st.

b) Name of children with date of birth if between May 6th and August 1st.

c) Sizes of Shoe. I am hoping to 'scrounge' a pair of Dunlop Greenflash Shoes (beach wear, squash etc.). No half sizes avilable and also a pair of Norvic Chukka 'Scallywags' (leisure wear) half sizes avilable.

d) I am giving notice that I require within 14 days or sooner from everyone 3 stories - Clean/Dirty/Sporting/Religious/Political etc. I will not take No for an answer, and they had better be good, as you will be listening to them many times on Tour.

Manager Alun Thomas's letter to the chosen few included an outline of the challenges ahead, a promise to try to 'scrounge' some trainers and a request for personal tour tales from the players.

MESSAGE FROM MR. ALUN THOMAS, MANAGER OF THE BRITISH LIONS TOURING TEAM

We are particularly happy to be back in Port Elizabeth where we were so kindly looked after during our stay earlier in the tour. It is indeed fitting that P.E. should be the scene of this great Test which means so much to both sides.

The Lions see this game as the day they can win the Test series. For the Springboks it is their last chance to salvage a draw from the series.

To our friends in P.E. we say thank you for all you have done to help us; and let us all now look forward to a great game of rugby football.

MILLAR, SYDNEY: Aged 39. Hon. Assistant Manager. General Manager — sand, gravel and concrete products company. Club — Ballymena. Capped 37 times for Ireland 1958–70, as a prop forward. A member of three Lions touring teams — to New Zealand in 1959 and to South Africa in 1962 and 1968. Also toured South Africa with Ireland in 1961. Will form a strong partnership on tour with Willie John McBride who also plays for Ballymena. Is now coach of Ireland's national team which won the Home Championship this season.

THOMAS, ALUN GRUFFYDD: Aged 48. Hon. Manager. Sales representative with family protective clothing company. Clubs — Swansea, Cardiff and Lianelli. Capped 13 times for Wales 1952–55. An all-round player capable of performing at fly-half centre, wing and full-back.

Syd Millar and Alun Thomas. In 1974, for the first time in Lions history, the coach – not the manager – was the de facto leader of the party.

The opposing captains. Both iconic figures going into the series, both tough as teak and both possibly past their best as players. The tour cemented one as a rugby legend and shattered the other's reputation.

1969/70, The Barbed Wire Tour. The Anti-Apartheid Movement's campaign mastermind Peter Hain makes his presence felt.

© Anti-apartheid movement archive

St Helen's, Swansea, 15 November 1969. The battle becomes a war as rugby vigilantes take on peaceful demonstrators.

© Anti-apartheid movement archive

Spring 1974.
Protests in
Cardiff and
London prior
to the Lions'
departure for
South Africa.

© Anti-apartheid
movement archive

Llanelli boys on tour. (Left to right) JJ Williams, Tom David, Roy Bergiers and Phil Bennett made the Scarlets the best represented side among the '74 Lions.

Vying to be number one at No. 8. Tour rebel Andy Ripley (right) was the hot tip to start the First Test. Lions veteran Mervyn Davies (left) had other ideas – so did his coach and captain.

Breaking records from the off. Tom David scores for the Lions in their opening fifty-nine points to thirteen victory over Western Transvaal. David's stellar start to the tour shuddered to a halt soon afterwards.

Boer Brotherhood. South Africa's captain Hannes Marais and coach Johan Claassen. Marais also led Eastern Province against the Lions in Port Elizabeth. Prior to that match, Claassen visited the home dressing-room. His exhortation provoked an explosive on-field response, and the myth of '99' was born.

MORNÉ DU PLESSIS

BY OEFENKAMP

Cultured and Cape Town-based, Morné du Plessis was captain of Western Province and a future Springbok skipper. In 1974 he paid the price for failure as the national team became increasingly entrenched in its Afrikanerdom.

Diplomacy has its limits. Fran Cotton knew from experience that the Proteas would offer a physical challenge. He responded in kind, despite the delicate political nature of the match.

As Barry John had done in the First Test against the All Blacks in 1971, Gareth Edwards did in Cape Town in 1974. His tactical genius helped the Lions dictate the course of the First Test at Newlands, securing an historic 12–3 win.

Heroes at the coalface. The dominant front row trio of Cotton (passing the ball), Windsor and McLauchlan in tandem at Newlands. As ever, Brown, Uttley and Davies are nearby offering vital support.

A tale of two bites. Mervyn Davies was one of the few Lions to have trouble in Rhodesia. For the rest of the squad, the visit proved a welcome respite.

The Lions starting XV for the first two Tests. Back row (left to right): Bennett, Slattery, JPR Williams, McBride, Uttley, Davies, Cotton. Front row: Brown, Windsor, McLauchlan, Edwards, McGeechan, Steele, Milliken, JJ Williams. Irvine for Steele (Third Test) and Ralston for Brown (Fourth Test) would be the only changes.

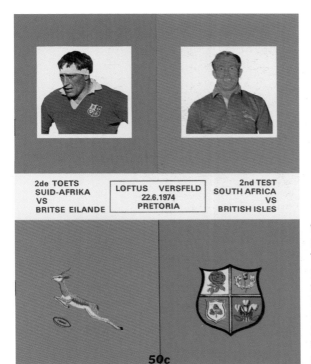

2de TOETS SUID-AFRIKA VS BRITSE EILANDE

LOFTUS VERSFELD
22.6.1974
PRETORIA

2nd TEST SOUTH AFRICA VS BRITISH ISLES

50c

Wait 'til you get to the Highveld. The Second Test at Loftus Versfeld proved to be a high water mark in Lions history. The teams are listed in traditional South African fashion, with the left winger wearing 13.

INTERNATIONAL/INTERNASIONAAL
LOFTUS VERSFELD - 22.6.74 - PRETORIA

SUID-AFRIKA/SOUTH AFRICA		BRITISH ISLES/BRITSE EILANDE
IAN McCALLUM (Natal, O/K)	15	J. P. R. WILLIAMS
GERRIE GERMISHUIZEN (O.V.S.)	13	J. J. WILLIAMS
PETER WHIPP (W.P.)	12	IAN McGEECHAN
JACKIE SNYMAN (O.V.S.)	11	DICK MILLIKEN
CHRIS POPE (W.P.)	14	BILLY STEELE
GERALD BOSCH (Tvl.)	10	PHIL BENNET
PAUL BAYVEL (Tvl.)	9	GARETH EDWARDS
NICK BEZUIDENHOUT (N.Tvl.)	1	MIGHTY MOUSE McLAUGHLAN
DAVE FREDRICKSON (Tvl.)	2	BOB WINDSOR
HANNES MARAIS (O.P., Kaptein)	3	FRAN COTTON
JAN ELLIS (S.W.A.)	6	ROGER UTTLEY
JOHN WILLIAMS (N.Tvl.)	4	WILLIE-JOHN McBRIDE (Capt.)
KEVIN DE KLERK (Tvl.)	5	GORDON BROWN
MORNE DU PLESSIS (W.P.)	7	FERGUS SLATTERY
DUGALD McDONALD (W.P.)	8	MERVYN DAVIES

Skeidsregter/Referee: Cas de Bruin (Transvaal)

Reserwes:		Reserves:
LEON VOGEL (O.V.S.)	16	ANDY IRVINE
DAWIE SNYMAN (W.P.)	17	GEOFF EVANS
ROY McCALLUM (W.P.)	18	JOHN MOLONEY
RAMPIE STANDER (O.V.S.)	19	KEN KENNEDY
PISTON VAN WYK (N.T.)	20	BOB CARMICHAEL
MOANER VAN HEERDEN (N.Tvl.)	21	TONEY NEARY

Two greats for the price of one. If Edwards was the controlling influence in the First Test, the Second was Bennett's chance to shine. His electric performance inspired the Lions to a 28–9 win, and secured his place among rugby's immortals.
© Getty Images

Smile for the cameras. The shot may have been stage managed, but the sentiments were genuine. The Lions felt that by playing non-white sides they were building bridges. The substantial crowd in the background may just add weight to that theory. Andy Irvine went straight from this game against the Leopards into the team for the Third Test.
© Colorsport

The defining moment. JJ Williams scores his first try of the match – his third of the series – in the Third Test at Boet Erasmus, leaving Springbok skipper Hannes Marais clutching at thin air. The non-white corner erupts in celebration behind them.
© Colorsport

Brothers in Arms. McBride and Brown, with Cotton behind, salute their comrades in the stand after their decisive 26–9 win in the Third Test. The moment summed up what made this Lions party so special.
© Colorsport

"Now I can die happy . . . . " Willie-John McBride

AT PORT ELIZABETH, JUNE 13
THIRD TEST
BRITISH ISLES 26, SOUTH AFRICA 9

Winners... and undisputed World Best

Dressing room congratulations from the Doc. Even Springbok legend Dr Danie Craven, who had watched them all come and go, admitted that the 1974 Lions were the best side he'd ever seen.

'Broonie, tonight you must be able to look me straight in the eye.' Brown and McBride, who never lost in five Lions Tests together, enjoy the chance to unwind after the win in Port Elizabeth. The Scotsman, with right hand bandaged, would be missing for the final challenge.

The one and only. JPR Williams, another of the tour's iconic figures, leads the Lions out for the first and last time as captain, holding the team mascot aloft. Stalwart prop Mike Burton follows the leader. This match against Eastern Transvaal is one of Williams's most treasured memories.

Hold on and don't look down. Ellis Park, Johannesburg – vast, imposing and downright dangerous. The Lions played to capacity crowds wherever they went, and the Transvaal Rugby Union enjoyed record takings for the Fourth Test, despite the fact that the series was already decided.

A try or not a try? The same question would be asked in the dying seconds of the game, but this decision by referee Max Baise undoubtedly went the Lions' way. Uttley was awarded the opening try despite photographic evidence suggesting that Springbok winger Chris Pope grounded the ball.

As he had all tour, Edwards played a decisive role, his elated reaction convincing Max Baise that the try was valid. The referee would later enrage the Lions by disallowing Fergus Slattery's seemingly legitimate effort, meaning that the final match of the tour ended in a 13–13 draw. The 1974 side remain the only Lions ever to emerge from a gruelling provincial schedule and a four-Test series undefeated.

The Lions were appalled by Craven's post-match behaviour. Roy Bergiers summed up their feelings on the matter bluntly: 'Craven was a proper bastard that day.' After they'd made their excuses and escaped the company of the self-flagellation society, the Lions showed what true friends were made of. They left the ground and headed straight for Alan Old's bedside. They found Lions selector Clive Rowlands already there ahead of them, talking Old through the day's events. Both the visitor and the invalid were immensely touched by the arrival of the victorious Lions: 'It said everything you needed to know about those boys,' opined Rowlands through misty eyes forty years later.

After the hospital ward came the bar. And that's where they stayed, long into Sunday the 9th.

CHAPTER 15

Low, High and UDI

'Culturally, we are different from other people
in this country, and we just want to protect our identity.'
Marina Haasbroek, Kleinfontein Afrikaner community, 2013

THE LIONS POURED and drank, then poured and drank some more, until finally they were ready to admit defeat for the first time on tour. Outside, it kept on pouring, and although the squad saw very little of Sunday in Cape Town, in truth there was very little to see through the rain. Some were still recovering on Monday, while others had succumbed to the flu, but there was a match to be played on Tuesday, so Mr Millar's exercise emporium was open for business again.

Andy Ripley had been chosen at 8 for the fixture against Southern Universities, Ian McGeechan was in at outside-half to give Bennett a rest. Both pulled out through illness. It was a fixture that had given the Lions problems in the past, and this time around the Universities had chosen nine of the Western Province side which had run the Lions close so recently. They included the whole back row, two-time try scorer Read on the wing, Whipp in the middle, and Snyman at 10.

If only the Springboks hadn't relied so heavily on those same Western Province stars a few days before, this match might have felt like a potential banana skin. But familiarity had bred, if not contempt, then a certain justified confidence, and despite the post Test comedown, the Lions approached the challenge without too many concerns.

The home side was made up of current and past students, including captain Morné du Plessis. He would be taking on the Lions for the third time in ten days, and the match would once again be played at Newlands. JBG Thomas had described conditions for the Test match as 'wet and muddy'. This time around one word would suffice – 'quagmire'.

The Lions fielded four of the Test match starting XV, Bennett in for McGeechan, Uttley multitasking in the unfamiliar role of 8 instead of Ripley, Brown having to fill in at lock and McLauchlan given the honour of captaining the side for the first time from prop. He was alongside Kennedy and Carmichael, Ralston took the other second row berth, while Uttley was flanked by Neary and the restored Tommy David. Moloney started at scrum-half, Evans and Bergiers got to re-establish their Test credentials at centre, while Grace and Rees on the wings and Irvine at full-back would also get a gallop.

For David, in particular, this was a strange old game. Only a couple of weeks earlier he'd been supremely confident of starting the First Test for the Lions at number 6.

Now he'd be playing alongside Uttley, the man who got the jersey in his absence. His admiration for the Englishman is obvious today, but David is also honest enough to accept that it was his lowest point and his darkest time: 'I'd started on fire, then I missed the next five games because of that pulled hamstring. So my Test spot went to Roger Uttley. And to this day it's all about playing in the Tests. So I was almost suicidal, I was so cheesed off I just wanted to go home. I couldn't run, I couldn't train. It was great seeing the boys winning of course, but I kept looking at the boy who was in my position, and being brutally honest I'd want us to win, but I'd want that player to play badly... But of course they were great players.'

Being injured on tour is one of the loneliest places of all to be, and it was difficult reconciling himself to someone else – Uttley in this case – having what he saw as his rightful place. Even as he jokes about it decades later, the sense of hurt is evident below the surface: 'I tried to get him drunk every night, but he wasn't a big drinker, and he never walked near enough to any high ledges either for me to give him a nudge... But he was a great player Roger, and a great character. As were all the other flankers by the way. They were very fine margins weren't they? Everyone wanted to be number one. If they didn't they shouldn't have been on the tour. One or two would react badly if they weren't picked, one or two were nuts in fact – but that competition is what made the squad so strong.'

How long did it take for David to pull himself together? Long enough – his time on the sidelines felt like an eternity, and he's had forty years since to try and put things into perspective: 'How did it feel? Devastating. You just don't feel a part of anything. The bottom line is that I'd have loved to have played in a Test match for the Lions. But I was injured and that was that – once I was fit it was too late, because once Roger got in he deserved to keep his place.'

Hindsight has helped immeasurably, but during that second week of June 1974, David had to deal with his demons as best he could. What tended to work best was having a rugby ball in his hands so that he could go on a rampage.

Except it wasn't really a rampaging kind of day.

The Universities, on a sunny day and on a hard track, might have stretched their opponents, but Newlands was anything but dry and hard, while the Lions were certainly the latter. Those without a vested interest felt that the match should never have taken place, so bad were conditions.

But the Lions were box office. Over 125,000 tickets were sold for their four-match, week and a half stay in Cape Town. Over 20,000 braved the rain on Tuesday, 11 June, because they had an inkling that these Lions were special, that they needed to be seen first-hand. Within the first ten minutes they had seen Moloney give and take on a loop from Neary, before sending Bergiers crashing straight through the middle for the opening try.

The Universities got a try back through an unstoppable charge by number 8 Dugald Macdonald. Durban-born, but Scottish in terms of background, Macdonald had been the only member of the Western Province back row to miss out on Test selection the previous week. His time would come soon enough, as indeed would that of his younger brother Donald, also Durban-born, also a number 8. But while Dugald would represent his native South Africa, Donald would go on to win seven caps for Scotland in the Five Nations campaigns of 1977 and 1978, as an international team-mate of McLauchlan, Carmichael, McGeechan, Steele and Irvine.

It was Irvine himself who steadied the Lions ship that day in Cape Town, place-kicking through the wind and rain as though practicing on a sunny spring afternoon at Herriot's. His early tour yips were by now long forgotten. His character, as well as his talent had come to the fore once again: 'Was I worried early on? Well, yes, you're always concerned about your form, but I was lucky in that I got a lot of game time – eventually playing the Saturday games on the wing, but also the midweek games at full-back. So it was brilliant from my point of view because you wanted to play as much as you possibly could.'

After another Scotsman, Brown, had scored his by now customary try from a short line-out, the win was assured. In fact, their progress was disrupted not by the opposition's players but by opponents of the tour. For the first time ever, anti-apartheid demonstrators took the battle to the enemy by invading a pitch on South African soil. Those brave protesters, both male and female, were Cape Town University students themselves, and as the Lions set up camp inside the home twenty-five at the far end of the field, they took to the Newlands turf and unfurled a banner proclaiming that 'WE'RE PLAYING WITH APARTHEID'.

Mud-caked players, who could hardly tell friend from foe in terms of their own colours, looked on in bemusement, as did the police until local fans took matters into their own hands. No, St Helen's didn't have the patent on rugby vigilantes – they were alive and well in Cape Town too, and they didn't need a '99' call to lay into what was still a peaceful demonstration. Protestors were man-handled and assaulted, one female demonstrator even suffered a broken nose.

For Morné du Plessis, this particular protest felt more personal than others. Trying to focus on winning a match was all the more difficult for a touch of empathy: 'You know we were students ourselves – myself for example just out of student life, and these were the circles we moved in. Some of these guys were friends of ours, so we understood that there was a deep unhappiness.'

So how difficult was is it being a rugby-playing South African with a liberal conscience during that time? And could he have taken a stand himself?

'Well I've asked that question of myself many times; "Why didn't you do more about it when you actually knew deep down in your heart of hearts that things were not right?" I've thought about it a lot – it's a very introspective thing. It's a regret that one has, that one carries, one that I deal with all the time… Rugby was a part of my heritage, so were the Springboks – my father being who he was – and, of course, I was a young man… But in truth there are no excuses.'

JJ Williams watched from the stands, glad he wasn't involved in the match: 'It was a tough day all around. They were nasty buggers in that sense… Yes, it was dealt with pretty harshly by the police. Badly, in fact.'

For the Lions, some unnerved, some embarrassed, some annoyed and some just miserably cold after the stoppage in play, the half-time break couldn't come soon enough.

They scored two more tries during the second half, both forward efforts from close range, rounded off by Uttley and Kennedy. That made it twenty-six points to four at the final whistle, a comfortable afternoon in terms of the rugby challenge if nothing else. Irvine had shown his acumen as a place-kicker in difficult conditions, and Tommy David was back to his bullocking best. The Lions had played four matches in Cape Town and won them all. They had found a perfect retreat – a home from home – at the famous Arthur's Seat Hotel, and they had enjoyed the most profitable of stays.

Any home comforts would now be left behind – they were headed back to the hinterland. Its modern name is Gauteng Province, back then it was the Transvaal, and its mushrooming capital Johannesburg was, in 1974, less than a century old.

*   *   *

In 1886 an Australian prospector named George Harrison – one of a clutch of speculators who had been drawn to the area by tales of 'El Dorado' actually found it, striking gold near the small farming settlement of Langlaagte. He didn't strike lucky though, selling his stake for around £10 soon afterwards without fully realising just what he had discovered. It turned out to be the richest seam of gold anywhere in the world, a reef that has by now given up around forty per cent of all the gold ever mined from the earth. The Witwatersrand gold rush had begun, and within a decade Johannesburg had exploded into the largest city in South Africa.

Thousands of prospective miners descended on the area, many complete novices; others, like Cecil Rhodes, had already made one fortune in the Kimberley diamond mines a few hundred miles to the south-west. Since the deposits at the Witwatersrand ran deep, the ones with money to invest were the ones who profited most. Boer controlled, but populated by citizens of the world, and largely funded by British money, Johannesburg soon became the focal point of political conspiracy.

As president of the Transvaal, Paul Kruger naturally valued the Republic's independence and determinedly protected Boer interests against the potentially overwhelming influx of 'Uitlanders'.

One result was the badly botched Jameson Raid of

Christmas 1895, when a Rhodes-funded party of 600 armed men invaded the Transvaal with the express intention of starting an insurrection and wresting power from Kruger and the Afrikaners. The raid was a disaster, Jameson and his party soon being out-thought and out-gunned by local commandos. But its effect was long-lasting, to the extent that it could be seen as the first, pre-emptive shot of the full-blown Anglo-Boer conflict that was to follow a few years later.

In rugby terms, as in all else, the Transvaal was a part of the Boer heartland. If Cape Town was the equivalent of Cardiff, cosmopolitan in attitude and free flowing in terms of its rugby philosophy, the Transvaal was the Gwent valleys, industrial, industrious, and hard. The antipathy was deep-rooted, and the locals had scoffed at the selection of seven Western Province players for the First Test. There followed a satisfying sense of schadenfreude when all went wrong at Newlands – despite the fact that there were only two Western Province players in the pack. There were none at all in the front five that was so comprehensively outplayed, whilst there were two from the Transvaal.

Suffice to say that the Transvaalers didn't think that the Lions had been truly tested so far. The Highveld would provide a rare old challenge in every way – at 6,000 feet up – altitude, attitude and attritional rugby would soon find the soft underbelly that even southern fists had failed to expose.

As the only provincial side to beat the 1968 Lions, they had a right to be confident. The fact that the flu was causing Lions to drop likes flies enhanced their prospects further – even unofficial team doctor Ken Kennedy was on the sick list. Added to those laid low by illness were those laid low by injury. Having left Alan Old behind in Cape Town, it was now Clive Rees's turn to have his tour jeopardised, due to a broken finger. Mike Gibson was by this time on his way out to reinforce the midfield, but more long distance phone-calls would be needed soon.

All those elements conspired to give this match a particularly tough look, and on a bitterly cold Highveld winter weekend, 68,000 fanatical Transvaalers flocked into Ellis Park to see what all the fuss was about. It was the second biggest crowd of the whole tour, eclipsed only by that for the Fourth and final Test at the same venue, when 75,000 crammed the place to the highest rafter despite the fact that the series was long gone.

And a full to the brim Ellis Park made for an awe-inspiring sight, row after fanatical row banked and jammed skywards towards the South African sun. The stadium itself was high, wide and downright ugly. Downright dangerous too according to many observers, who were terrified by the rickety old scaffold stands, overcrowded benches and gridlocked gangways. Quite simply, it was a recipe for sporting disaster – although the locals seemed perfectly at home.

The Lions were not. They came close to their own sporting disaster on that cold, sunny Saturday afternoon at Ellis Park. It was their hardest match yet.

Transvaal had Test match candidates aplenty aiming to stake a claim. Muller on the wing, Sauermann at prop and De Klerk in the second row had all played in the First Test, but their star players were the half-backs – Paul Bayvel at scrum-half, and outside-half Gerald Bosch. If the Western Province combination of McCallum and Snyman were picked for sharpness and speed only to be ground into the sodden turf of Newlands, then Bayvel and Bosch were their antithesis. Bosch the boot would surely capitalise on his pack's expected dominance, and the Springbok selectors would be there to take note.

The home side also had a man of fearsome reputation at prop. Johan Strauss would finally win his first cap against New Zealand in 1976, but he was already making a name for himself within South African provincial rugby.

The Lions fielded whoever wasn't lying prone on his sick

bed – and some that were. JPR Williams was one such. He shouldn't really have left his hotel room, let alone ventured into a rugby changing room, but there he was, and others took strength from his commitment. Grace and JJ Williams would cover for him as best they could on the wings, Milliken and Bergiers would take up his physical burden, and Bennett and Moloney would attempt to keep the ball pinned as far away from his end of the field as possible. Williams, even today, is stoic: 'I felt dreadful but then again so did everyone else. We were at altitude as well... I think that was one of the greatest performances of them all, simply because a lot of us shouldn't have been playing at all.'

Bennett, Gordon Brown and Bobby Windsor were suffering too, but out they came. Windsor would be glad of being (sometimes literally) carried by McLauchlan and Cotton in the front row, but still found time before kick off to ask Transvaal's number 3 if his name was Strauss. When the rough-house Afrikaner answered in the affirmative, Windsor showed a previously unknown appreciation of classical music with the response: 'Well Mouse is going to give you a real tuning.'

And did he? Forty years later this was McLauchlan's own recollection: 'I played against Johan Strauss again a few years later for Natal against Transvaal. And all the papers were full of this stuff about Johan's chance to get even, and Strauss will get his revenge. Well he went away with his tail between his legs that time as well.'

If the front row trio were ready for a challenge, then Brown, playing his fifth match on the trot, was finding life fatiguing. He was joined by skipper McBride in the second row while the English triumvirate of Uttley, Ripley and Neary combined at the back of the scrum. It was a pack to take on Test match opposition, and it would need to be.

* * *

The first half was all about the Transvaal, and largely about Gerald Bosch, who kicked the home side into a six-point lead and then to 9–3 after Bennett had finally responded. The irony about Bosch was that he was a kicking outside-half playing on possibly the firmest, fastest pitch in South Africa, ideal for flinging a pass. The Transvaal could really have been further ahead at the break. The fact that they weren't gave the Lions hope.

When they needed big characters to step up to the plate, they found them. Firstly Milliken, all brawn and bustle in his now familiar number 11 shirt, took a pass from Bennett on the opposition twenty-five and with a dummy and a step inside, found his path to the try line open.

The Irishman's confidence was as obvious as it was infectious, and Bennett's conversion brought the scores level within minutes of the restart. Bosch put the Transvaal back ahead with a drop goal before Ripley scored a legitimate try only for the referee to miss his grounding of the ball. By now though the Lions had worked up a head of steam, and from the resulting five-yard scrum they took the lead for the first time. Again it was Milliken's try, even though he didn't actually score it.

Taking the ball on a scissors from Bennett, the centre started to sidestep off his right foot, and started to elude white shirted opponents as he did so. One, two, three, four grasped and missed – and as Lions forwards emerged from their scrummaging efforts, they too were forced into evasive action as Milliken angled for the corner. He was finally collared two yards short, only for JPR Williams to find something from somewhere and come galloping up on his shoulder. Milliken heard the hoof-beats and off-loaded in the tackle, Williams crossed in the left hand corner for a try his namesake on the wing would have relished.

All that effort had left Milliken utterly shattered. He remembered afterwards that: 'The Transvaal match more so than any other was the one where I felt most affected by altitude... I was so exhausted that I had to lie down and feign injury at one point.' He'd deserved his lie down – this was his match to all intents and purposes.

That second try made it 13–12, and Bennett soon extended the lead with another penalty. Whenever the Lions looked as though they might just close the match out though, back came Bosch – another drop goal closing the gap once again, to 16–15.

Finally, in the dying minutes, the Lions got the breathing space they craved through Bennett's third penalty, then a third try. Moloney – almost always the instigator – put Ripley away, and the number 8 with arms and legs flailing like a wounded wildebeest, was finally surrounded and brought to ground by a pack of Transvaal hyenas. As he fell, he managed to pop the ball one handed to the on-rushing Neary. The flanker out-sprinted not only the cover defence but the supporting Grace to round things off at 23–15.

The tourists were thrilled to run down the clock and tick off another 'w' – one that put them into double figures for the tour. They had found the answers yet again, and coped not just with a decent home side, but with sickness and altitude. And they had scored three tries to none. JPR Williams saw it as: 'A big match in terms of the tour, because it showed our mental strength as well as our physical ability. We were a tough old lot.'

According to Bobby Windsor's recollections, they also got an unexpected bonus on their return to the dressing room, with one generous local distributing bundles of Rand notes among the players, amounting to around £200 each. All off the books of course, all strictly illegal in terms of rugby's amateur laws, and something that could have seen the whole party banned for life.

Decades before the game finally admitted that it was professional in all but name and decided to bend with the breeze, the odd back-hander served rugby players the world over well enough. As long as certain officials were happy to look the other way, and the blazers at home didn't find out, all charity was more than welcome. In this particular instance, it beat the hell out of the usual post-match reward, a couple of packs of Rothmans cigarettes and a case of Castle lager.

Generous off the pitch, the Transvaal had been tough – if limited – in their approach on it. But the watching Springbok selectors were impressed enough by what they saw, and the home half-backs had played themselves into the starting line-up for the Second Test.

If Bayvel and Bosch were on their way, so too were the Lions. They were leaving Johannesburg once again, and leaving South Africa once again. This time their destination was Rhodesia.

* * *

Today it's known as Zimbabwe, and its capital city is Harare. But before the country became the basket case of Africa, it was known as the continent's breadbasket, rich in natural resources, fertile in terms of land, and hospitable in terms of climate. Back then its capital was called Salisbury, and it was the most British of destinations in terms of the 1974 Lions.

And yet Rhodesia's relationship with the mother country was even more fraught than South Africa's. In fact, whereas South Africa – even under the Apartheid system – still had its political uses, Rhodesia wasn't even recognised as an entity by the UK in 1974.

As ever in Africa, the history was complex. Before Cecil Rhodes got his hands on the land in the 1890s, it was Matabeleland and Mashonaland. Later it was Southern Rhodesia, a self-governing British colony from 1923 onwards.

But when its neighbour Northern Rhodesia became Zambia in the aftermath of independence in 1964, the south saw no reason to keep its Southern prefix and took to calling itself plain old Rhodesia.

But while Zambia's move to self-rule had been relatively straightforward, Rhodesia's was anything but. The British government refused to grant the colony independence like its northern neighbour until it accepted the principle of majority rule. Since the majority was overwhelmingly black, the white minority – less than ten per cent of the population – determined to hold on to power by going it alone.

Prime Minister Ian Smith made his Unilateral Declaration of Independence in November 1965, somewhat spuriously claiming America's Declaration of Independence as his precedent and inspiration. It was greeted by the UK as an 'act of rebellion against the Crown', leading swiftly to condemnation and sanctions. By the time Smith led Rhodesia out of the Commonwealth and declared the country a republic in 1970, Joshua Nkomo's ZAPU and Robert Mugabe's ZANU were already making their presence felt. By the time the Lions toured in 1974, they were making any notion of a future Rhodesian republic being successfully run by the white minority completely fanciful.

Isolated from the outside world and beset by guerrilla warfare within its own borders, white Rhodesia came to rely more and more heavily on Apartheid South Africa.

Ironically, those white Rhodesians counted themselves very much as British in terms of heritage, tradition and allegiance. Per-head of population, more white Rhodesians had fought in the two World Wars than from any other part of the British Empire. Ian Smith himself was a World War II fighter pilot, shot down over Italy and aided in his escape by Italian partisans. The ties were still strong in both directions, so the Lions were going to visit the country whether the Government at home liked it or not.

On their way though, they had time for a stop at one of the world's natural wonders – Victoria Falls. Some appreciated the sights, others the ample food and alcohol, but all enjoyed the visit in their different ways according to JJ Williams: 'Roy Bergiers had this cine-camera stuck to his face; I think he filmed every impala in the whole of South Africa. Then you had the other extreme – Bobby, who wouldn't even get off the bus at Victoria Falls. "To see water? Who cares?"'

They visited a crocodile farm along the Zambezi, pausing long enough for a variety of snaps, some of them painful. Mervyn Davies's camera fell into the water at one point, and after reaching in to retrieve it, he withdrew his hand sharply to find a baby croc attached firmly to his fingers. The players also managed to visit the nearby Livingstone monument, where one Scottish international second row claimed in all seriousness to be related to the great missionary – Gordon Brown, I presume.

His fellow team-mates absorbed this news as they re-boarded for the last leg to Salisbury, a fair number having already acknowledged that Brown was touched by greatness long before this latest claim to fame.

For another, non-Livingstone related Scot, Rhodesia marked a change for the better from Johannesburg, both in terms of weather and welcome. Andy Irvine remembers that: 'Victoria Falls was great, and Rhodesia was a really nice place... The best place we went to from a political point of view. The local black population there seemed a lot more contented with life than they were in South Africa, and it's rather sad to see how that country deteriorated later, because it's in a bad way now... From what the hell happened to the country afterwards, I think they'd have been far better off if Ian Smith had still been there.'

Roy Bergiers is another who remembers Rhodesia with fondness: 'Rhodesia was like going back into the Thirties, a step back in time. And for me, coming from deepest Carmarthenshire in the Seventies that's really saying something... But Salisbury felt like a home from home, there were lots of excited Welsh exiles.' The Rhodesian team even had a Lloyd-Evans playing at centre, just to make the Welshmen feel even more at home.

As with South West Africa, Rhodesia played under the banner of the South African Rugby Board, and the country's players could aspire to become Springboks.

But in fact Rhodesia had achieved something quite remarkable as far back as 1949, something that even established international teams such as Scotland and Ireland have failed to do to this day. Because in 1949, Rhodesia beat the touring All Blacks, the undoubted highlight of the region's rugby history.

Unfortunately, the 1974 vintage weren't quite in the same class. Despite having been recent Currie Cup semi-finalists, this particular Rhodesia side offered little in terms of a challenge to the tourists' record. With a decisive Test match looming, many of the Lions' big hitters got to relax and enjoy the sun.

One of the few who didn't was Mike Burton, who'd picked up an eye infection which necessitated the wearing of an eyepatch. All bandage and plaster, it made him look like possibly the first – and worst – Rooster Cogburn tribute act in history, though he was feeling more Dear John than John Wayne. Having missed the opening exchanges of the tour through injury and having been stood down before the Transvaal game because of his eye, he was eager to make up ground. Now he missed out again, having to watch Carmichael, Kennedy and Cotton do front row duty.

Chris Ralston was glad of a game in the second row, but Roger Uttley, back at lock after stints at 8 and 6, was playing his fifth match on the bounce. McKinney, Davies and Slattery rounded out the pack, with Edwards captaining from scrum-half.

The Welshman had played against – and scored against – Rhodesia two years previously when his club side Cardiff had toured the country and won their unofficial Test match in Salisbury. If Edwards was the acknowledged star turn, the rest of the back line this time around had the look of dirt-trackers for the most part, McGeechan doing duty at 10, Evans and Bergiers in the centre, Steele and Grace out wide with Irvine at full-back.

Twenty-two thousand spectators crammed The Police Ground, including Prime Minister Smith. There were rows of boater-hatted and blazered school boys and any number of rheumy-eyed colonial romantics – all shadowed by an aerial guard in the skies above. The presence of this 'safekeeping squadron' from the Rhodesian Air Force added an extra element of the surreal to what was already a unique atmosphere.

The afternoon soon got even more surreal when Rhodesia full-back Ian Robertson answered two Irvine penalties with a couple of his own early on. That autumn, the talented Robertson would win his first Springbok cap in a victory over France, and two years later he would be doing the unimaginable – defeating New Zealand as a South African international.

Other Zimbabweans have gone on to shine in Springbok colours since, including captains Gary Teichmann and Bobby Skinstad, and of a more recent vintage 'The Beast', Tendai Mtawarira. The most important man in South African rugby, and ZANZAR's current chief operating officer is also a Zimbabwean – with a little bit of Welsh thrown in – Andy Marinos.

So Robertson wasn't the last Springbok from north of the border, but he was the last to play for Rhodesia against the Lions. After his two early strikes, reality reasserted itself, the Lions pack dominating and the backs profiting, first Steele then Grace, then Edwards with the try of the game from long range.

Unless Luis Suárez runs out of options in terms of football clubs and turns his attention to rugby union, biting will always remain something for the game's shadowlands. Very seldom do alleged bites get caught on camera because they invariably occur in the recesses of a ruck or a maul, and in the twilight zone where gouging is regarded as the cardinal sin, biting is almost the lesser of evils. There are some famous instances nonetheless, including the Lions' very own Danny Grewcock, banned for two months in 2005 for nipping at New Zealand's Keven Mealamu in the First Test. Then there's Dylan 'Dentures' Hartley, banned for sinking his fangs into Stephen Ferris of Ireland. The Springboks themselves can boast Johan Roux, famous for taking a chunk out of All Black captain Sean Fitzpatrick's ear in 1994. Even the latest Lions tour had an accusation of biting, Irish prop Cian Healy cleared of any offence during the match against Western Force.

There are plenty of other examples of course, including on one sunny Tuesday afternoon in 1974, a Rhodesian prop named André Van Zyl. The recipient of his unwanted attention was Lions number 8 Mervyn Davies, who was more than happy to show the bite marks on his arm to any interested parties.

First the croc, then Van Zyl – Davies could be forgiven for wanting out of Rhodesia on the first plane back to Jo'burg. His consolation? All the major chunks were being torn out of the Rhodesian side.

Grace scored a second try early in the second half, Slattery added another, and Irvine brought the curtain down with an eye-catching, sidestepping dart to the line to make the final score 42–6. It capped a generally impressive showing from the Scot, he'd dropped a goal too, and twenty-two points from a total of forty-two was some return. As both a runner and a kicker, Irvine was planting seeds in the minds of the management team.

For Rhodesia's young coach, Ian McIntosh, this match was a major learning experience. He would go on to coach Natal, South Africa and eventually Newport in Wales. He is still a national selector for the Springbok team. His memory of the tour was of friendships and connections made, and lessons learnt: 'We were Currie Cup semi-finalists in 1973, and we were a good side. But we lost our outside-half Stuart Dunbar the week before the game – which was a huge loss. Every coach must think he has a chance in any match, and afterwards I was really down, but in retrospect, we didn't have a hope in hell against that side. They were one of the best ever.'

In political terms it was the last hoorah, the next tourists – the All Blacks of 1976 – didn't visit Rhodesia. McIntosh was grateful for the opportunity to welcome the best – and build relationships with McBride, Millar and the Welsh contingent that would stand him in good stead. When asked for his thoughts forty years later, he still maintains that: 'Those Lions are revered like no other side here in South Africa.'

Prime Minister Smith put his daily travails aside for a few hours afterwards to mix with the tourists, and apparently even enjoyed the experience of seeing Irishmen Milliken and Slattery taking an unauthorised spin in his Bentley. He had his mind on far more important and pressing matters anyway. The following day Rhodesia's prime minister announced a general election that would go some way to deciding the country's future.

The Lions too turned their thoughts elsewhere. They were halfway through their tour – and would fly out the next day for their date with destiny, and the match that would define their lives.

CHAPTER 16

Bring on your Wrecking Ball

'And those you are with, in the presence of miracles, you never forget. Life does not separate you. Time does not separate you, Animosities do not separate you. Death does not separate you.'

Bruce Springsteen, 2009

THE LIONS HAD been away from home for almost seven weeks. They had played eleven matches and won them all. They had totted up thousands of air miles and a dozen different hotels. They'd been watched by over 300,000 people, and scored almost 400 points. Having landed yet again in Johannesburg, they made the trip of just over thirty miles downhill to Pretoria in contemplative mood.

Despite being in the shadow of Johannesburg in terms of geography, Pretoria was a different place in almost every way. Lower and warmer, it was also much smaller and prettier than its colossal industrial neighbour. It was, and is, South Africa's administrative capital, a place of politicians and students.

Any danger of enlightened thinking though was stamped out soon enough in 1974. Pretoria was the epicentre of apartheid, and a Boer stronghold. Whereas Johannesburg had been diluted by the influx of 'Uitlanders' over the decades, Pretoria was the cutural and historical bastion. Nowhere was that more applicable than Loftus Versfeld, home of national champions Northern Transvaal and of South Africa's rugby consciousness.

The referee chosen for the all-important Second Test was an interesting one. There was no Max Baise – struck off the candidate list – so the Lions opted for Cas de Bruyn, who'd refereed their match against South West Africa. He'd also subsequently had to endure the embarrassment of Springs, where he'd abandoned a match between Eastern Transvaal and the French champions Tarbes because of the unrelenting violence. JBG Thomas saw the selection of de Bruyn, the man who'd apologised to Syd Millar for his poor performance in Windhoek weeks before as a vindication of the management's strategy: 'One believed how much thought the management and captain had given to the matter.' Millar was sure he would get a referee on best behaviour, which in effect meant as level a playing field as he could hope for.

The Springboks meanwhile had made wholesale changes to their starting line-up. Six had become seven after the Transvaal's winger Gert Muller pulled out with an injury. He was replaced by Gerrie Germishuys of Orange Free State who would win his first cap. The other six changes amounted to a total rethink in terms of approach. Dawie Snyman's younger brother Jackie, also a fly-half by trade, was the second Orange Free State player brought into the backs, and the second new cap. He was selected at centre instead of the injured Oosthuizen, but sadly wouldn't be partnering his brother.

The elder Snyman was dropped, along with his Western Province partner Roy McCallum, in favour of the Transvaal half-back pairing of Paul Bayvel at 9 and Gerald Bosch at 10 – new caps both.

Gareth Edwards looks back now and feels particularly sorry for McCallum: 'Roy was the best scrum-half I played against on that tour. I saw him a year or two ago and told him too. I said; "Roy I'm not blowing smoke, but the worst thing they did was get rid of you. If they'd stuck with you we'd have had a far more difficult series." And I meant it. But we created that uncertainty in their minds, forced the panic, purely because they'd never been in that situation before... Never.'

The revolving door policy was also in full swing up front. Out went one Transvaal prop – Sauermann, and one local favourite, Northern Transvaal hooker van Wyk. In came Northern Transvaal prop Nic Bezuidenhout, and the Transvaal hooker Dave Frederickson, new cap number five. If that was confusing, so was the retention of a clearly struggling Marais as prop and skipper. Williams and De Klerk were also given a second chance in the second row, while Dugald Macdonald became the sixth new cap at number eight. Out went Boland Coetzee, and with Jan Ellis's place at 7 sacrosanct, the athletic, free-ranging Morné du Plessis – used to playing numbers 8 and 7 and well-suited to either role – was moved across to 6.

As though getting used to playing in blind-side shackles wasn't tough enough for du Plessis, he and the rest of the side were now literally incarcerated as well.

Rugby fans of a more recent vintage will recall coach Rudi Straeuli's infamous boot camp prior to the 2003 World Cup. Straeuli took his Springbok squad to Kamp Staaldraad – Camp Barbed Wire – where among other indignities the players were forced to strip naked and jump into lakes and fox-holes at gunpoint. It did not have the desired effect of building bonds. When news of the exercise broke, it forced Straeuli's resignation. That was sad but the tragedy came two years later, when the whistleblower – video analyst Dale McDermott – committed suicide.

If Straeuli's tactics were brutal in the extreme, they were not entirely without precedent in terms of Springbok rugby. In 1974, coach Johan Claassen – yes the very same Claassen who had ventured into the Eastern Province dressing room to encourage a bit of fisticuffs – decided that the best way to bring his side together was to lock them up in Pretoria's maximum security prison.

They slept in cells, weren't allowed to read papers, and had no contact with the outside world. It failed to focus minds as had been intended, unless they were focused on hatching escape plans.

Whether they were vastly experienced or complete international novices, the players found the whole experience disconcerting: 'The Second Test in Pretoria, we were nervous wrecks before we even ran onto the field,' admitted centre Peter Whipp in a television interview years later:

'It was ludicrous, grown men being told when to go to bed, and not being allowed to read newspapers, not being able to mix with the public, being spirited away to secret training locations.'

Maybe modern-day professionals in their intensive and self-contained training bases would be less surprised by some of those extremes. Wales's Vale of Glamorgan base has, at times in recent years been dubbed 'The Jail of Glamorgan' for example. But in 1974, just when they needed to be inspired and offered encouragement, South Africa's players were being mentally dismantled before they even faced the Lions.

Meanwhile, the real team bonding was being done elsewhere. The Lions picked the same side for the Second Test on Saturday, 22 June, as they had for the first. The day was warm and sunny, and as the Lions team bus drew up outside Loftus Versfeld Stadium, the squad was caught up in a moment which has stayed with each of them ever since.

Scotsman Billy Steele was the tour's choirmaster, and he managed to do with one song, 'Flower of Scotland' what the Pretoria Prison experience failed so utterly to do for the Springboks, re-ignite a fire.

Scotland versus England at Murrayfield in 1990, with the Grand Slam at stake, is perhaps when 'Flower of Scotland' really entered the public's consciousness. David Sole's long walk to the field, a stirring tune becoming an anthem over the course of one spine tingling rendition, and Scotland turning in a rampaging, unstoppable performance to break English hearts.

But the song itself had already proved inspirational, had already become an anthem, seventeen years previously, with the 'Springbok Army' replacing that of 'Proud Edward' so as not to offend English sensibilities.

The Lions were right in the middle of singing 'Flower of Scotland' as their bus arrived at the ground. The doors opened, hundreds of expectant fans waited to catch a glimpse, to size them up. Nothing happened. Inside the bus no-one had moved a muscle, no attempt had been made to stand up, to reach for bags, to head for the door. They just sat and sang the song to its finish, wrapped up in the moment.

According to Gordon Brown: 'We sat there and we sang it to the end… Do you know, if you'd have taken us off that bus and dropped us into Vietnam, we could have sorted it all out. The togetherness was incredible.' When they did finally finish, and as they started to make their way for the exit, they knew – just knew – that there was something special afoot.

By the time they got into the dressing room, the captain felt that they were plainly motivated enough as it was.

But McBride wanted them to take in the sense of history, and appreciate what was within their grasp: 'I didn't feel the need to say too much. I remember telling them; "I just want you to think about coming back through that door in eighty minutes' time. How do you want to feel? Where do you want to be?" But I remember thinking as I went around them, just looking into their eyes, feeding off what they were feeling that they didn't need any more. You could see it coming… So when I led them out, I knew there were fourteen guys coming out behind me who wouldn't let us lose that game. We just weren't going to lose. It's an amazing sensation looking back on it now, just one of those rare moments in life that you hold on to.'

Loftus Versfeld was South Africa's most impressive and most intimidating stadium, famous for unnerving visiting teams and putting them off their game. Not this time. In front of 63,000 expectant fans, Phil Bennett once again got a Lions versus South Africa Test match under way.

Considering that this is the match – even more so than the Barbarians versus New Zealand encounter the year before – which defined Bennett's career in many ways, he is surprisingly ambivalent about it today. In true Dickensian fashion, the day would turn out to be the best of times and the worst of times because it cemented the outside-half's reputation, yet left him unable to touch those heights again: 'It's one of the great days of my life, and also one of the saddest... It was a day that changed my life forever in some ways, but it changed my tour too, and not for the better.'

The early momentum was with the Springboks, with the third John Williams on the field – the Northern Transvaal second row – making his presence felt to good effect. Tall, athletic and an expert line-out jumper, Williams was a constant source of possession, and a constant threat to the opposition's ball. He was therefore targeted unremittingly. The Lions had even resorted to talking up other prospective Springbok second rows in a bout of pre-match kidology, and once the match was under way Gordon Brown took it as his sworn duty to disrupt Williams as best he could.

The one thing that Williams seemed to lack in terms of being a world-class second row was the mean streak so prevalent in his countrymen. Subsequent Springbok hard nuts like Kobus Wiese, Mark Andrews and Bakkies Botha would have been appalled that a 'Bok lock could be anything other than explosive with his fists. But even the mild-mannered Williams was forced to retaliate in the face of Brown's provocation, the Scotsman taking a clout on the chin which might just have discouraged him for a minute or two.

If Williams surprised the Lions with some quick hands, so did outside-half Bosch, who chose to run and pass effectively early on. In fact South Africa were looking both penetrative and physical. Except at the scrum that is. There the Lions took

217

solace, and from there they launched their first meaningful attack.

The scrum had settled just inside the Springbok half, about ten yards in from the left hand touchline. The move was pre-planned to such an extent that Edwards didn't even need to look up and assess his options. He picked and kicked in one movement, and as he did so JJ Williams started to sprint from ten yards back.

By the time the ball was in flight, the winger was perfectly level with his scrum-half – not an inch in front, not even a hair's breadth – but Williams was lightening quick.

Springbok winger Pope started to turn and chase back, McCallum at full-back came across to cover. The ball bounced once, and as the two South Africans hesitated, Williams was between them, getting his left foot to the ball. It flew wide of the grasping McCallum, and Williams was past him like Gareth Bale skinning an unwitting opponent with a push and run. As the ball bounced again on the try line, the Welshman dropped and smothered it. The deadlock had been broken in startling fashion.

Anyone who's ever seen footage of JJ Williams score his Test match tries in 1974 and expressed amazement – amazement at his downright luck, amazement that a rugby ball can be kicked by a man in full-flight and yet bounce so favourably each time into his out-stretched hands – should remember one thing: Williams kicked like a fly-half. In fact, he had the hands of a centre, the speed of a sprinter and the touch of a number 10 with his boot.

As a boy he had starred for the Welsh Schools XV at outside-half, and in one grudge match against the Welsh Youth side, had dropped a goal in the dying minutes to win the fixture. The opposition's number 10 that day – the losing outside-half – was one Phillip Bennett.

So if Williams ever 'did' luck, he combined it with electric pace, perfect timing and the sweetest of skill. He also threw in a killer instinct and a steely competitive edge for good measure. As he climbed to his feet in Pretoria, with the ball clutched in two hands like a trophy high above his head, he was announcing his arrival as a world-class player.

He was wearing the number 13 jersey that day, with Dick Milliken wearing the winger's traditional 11.This had become the norm during that tour to South Africa, prompting people to ask Williams over the years why he was playing at centre.

The confusion according to Williams was down to a simple South African custom: 'The programme notes read downwards, 15, 13, 12, 11, 14. What they did in South Africa was put 14 right wing, 13 left wing, and 12 and 11 at centre. It was the way they listed us, so that was the way we went. You know, it never even occurred to me – it certainly didn't bother me. As long as they were only seeing the back of my jersey the number was irrelevant.'

In fact some players refused to wear 13 on superstitious grounds. If it was an unlucky number for some, it was the making of JJ Williams.

The Lions still couldn't get to grips with the match though. Bennett was missing penalties, they were playing good stuff without finding the killer touch. They had what seemed like a perfectly good try disallowed when Bennett broke blind-side inside the 'Boks twenty-five and jinked his way towards the try line. He'd skipped his way past most of the pack when he ran out of room. Instead of selling one last dummy, he floated out a perfect pass towards Williams's wing. His Llanelli team-mate arrived at pace and crossed in the corner, only for Bayvel's last-ditch lunge to nudge him into the corner flag. No try, still too tight to call.

If the Lions were fluffing their lines, then the Springboks were failing to take advantage, especially considering the prodigious penalty count in their favour. Whether out of hand or off the sand, their kicking was poor, and eventually it would cost them.

The kick that eventually did so was launched by Ian McCallum, charging along Williams's touchline before hoofing high and long into the Lions twenty-five. Bennett took it over his shoulder, within yards of his own try line – not under his own posts as he had for the Barbarians in 1973, but close enough. And then he started to run.

Speed off the mark took him clear of the initial melee, and a split-second sidestep took him up and away towards halfway: 'I was in good nick, feeling confident' he remembers: 'I knew that with the ground like it was I could sidestep my way past anyone, I could beat people easily if I'm honest. Even if they knew it was coming, they couldn't stop it.'

Bennett was finally collared by a diving Marais, who deserved plaudits for even getting near the Welshman, but not before Bennett had managed to offload to the nearest Lion, who just happened to be McBride. The startled skipper got rid of the ball almost as soon as he had it, but the recipient, Davies, was taken almost immediately, so passed back to McBride. Ulster's finest then took a couple of steps, hardly a charge, before finding Brown, who in turn sensed Edwards steaming up on his outside in familiar fashion.

By this time the move had advanced into Springbok territory, and developed from one flank to the other, but its promise seemed to have petered out when Edwards was brought to ground on the touchline.

Yet somehow the scrum-half managed to flick the ball hopefully inside as he hit the dirt, keeping the move alive. Roger Uttley was the nearest man, but at almost 6' 5", the bending of the knee in co-ordination with the taking of the pass proved too much for him. He simply couldn't get down quickly enough.

In the commentary box, former England scrum-half Nigel Starmer-Smith caught his breath and described 'Uttley just knocking the ball forward'. It looked as though he had, but the flanker knew better. The ball had in fact bounced off his knee – no knock-on therefore, and the move was still very much alive.

Uttley described what happened next years later: 'When

you look at it, it looks as though I made a complete hash of it. But I thought it was a brilliant bit of skill at the time... And I still do actually in my own mind.'

In fact, on second, third and fourth viewing, Uttley is right – it was a brilliant piece of skill. He managed to hook his right foot around the ball as it bobbled towards the touchline and tap it back in-field. There, lurking was JJ Williams, who had followed the move across the field, away from his own wing: 'I had played with Benny long enough at Stradey to know that if he set off from deep, and play was broken, I should go after him. So I just followed. And I'll tell you this – if the camera angle had been better – up high instead of too close – it would have been ranked as one of the great tries of all time.'

Williams tapped the ball past covering outside-half Bosch, beat him to the bounce, and this time chipped ahead right footed. Once again the ball bobbed up and into his grateful arms as he crossed the try line.

The next Lion to Williams as he touched down was Gordon Brown – no wonder he scored eight tries in his twelve appearances on tour.

All in all, the move had involved seven players and gone the length of the field. It might not have had the precision or cleanliness of the JPR, Mike Gibson, Gerald Davies try in the Second Test in 1971, but this one was in a winning cause, when the pressure was at its highest. It was in many ways a more worthwhile effort – and it put the Lions into a 10–0 lead after a half-hour of the game.

Morné du Plessis, likens that try not to that scored by Gerald Davies in 1971 but to another, more famous effort: 'We'd watched the Barbarians game from 1973 over and over – Dugald Macdonald was a friend of mine, and he actually had cine-footage of that match, so we'd studied it. And we'd watched that try where Phil Bennett started everything off and Gareth finished it, probably a hundred times, replayed it over and over. And then there we were playing against them in Pretoria and it actually happened to us.'

JJ Williams is one of a number of '74 Lions who feel that they have never been accorded the respect they deserved for their play, especially among the backs: 'It was the brilliance of one or two backs that actually won the Tests in terms of tries scored – you should remember that. All the talk of forward domination is fine – and they did dominate no doubt – but they needed us too. We scored some very special tries. I think nowadays, when people look back at those tries they think, bloody hell, they were good. But maybe not so much at the time.'

A drop goal and a penalty by Bosch either side of half-time brought the Springboks back to 10–6, but the Lions were just getting into their stride. If Williams's brace was historic, the game's true star was Bennett, who, having started the last try, engineered and executed the next.

It began with Slattery collecting a loose ball on his own ten-yard line. He headed off towards halfway before switching the ball back inside to Bennett, and from there things became something of a blur.

Once again Bennett's blistering acceleration took him past the first man – opposite number Bosch, but the magic was in the sidestep that followed. As he tore towards the South African twenty-five-yard line to be confronted by full-back McCallum, Bennett shifted the ball briefly into both hands, as though shaping to pass to Steele outside. It caused just enough hesitation in McCallum's mind, and when the step came, he was left completely wrong footed, grasping at thin air as Bennett vanished towards the try line.

As ever, it was a step off the right leg, as ever, it seemed to come out of nowhere, and as ever, the covering player was left sprawling. McCallum did though stick out a leg as Bennett breezed past, clipping the outside-half's shin and drawing blood. The cut would require stitches post-match, but as Bennett hobbled back towards halfway and Edwards prepared to take over kicking duties, McBride told his star player in no uncertain terms that he was staying on the field of play, no matter how painful the knock.

When Bennett talks about that try forty years later, from the comfort of his armchair, there are mixed emotions. Certainly none of the misty eyed romance that one might expect: 'Fergus was a good footballer and he'd made some space, but when I got the ball I still had about fifty yards to go. So I managed to get clear, get into open ground, with the full-back now in front of me. And I'm looking at his eyes, and I know that he's coming too quickly, so I've got him... But as I step past him, I feel what I can only describe as a knife going into my leg... There's blood pumping out, my sock is absolutely soaked through, and I'm saying to anyone who'll listen; "If I die here make sure I get buried with those Welsh boys up at Rorke's Drift... don't let these bastards bury me here all right?"'

McBride saw the injury and decided to put a lesson learnt to good use. Using the same line Carwyn James had used on him three years previously, he told his outside-half: 'Benny, I need you.'

Bennett's reaction? 'Well Willie looks at it and says: "Jeez, it's only a scratch." Of course when he asks you to stay on, to be brave, that's exactly what you do, no matter what state you're in.' And Bennett was in a state. Not just the deep gash, which Ken Kennedy would stitch up later, but a wrenched knee that would cause even more problems over the coming weeks. That try would be his career highlight in many ways, but would also lead to the deepest of troughs.

For the illustrious McCallum, one of South African rugby's poster boys in years gone by, the torture continued. Within minutes of Bennett's try, the full-back was involved in yet another for the Lions.

There was still a quarter of the match left to play at this point, and with Edwards refereeing the put-in, the Springbok scrum was in a mess. Poor ball was shipped backwards towards Bosch deep inside his own twenty-five, and the outside-half had nowhere to go.

Bennett had recovered enough to close him down and hold him, forcing a wild pass which found McCallum. The full-back's clearance kick found only trouble in the shape of the covering Edwards, now bursting down the touchline towards glory. He stepped inside one defender as though taught by his best mate Gerald Davies, but was caught by the next. Who should be there on his shoulder working up a huge head of steam, but Gordon Brown.

Had he been at Khe Sanh, no amount of General Giap's North Vietnamese foot soldiers could have stopped him. He brushed past the last remnants of Springbok defiance, ball clutched to his chest in both hands like an American Football running back, and stormed over for the try. At 18–6 it was all over.

So too was Ian McCallum's international career, which came to an ignominious end. He was physically shattered, and limped away to be replaced by Dawie Snyman. After a hiatus of two decades, the Springboks had now fielded two different sets of brothers in two consecutive internationals, firstly the McCallums, now the Snymans. Dawie's cameo soon ended in farce though. He lasted less than ten minutes before being forced off himself through injury, replaced by one-cap wonder Leon Vogel – it summed up South Africa's misery and misfortune completely.

Amidst the chaos, Bosch landed his second penalty, McGeechan scored his first points of the tour with a booming left footed drop goal on the run, Bennett picked himself up after being floored late by Vogel to kick a further penalty, and centre Milliken landed the coup de grâce.

Spotting the Springbok defence on the back foot near its own try line, Bennett darted down the narrow side before handing on to the Irishman. He still had plenty to do, but dummied to JJ Williams outside and headed for the line. By the time he got there he'd worked up enough momentum to crash not only into but through the cordon of green jerseys. Jan Ellis, Springbok legend, was among the bodies scattered to the winds by the charge. The rout was complete, at twenty-eight points to nine.

* * *

If the First Test had been a marker, the Second was plain monumental. Fran Cotton relished the whole experience: 'It had been a really important performance in that First Test in Cape Town, because we hadn't won down there in so long. But in fact we found the Highveld even easier. It suited us more, it allowed us to scrum and to run... Pretoria was the centre of rugby in South Africa, and no-one expected us to win there, even though we'd beaten them at Newlands. They thought the altitude, the dry conditions would give them the upper hand. It actually worked the other way.'

The Lions of 1971 had lost their Second Test decisively in New Zealand. The Lions of 1974 posted a record score in Pretoria – the Springboks had never been beaten that badly in their illustrious history. McBride's men had also scored five tries, two of which would be considered as classics by generations to come. After Newlands, they had been told to expect a different challenge altogether on the Highveld. If anything, this experience left their opponents feeling even more chastened.

Morné du Plessis would be one of the casualties of that performance, but he feels now, as he did then, that they came up against something special, something unique: 'If anything it suited the Lions even more up at Loftus with its hard ground, dry conditions. I remember Phil Bennett was sensational that day. But you also had JPR, JJ, Gareth – they ran rings around us frankly.'

Even from the one position on the pitch which made a judgement difficult, Fran Cotton could appreciate what the side's backs had brought to the party: 'Our backs never got their just desserts throughout. There was only one try scored in the Tests by the opposition backs. Look at the number we scored behind – four in this game, seven in all was it? And that's not even counting the provincial matches and all the records they broke.'

If there was any lingering doubt that these Lions could play rugby, then it was finally dispelled at Loftus. Terry O'Connor was moved to write later that: 'Anyone who watched this game would know that only a blind or bigoted observer could accuse the 1974 Lions of playing ten-man rugby. Bennett produced a performance which for most men is confined to dreams.'

Despite the heroics up front, despite the history making by JJ Williams, it had been Bennett's game. Six years previously Jan Ellis had shattered Lions' hopes, and Barry John's collarbone on this very ground. Now, according to John Reason: 'He did not touch Bennett all afternoon.'

Hannes Marais was one of many who had underestimated Bennett: 'The one who really surprised us was Phil Bennett. We thought he was this little jack-in-the-box, a real weakness in their side. Instead he was our main problem.'

Clive Rowlands, watching admiringly from the stands felt that: 'He was outstanding – pace, skill, and nerve – one of the great performances of all time. How did he compare with Barry? Barry was a great attacker from set-pieces as well as loose play. Better than Phil. Phil was different, he needed it loose. But tactically he was brilliant, and in South Africa you couldn't have picked a better fly-half. That's including Barry, by the way. Everything he did was perfect. It's a hell of a thing to say, but it's true.'

Gareth Edwards concurs, and feels that maybe people didn't quite appreciate just how good Bennett was at that time: 'Phil was simply outstanding – quite sensational. In fact, on the Highveld he was nigh on unplayable. Like a great spin bowler, you might think you know what he's going to do, and yet he'll still bamboozle you. He was just brilliant. Different to Barry, who was unique in other ways, but brilliant nonetheless. The pity today is that there isn't that much film of what he did, and what we did. Out of sight, out of mind, to a certain extent... But when you went to South Africa all they talked about was Cliff Morgan and that 1955 tour. He was a legend out there. Now for Benny to supersede that memory for South Africans says everything about how good he was.'

The one man who couldn't seem to appreciate and enjoy what he'd done was Bennett himself. The outside-half was sure that his South African adventure was at an end: 'If I'm honest my tour was almost over there and then. Really they should have sent me home, because I couldn't play for weeks – I was useless... Of course I was glad to contribute later on in the Third Test – two drop goals was some sort of help to the team cause. But in a split-second I'd gone from being a man who could rip people apart to this hobbling, battered wreck... It was a turning point, and not in a good way. Even when I came back into the team, I knew I could do a job for the Lions, but I wouldn't be the same. I just wish I could have carried that fitness and form from Loftus into the Third and Fourth Tests.'

As Bennett gingerly made his way towards the changing rooms at the final whistle, fans poured onto the field and there was one last piece of drama. An unfortunate Afrikaner, over-enthusiastic and uncoordinated, got in the way of another and was clipped accidentally at the ankle. He fell into the back of Gareth Edwards, executing a near perfect if completely innocent tackle. The scrum-half naturally suspected foul play and reacted accordingly, landing two swift right hooks on his assailant before turning for the safety of the stands.

That startled South African fan had managed something none of his Springbok heroes could do all afternoon. He had flustered the Lions talisman, as well as flooring him. But by then, Edwards and the rest were in celebratory mood, and nothing could sour the occasion.

Not even being taken to jail themselves. There was one last twist to that most memorable of days. The post-match dinner was to be held at the very same prison which had been a pre-match home to the Springboks. 'They'd been a bag of nerves coming out for the match' said JJ Williams: 'Now after the game, we were all back there. It was a long table, them on one side, us on the other, they didn't want to talk, they were plain unfriendly actually. And we're being brought our food by the prisoners. It must have been tough for the South African players – they hated us, they were embarrassed, and they were stuck in this bloody prison for supper with us.'

The bad feeling and mutual antipathy was most certainly reciprocated. Peter Whipp and others have been happy to brand the Lions as an 'unfriendly bunch'.

Hannes Marais went so far as to call them: 'Extremely unsociable.'

The Lions by that stage didn't care what anyone thought. Andy Irvine felt the shift in mood: 'The feeling after the First Test was relief, because that game had been close, and we still weren't really sure if we were a better side than them or not... But once the Second was in the bag, well you knew that you couldn't lose the series, so immediately the tour was massively successful... In fact I felt as though we could walk on water.' And he hadn't even been playing.

When Ian McGeechan coached the Lions to their historic series victory in South Africa twenty-three years later, he would remember those precious moments. Before their very own date with destiny, the Second Test match in Durban in 1997, he spoke movingly to the players, spelling out why the occasion was so important.

His pre-match speech is still talked of today, and included these words: 'These are the days that you never believe will come again. This one has. It's been a privilege. You will meet each other on a street in thirty years' time and there will just be a look, and you will know how special some days in your life are. If you get it right today, your lives will be different from this point on.'

The words still resonate today, as they did for Martin Johnson, Keith Wood, Scott Gibbs, and Jeremy Guscott back then, because McGeechan spoke from the heart. He knew exactly what it meant because he'd done it, and his own life had been changed forever.

The Lions were two up with two to play.

CHAPTER 17

Party like it's 1968

'Just do what must be done.
This may not be happiness, but it is greatness.'
George Bernard Shaw

IF THE VICTORY was monumental, then so were the celebrations afterwards. They went on for days, and were allowed to, because the Lions were on a well-earned sabbatical. Their destination for a bit of rest and relaxation was the world-famous Kruger National Park, but for every single leopard or elephant spotted, the legend goes that the players saw double their number – such was their state of inebriation.

It began early, as they boarded two old Dakota planes at Jan Smuts Airport. JJ Williams remembers one or two of his Welsh colleagues in particular leading the way: 'As we were boarding, Merve was loading crate after crate after crate of beer onto the plane. He was just this mess in a straw hat, T-shirt, flip-flops, fag in hand. He looked like Robinson Crusoe.' At this point Williams pauses, grins and takes on an air of mock seriousness: 'And I was just thinking – you know, me being a proper athlete and all that – Christ, four days of solid drinking. I wasn't ready for it... Merve most definitely was, JPR too. If you were up til 1 a.m. he'd have to be up til 2 a.m., he was that competitive.'

They also celebrated the arrival of reinforcements, in the shape of Mike Gibson, fresh off the plane from home. On arrival at Kruger, the hobbling Phil Bennett was ferried from

230

roundeval (essentially a mud hut) to bar to jeep to bar to bed on the backs of various willing forwards. This was fine in daylight, but at night, in savanna darkness, with no electric lights, this became a concern. Especially when the willing donkey, Willie John McBride, heard a lion which wasn't one of his own pride nearby, prompting an ambling sprint for his hut. A low-slung branch caught the jockeying Bennett flush in the face, and dislodged him from McBride's back. For once – the only time on tour in fact – the captain declared that it was 'every man for himself' and kept on going.

In a park famous for its game, the game that most captured the imagination involved beer. At least one first-teamer – Billy Steele – never quite got over an attempt to match JPR Williams bottle for bottle over the course of a single day. The full-back takes full responsibility: 'I was sharing a room with Billy, and I'd said that I'd make sure he had a good time if we won the Second Test. So at Kruger, I did – and he never recovered. It was a great few days – I smile about it even now.' Some were reminded of the worst excesses of the previous Lions tour to South Africa, that of 1968. The infamous 'Kippers and Wreckers' tour had blazed – quite literally at times – a trail throughout the land, prompting unfavourable newspaper headlines, hand-wringing and a fair bit of amusement.

The Johannesburg *Sunday Times* labelled them the worst team ever to tour South Africa: 'They have left a trail of havoc and stunned incredulity after three days in East London... marked by severe drinking bouts, riotous behaviour at hotels and nightclubs. They left broken hotel doors, broken glasses by the dozen, unpaid liquor debts and girls in tears because of outright rudeness.'

That tour party of '68 was essentially divided into the party animals – the Wreckers – and those who chose to steer clear – the Kippers – with another off-shoot of the Wreckers becoming known as the Burners because of their propensity for pyrotechnics. Yes, it was a tour of broken bottles, beds and hearts – as well as burnt shirts, trousers and underwear, some of it male.

Since one of the main Wreckers was tour manager David Brooks, who paid for the damages as well as the bar tab, essentially sanctioning the carnage, those like Gerald Davies and John Taylor who were firmly among the Kippers felt particularly uncomfortable. There was a *Lord of the Flies* mentality at work, so you either joined in or lived in fear. Taylor for one confessed to being anxious at times, while fellow tourist Jim Telfer felt the excess was a form of public school arrogance – in effect rugby's equivalent to Oxford's Bullingdon Club. Nervousness bred tension, which bred division. Even those, like Willie John McBride himself who enjoyed the wrecking element very much, admitted later that things had gone too far.

During those few days in Kruger, and later in Port Elizabeth, the Lions of '74 attempted to emulate the notorious behaviour of their predecessors. Thankfully, they didn't come close. The Lions of '68 weren't remembered fondly in South Africa, the Lions of '74 are still revered to this day.

By midweek, they were back on the bus and back in Johannesburg, at least in body. Mentally though the break would take some getting over, and it showed. The Lions had climbed their Everest, and having come back down to base camp, were now being asked to climb it all over again.

* * *

Next up were the Quaggas, an invitational side in the Barbarian mould, named after an extinct type of zebra. Only three of the Test match XV started, McGeechan stepping in at outside-half for the crocked Bennett, the ever willing Brown up for a challenge yet again at lock, and Fran Cotton, given the ultimate compliment of captaining the side for the first time. He would be the only novice tourist to lead the Lions throughout the tour.

Irvine at full-back was flanked by Grace and a far from fully fit Rees. With Billy Steele still feeling the after-effects of Kruger – along with a few genuine niggles – and JJ Williams now wrapped in cotton wool until a fixture demanded his presence, Rees was rushed back into the fray. The gamble didn't pay off. It would be his last match of the tour.

Mike Gibson played his first match alongside Bergiers in the centre – the wonderfully gifted Ulsterman would eventually play sixty-eight matches for the British and Irish Lions, putting him second on the all-time list. Behind him, in joint third are Delme Thomas and Syd Millar with forty-four appearances. Ahead of Gibson, with seventy appearances, is Willie John McBride.

Moloney partnered McGeechan at scrum-half, Burton – fully focused in every sense without his eyepatch – was back at prop alongside Kennedy and Cotton. Ralston partnered Brown behind them, while Tommy David was given his first start since Cape Town in tandem with Ripley at number 8 and Neary on the open-side.

There was talk of the Quaggas fielding one or two of the non-white players who'd starred for the Proteas. It would have been a major step forward – too big a step as it turned out, because when the team was announced, it was all white.

In rugby terms, it was all right too, with Bayvel at scrum-half and captain, partnered by a rising star, Western Province's Peter Kirsten. The youngster's rugby career would be cut short through injury before he could become a fully-fledged Springbok, but he would go on to star for the South African cricket team instead. Kirsten would eventually play his first Test match when South Africa was welcomed back into the international fold in 1992. By the time he pulled on his pads against the West Indies in Bridgetown, fully eighteen years after he'd dazzled the British and Irish Lions in Johannesburg, Kirsten was thirty-seven years old.

There were others who shone that day in Ellis Park. A number of the starting line-up came from the Transvaal,

233

and some, like centre Peter Cronje and number 8 'Klippies' Kritzinger were putting their hands up for national selection.

Amazingly, despite two Test defeats, or possibly because of them, 55,000 fans, a world record for a midweek match, came to Ellis Park to watch the bits and bobs of South African rugby attempt to topple the Lions.

* * *

Irvine and Kirsten exchanged early penalties before the Lions registered their opening try, a simple kick and chase by Ripley, who charged, knees pumping high towards his chest, and managed to beat all comers to the touchdown. In full flight he was an awesome sight.

When I asked Clive Rowlands about Ripley, he inevitably compared him to Mervyn Davies at number 8: 'He was a super player. But Ripley didn't work enough on his game. He had natural pace, natural strength. But natural pace for rugby football is totally different to natural pace for bloody hurdling. Quick, big, he could get you a score from ten, twenty, thirty yards out sometimes. But those chances didn't come around that often. Merve did everything else.'

Ripley's try wasn't in fact as straightforward as it seemed. There was an element of doubt about his grounding, enough to stir South African blood when it was awarded. The crowd's ire was further provoked when their own side's claims for a try were turned down by referee Ian Gourlay of Natal. When he'd refereed the Lions match against Western Province in Cape Town earlier in the tour, he'd been fine. Here his affiliation meant that he was already lacking in friends before the match began. He would be public enemy number one by the time it ended.

The Quaggas scored the next try – awarded – to winger Stephenson, before Gordon Brown – the only veteran of '71 in the Lions pack that day – took a decisive hand. Again it was a controversial try – not only was the grounding suspect, but there were also claims of a knock-on. The home crowd felt aggrieved enough to act, and had plenty of ammunition to work with. There was a tradition of selling oranges outside rugby grounds in South Africa – they were known locally as 'naartjies'. These were now used as missiles, all hurled in Mr Gourlay's general direction. Half-time was a welcome respite, a chance for the players and referee to huddle in the safety of midfield.

At that stage the Lions led by thirteen points to seven, but it was becoming an uncomfortable afternoon's work: 13–7 became 13–10, became 16–10, became 16–13. Rees departed after compounding his hand injury to be replaced by JPR Williams, Bayvel departed too but the Quaggas didn't seem to miss him. Kirsten was landing everything, the pressure was on, the crowd sensed it, the players sensed it – this could be the South African equivalent of the Barbarians vs New Zealand in 1973. There were ten minutes to go.

Then Brown turned the whole world orange once more with another controversial score to ignite the crowd. His second try was as dodgy as the first as far as the locals were concerned, and again the referee, the pitch and the Lions players were pelted with half eaten fruit, and anything else that would fly. Irvine even had to delay his conversion – unsuccessful – as the locals vented their fury. At 20–13 the Lions finally seemed to be home if not entirely dry. But injury time dragged, Kirsten kicked another penalty, and the Quaggas were back within range at 20–16. Finally Gourlay called a halt to the play, and called a start to the riot. As he and the players sprinted from the far side of the pitch towards the safety of the dressing rooms, Ellis Park was overrun by irate Afrikaners.

The referee was swiftly surrounded, knocked to the ground and only managed to get away with the help of a police escort and some red-shirted out-riders. As he had been during the preceding eighty-plus minutes, Gordon Brown was again to the fore in this regard, and accepted a personal thank-you from Mr Gourlay during the after-match reception. By then the referee was sporting a black eye to make a cruiserweight proud, and he would suffer further indignity when attacked verbally by the head of South Africa's referees later on. He did find support back home in Natal at least, and the storm eventually blew over. Two years later Gourlay was refereeing a Test match between South Africa and New Zealand.

If the referee had a lucky escape that day, then so too did the Lions. The post Test comedown, the Kruger hangover and the lack of respect afforded the tourists by the free-running Quaggas had almost proved their undoing. Clive Rees was actually done – he was soon replaced on tour by Alan Morley of Bristol, the man who'd scored the winning try when England beat the 'Boks at that very ground back in 1972.

There had been efforts made to persuade Gerald Davies to join the squad. His best friend Gareth Edwards was charged with that responsibility: 'Syd asked if I'd phone Gerald to see whether he'd come out. So I did, but Gerald said; "It's after the Lord Mayor's show by now. You've done it haven't you? There's no point in me coming out this late." I'd been upset that he hadn't come initially, so I was telling him; "Look you'll enjoy it, the boys are great, we're playing fantastic stuff. Come on."'

Davies admits that he was tempted due to Edwards's intervention: 'The Lions rang up and asked and I said no. So then they got Gareth to ring from South Africa. I wavered – it was Gareth asking after all – a good friend, and he talked to me about how well things were going, and told me I must come out and join them... So yes, I wavered. I thought about it for a couple of hours, but decided that I couldn't change my mind. I told him eventually that I was sticking to my guns.'

But would he have enjoyed it, the style, the achievement? 'I never look back. I never thought afterwards that I should have gone, I just don't look over my shoulder and think; "I should have done this or that." I didn't envy them their achievement or their success, and there have been no regrets.'

Edwards for his part feels that there's an element of fate in these things: 'It was just too late for Gerald. I was disappointed, but then you look at Andy Irvine, and how he played, well he was fantastic. And it helped create his own Lions legend didn't it? Some things are meant to be I suppose.'

The squad left Johannesburg battered, bruised and chastened. Worryingly they had just one day between matches this time to get their 'game heads' on. Having found themselves in a state of free flowing oranges on a Thursday, they now had to prepare for the Orange Free State on a Saturday.

* * *

There are some stories that become legends, and those legends become blurred with the passage of time. The original event, what actually happened and where, almost becomes incidental – the tale is told and retold, it grows, it is tailored for an occasion, until the legend bears little resemblance to the actual truth of the matter. In terms of the Lions of 1974, there are many such legends. Willie John McBride's pipe-smoking response to imminent arrest in Port Elizabeth is one, and will come later.

Then there is the story of the 'phantom phone calls'. The Lions had allocated 'duty boys' for every stay, for every different hotel. Their duties involved counting heads, looking after baggage, making sure hotel bills were accounted for and paid, and generally making sure that everything ran smoothly for the rest of the squad. When Bobby Windsor took his turn as duty boy during a stay in Cape Town, he decided to take advantage of his position by making a few long-distance phone calls home and conveniently losing the paper work. He almost got away with it too. The Lions were on the bus and about to depart their hotel when manager Alun Thomas boarded in high dudgeon. He had been accosted by the hotel manager who'd insisted that there was an unpaid telephone bill. It ran to almost £100.

Thomas asked for the culprit to step forward. No-one did. Thomas then played his trump card, explaining that all the calls were made to one number in Newport, south Wales.

Suspicion naturally fell on Windsor, and, as ever when challenged, the hooker rose to the occasion. In a response that has since become a part of Lions folklore, Windsor turned to his team-mates in indignation, and asked: 'Which one of you bastards has been phoning my wife?'

His quick thinking tickled his coach so much that Millar informed Thomas to inform the hotel manager that the South African Rugby Board was picking up that particular tab. 'So I got away with it after all' laughs Windsor now – on tour, every small victory over authority is worth its weight in gold.

Another tour legend revolves around the Orange Free State's giant lock Johan de Bruyn, the man with the glass eye. The setting for the story is usually the Third Test in Port Elizabeth, where Gordon Brown is said to have hit de Bruyn so hard that his glass eye flew out. This prompted the most comical interlude in what was a brutal match, as players from both sides scrabbled around in the dirt trying to find the missing eye. When it was finally recovered, de Bruyn simply stuck it back in its socket, grass and all, and carried on with the game.

Now here's where myth and reality become blurred. Bobby Windsor has claimed that the incident took place in the match against Orange Free State, a possibility because de Bruyn was also putting himself about in that particular game. Less plausible is the claim that it was Mike Burton who dislodged the glass eye. Burton would have had difficulty punching de Bruyn for the simple reason that he didn't actually play in either the Free State match or the Test that followed!

The general consensus, and the story presented in pages of *The History of the British and Irish Lions* concludes, in Cluedo fashion, that it was Mr Brown in the Third Test with a right hook. JPR Williams among others is adamant that the story is fact not fiction: 'It's a true story, it happened in the Third Test. I remember wondering what all these fellows were doing on the floor by the touchline, and they were genuinely looking for his glass eye. You can't make that up.'

As though to confirm the story, the eye itself, encased and enshrined, was presented to Mrs Brown after Gordon's passing by de Bruyn himself. Such is the fraternity of rugby.

Except that there wasn't much fraternity on show on Saturday, 29 June 1974, in Bloemfontein, when de Bruyn and the rest of his Free State cohorts almost ruined a perfect touring record.

* * *

As losing Currie Cup finalists in 1973, 1975, 1977 and 1978 – and winners in 1976 – the Free State were among South Africa's teams of the Seventies, and as such were expected to offer a particularly stern challenge. If the South African Rugby Board had scheduled their match, as well as Northern Transvaal's, towards the beginning of the tour, then history might have been different. Rather than top-loading the schedule, the heavy hitters were kept back, and by the time they took on the Lions it was too late – the tourists were well into their formidable stride.

That at least was the theory of Lions liaison officer Choet Visser. A Bloemfontein native, he was naturally keen that his Free Staters do well, but also grew to be an integral part of that close-knit Lions party in 1974. Andy Irvine recalls him warning the squad to be careful on his home patch: 'He told us that "The one game where you'll be really tested will be the Free State" and that was the game we came nearest to losing.'

Forewarned, the Lions now forearmed, with a side fit for a Test match. The two Williamses and Steele formed the back three, Milliken and Evans were in the centre, with McGeechan and Edwards at half-back. The front row consisted of McLauchlan, Windsor and Carmichael, with McBride and Ralston behind them, and McKinney, Slattery and Davies filling out the back row. Both McGeechan and Ralston were playing their second match in three days, but surely the Lions collective would have shaken off their mid-tour lethargy by now?

The one issue that did cause real concern beforehand was kicking for the posts. With both Bennett and Irvine rested, the pre-match training shoot out between JPR Williams, McGeechan, Edwards and Stewart McKinney proved far from satisfactory. The lottery would continue during the course of a tense encounter, and would almost cost the Lions dear.

Once again the crowds came in their tens of thousands, and they still travelled with a fair amount of partisan expectation. And as always, wherever the Lions went, a holiday mood took over. The squad had been convoyed into the city by a fleet of vintage cars – a sight in itself – and it seemed that the whole of Bloemfontein had turned out to greet their arrival. Now they turned out again, 60,000 of them, and of all the fans at all those matches throughout the tour, they came closest to seeing an upset.

'They came down the tunnel like maniacs' recalled JJ Williams of the Free State side: 'They were going to kill us, these Dutchmen from the mountains. And it was hard – the hardest match of the tour.'

A half-hour of stalemate was broken when Springbok new boy Jackie Snyman kicked a penalty, provoking the by now customary Lions response. Adhering to another custom, they launched their attack from the base of the scrum. Five yards out, rock solid, momentum gained, Mervyn Davies picked up and drove – try. Not pretty, but pretty effective. Less so was their kicking – McGeechan and Williams both missed shots at the sticks, and when, early in the second half, Snyman dropped a goal to put the Free Staters back ahead by six points to four, things really started to hot up. Happy to kill ball, to slow play and to mix it physically, the local side were looking good value for their lead.

Then up stepped Stewart McKinney, making his second vital contribution to the tour's success. Another penalty award, another conference to see who might fancy a pop at goal, and this time it was the Ulster flanker who got the nod. He'd kicked a crucial penalty in Ireland's win over Scotland back in March, and this time around, while all about him were losing their heads, McKinney remembered his Kipling. He hit it long, straight and true, and the Lions were back in front, by seven points to six.

Into the frantic last ten, and Orange Free State still fancied their chances. When they were awarded another penalty, duly slotted home by the nerveless Snyman, the home fans could barely contain themselves. Here it was at last, they would bear witness to their own piece of rugby history, a win that would bring their nation hope for things to come. Down by nine points to seven, with only seconds remaining, the crowd screaming for the final whistle, the Lions launched one last desperate attack.

They didn't score, they didn't even get a penalty. But they did get a scrum five yards out from the Orange Free State line. There was only one catch – it wasn't their own put-in. Play stopped as a Free State player took time out. One of the home stalwarts, de Bruyn's second row partner Botha, had been hit so hard in the previous engagement that he was staggering, dazed and bloody – unsure of his surroundings. He would have to leave the field.

He was helped away by McBride himself, ever the old fox. They were in the furthest corner of the ground, as far away from the grandstand touchline, the reserves and match officials as they could be.

In those days a replacement could be sent on only after the match doctor had certified that the original injury was genuine, that the injured player really was in no condition to carry on. Said match doctor was nowhere in sight, and as the Free State replacement charged across the pitch to join the fray, Gareth Edwards knew exactly what to do. He reminded referee Bezuidenhout that the doctor hadn't yet seen Botha, in effect forcing the referee to send the new player back off.

It was one of the tour's key exchanges according to the scrum-half: 'You can't imagine how difficult that game was. We were working our way downfield, working all the way until we'd get into their twenty-five. Then ping. Whistle goes, and we're penalised, and Snyman puts us back sixty yards. And we start again, get down there... and the same happens. We were in control, but every time we'd get close, we'd get pinged. So we got down to those last few seconds, with that big old clock at the end of the ground showing exactly how much time we had left, and we knew we were being tucked up. So when this happened before the last scrum I turned to the ref and said; "Hang on, he can't come on. The doctor hasn't seen the guy yet." And I can remember the ref's face now. He'd had us all game, and there he was caught out himself right at the very end. And he says in this broad Afrikaner accent; "You're rrright. He must go and see the doctor." And that was it. Still their ball, but we had a chance.'

It was enough.

Having failed to get the doctor on soon enough, home skipper Swart now missed another trick, and in the process presented the Lions with more than a glimmer of hope.

The Free State could have brought one of their bigger backs into the back row, thus making up the numbers and freeing up their number 8 Grobler, who could have moved forward to lock. All they had to do was guarantee their own ball, heel safely and hoof to touch. Those Free Staters would be history makers.

But more than eighty minutes of absolute commitment, of unrelenting effort, of physical pain, had taken its toll. Swart couldn't think straight, and no-one else stepped up to remind him of his options. Orange Free State packed down with seven men. Willie John McBride gathered his forwards and told them that this was it. This was their one shot, their chance to show what they were made of. In the stands, Messrs Burton and Cotton, who could have been forgiven for not wanting their front row rivals to grab too much of the glory, turned to each other and nodded. They had propped with and against these boys for two months, sixty, seventy times a day in training, and then against the best that South Africa had to offer. They knew what came next, and more to the point, they were grinning with excitement at the prospect.

The biggest irony of all was that Orange Free State had a ready-made number 8 on the pitch already in Gerrie Sonnekus. A useful one too – good enough to play for the Springboks in that position in future. The problem was that Sonnekus was at that time playing scrum-half, and was entrusted with making sure the put-in went the right way. He did, but it was irrelevant.

As the ball shot towards the back of the Free State scrum, the Lions put on an almighty squeeze. Both front rows came up, but crucially the ones in red were moving forwards at a rate of knots.

With the Free State seven back-peddling towards their own try line, the ball shot back in the opposite direction, with Windsor heeling towards the feet of Mervyn Davies.

The number 8 picked and passed, in one movement almost, to Edwards rushing full tilt for the blind-side corner. A trademark dummy got him past the initial cover, but as he sprinted for the line, he realised that he would be bundled into touch. It happened in the blink of an eye, but remains one of the greatest pieces of rugby skill under pressure ever seen. Edwards threw the ball over his head – except that 'threw' doesn't do it justice at all – he passed the ball over his head, towards the spot JJ Williams had instinctively angled for when he saw his number 9 running out of space.

There were plenty of white shirted defenders in the vicinity, but none had been prepared for Edwards's moment of genius. Williams was – he gathered the ball in his fingertips and crossed the try line unopposed.

Williams is matter-of-fact in his assessment: 'Wingers are there to score crucial tries at crucial times. That's what top rugby players are supposed to do isn't it? It's called skill. I preach skill these days and no-one listens. They don't get taught like that any more.'

If they don't they should watch the video. That try is one of the few scored in the provincial matches that has survived on tape, and when you watch it for the first time it's hard to grasp just how extraordinary the whole thing is, that anyone should dare to try something so outrageous, and that it should actually come off, under those circumstances. It was, and still is quite simply a work of art, just a few seconds long, but in that particular context, a masterpiece.

When I asked him whether greatness was all about context, and whether that try encapsulated his own greatness, Gareth Edwards had this to say: 'Well, it was the one chance we had. That's why it gives me huge satisfaction to this day. It still makes me smile when I think about that one, how it worked, and that it worked in a particularly tough situation. Sometimes it doesn't come off. The fact that it did right then, under such extreme pressure was special. I can't tell you how satisfying that try was just because of the circumstances.'

Two weeks later, on the eve of the Third Test – 12 July – Gareth Edwards celebrated his twenty-seventh birthday in Port Elizabeth. Veteran journalist Neil Cameron, writing for *The Herald*, marked this personal milestone with a column that celebrated Edwards's genius: 'I have not seen a finer player than this dark, curly-haired Welshman' he wrote. Looking back at that monumental finish in Bloemfontein, Cameron concluded that: 'The record books give the final credit to Williams for saving the day, but in the Lions' heart of hearts they all know it was Gareth Edwards.'

McKinney missed the touchline conversion but it was too late for any reply from the Free State. It ended 11–9. The home players sank to their knees at the final whistle, bloodied and broken. Syd Millar commented later that this was the hardest match the Lions played during the whole of the tour. Forty years afterwards, Willie John McBride still insists that it was the toughest. The innate ability to react when under the most extreme pressure – the true mark of champions – had seen them through. That, and a piece of magic from the most gifted player on earth.

When the players gathered for a celebratory evening at a local restaurant, JJ Williams noticed that his Llanelli team-mate Phil Bennett was quiet, to the point of being morose: 'We were in this restaurant after the game, and he was on the verge of tears. Now we'd just won this tough game, and I'd scored the try, so I was "up" as you can imagine, but Phil was down in the dumps, really miserable. He felt he was missing out – I'd never seen him like that before.'

Williams recognised that the combination of physical pain and mental torture was affecting his friend, and, in his own inimitable fashion, decided to act: 'I just said; "What the fuck's wrong with you – you've got to get on with it." That's how it was, and that's how we were together. There was no time for beating around the bush. The Third Test was coming, we needed him ready mentally and physically.'

Bennett admits that he was at his lowest ebb during those weeks: 'There were some matches that I just couldn't watch, and others where after saying well done to the boys in the dressing room, I'd just have to vanish for a half-hour. I'd have to go for a walk behind the stands, stuff like that. I was in a mess really, and I just couldn't see myself contributing again.'

As well as Williams's blunt pep talk, one more conversation had the desired effect according to Bennett: 'After that Free State game I talked to Syd and he said; "Benny, we've got no control at number 10." So they still needed me. For him to say that gave me a big lift. I thought then I'd get back in, I'd still play a part.'

One last postscript to that visit to Bloemfontein. From that day on, the Lions made sure they picked a specialist goal kicker for every match.

* * *

They still had another two weeks before the Third Test in Port Elizabeth, but now that they were back on the road, matches were coming thick and fast. The Lions next drove to Kimberley, famous as the diamond mining capital of Africa and for a protracted siege during the last Boer War. This time around, it was the Griqualand West team that came under siege, and it was the Brits who had all the big guns. The relaxed approach to the match was reflected in the XV selected. Irvine at full-back, Steele and Grace on the wings, Milliken and Evans at centre. The all-Irish partnership of Gibson and Moloney were at 10 and 9, with what was by now the recognised second string of Carmichael, Kennedy and Burton in the front row. Ralston, belatedly getting a run of games at second row played his third in succession alongside Uttley. Ripley at 8 was flanked by David and Slattery, who once again got to lead the side.

A few first-teamers enjoyed the chance to relax. Windsor and McLauchlan went on safari, joining a hunting trip which was contributing to the annual cull of local springbok. The group they accompanied eventually bagged sixteen in all, prompting Windsor to tell one journalist that they'd got the whole South Africa team.

When it was pointed out that the total number was sixteen not fifteen, he quipped that: 'We shot the ref as well.' The joke was lost on Alun Thomas, always a stickler for protocol. They couldn't afford to alienate the local referees any further because they might still have need of a favourable on-field decision here and there. So thought the manager, but Windsor was beyond caring. He had learned to expect no favours in

South Africa, and didn't feel they needed any by that stage anyway.

Back on the pitch, the midweek side was experiencing its own version of 'shooting fish in a barrel'. Having become accustomed to the huge crowds on the Highveld, the De Beers Stadium, with its capacity of less than 10,000 seemed miniscule in comparison. Wherever they went though, the Lions put on a show. It was fast, it was open, and for the Griquas it was murder. England had put sixty points on them two years previously, so the only real pressure on the Lions was to surpass that mark.

It turned out to be the day of the Irish. Of twelve tries scored, Grace accounted for four, with Kennedy, Slattery and Moloney all chipping in with one each. The scrum-half got the ball rolling within minutes of the start, capitalising on a bullocking charge by David which left gaping holes in the home defence. Moloney swept through the open door and sprinted past full-back Smith for the try.

Evans jinked past three men to touch down for the second – the deftest of passes from Gibson having opened up the initial space. Gibson had been at number 10 the last time the Lions had played this fixture, back in 1968. They'd won 11–3 that day, this time around things were a lot easier.

And it got easier still when David got on the score sheet, brushing, shrugging, pushing, barging and eventually crashing his way through five different players to score under the posts.

The Lions were eighteen up within as many minutes, and that was before the other Tom – Grace – got going. His first came just before half-time, his second just after. Slattery then sprinted half the length of the field, showing both David and Ripley how to travel at full tilt with the ball carried in both hands. As it happened he didn't need to pass, as he rounded Smith, the forlorn last line of defence again, with some ease.

Grace, having seen his skipper score a winger's try, decided to take back the initiative, and promptly scored two more, the last of which saw him waltz through six covering Griquas as though they were playing a game of two handed touch. It mirrored Billy Steele's effort against Eastern Province weeks before, a step infield off the right foot followed by a burst outside the remaining cover.

Ripley's first, the team's ninth, took the Lions over fifty points. Billy Steele on the opposite wing got a late brace of his own, before the afternoon was rounded off in popular fashion by Ken Kennedy.

In between the glut of tries, Irvine had landed eight conversions and a penalty for a grand total of nineteen, and Gibson had registered his first points of the tour with a conversion. The Griquas had scored two tries of their own, both scored by winger Wiese. He also added a conversion and a penalty for a personal tally of thirteen. Another penalty from outside-half Van Eck meant that the home side ended the match with a respectable sixteen points, but the Lions' sixty-nine had exceeded England's total two years previously, and would be their second highest tally of the whole tour.

It was a well-timed lift. The Lions were in the middle of their most gruelling run of fixtures. Five matches in twelve days followed by the biggest match of their lives. They had already accounted for the Quaggas, Orange Free State and Griqualand West in less than a week. Now they faced Northen Transvaal and the second 'non-white' team of the tour, the Leopards, before the massive Third Test in Port Elizabeth. Unbelievably, the toughest of their challenges were yet to come.

CHAPTER 18

The Battle of Boet Erasmus
— Part II

'Today is a good day to fight, today is a good day to die.
Cowards to the rear, brave hearts follow me.'
Crazy Horse, War Chief, Oglala Sioux, 25 June 1876,
Battle of the Little Big Horn

'Treat your men as you would your own beloved sons.
And they will follow you into the deepest valley.'
Sun Tzu, *The Art of War*

AND SO IT was back to Loftus Versfeld, Pretoria, and back
to another throng of agitated Afrikaners, 55,000 strong.
Northern Transvaal were undoubtedly the South African team
of the decade. They won the Currie Cup five times between
1973 and 1978 and were always there or thereabouts in terms
of contesting the provincial final. The cauldron would be
bubbling again this time, and the Lions needed all hands on
deck. That meant JPR Williams at full-back, Irvine – a place
kicker, no less – chosen on the right wing with JJ Williams on
the other. Gibson and Milliken played together at centre – the
last time they'd done so was back in March, when Milliken
had scored the only try and Gibson had converted in Ireland's
Five Nations win over Scotland. The young tyro from Bangor
had come a long way since then.

While Bennett missed his fourth game on the trot, McGeechan started yet again, his fifth outing in six matches, this time alongside Edwards. Up front seven of the eight were Test match starters – McLauchlan, Windsor, Cotton, McBride, Brown, Uttley and Davies. Slattery, who'd been almost as busy as McGeechan in a more physical role, was given the day off, with Neary drafted in.

Northern Transvaal possessed a core of formidable forwards, including the estimable John Williams at lock alongside self-confessed hard nut Moaner van Heerden. If the Lions expected a slog, they got that and more, and at times it was downright ugly. An exchange of early penalties left Northerns 6–3 up, but they were caught by a sucker punch late in the first half which gifted the Lions a lead. Faced with a line-out virtually on their own try line, the local side switched off. Maybe they felt that their own powerhouse, Williams, could contest anything thrown to the middle and disrupt possession. And maybe that's why Windsor threw long towards the tail. Davies leapt unopposed, caught and crashed over. Irvine converted for a 9–6 lead to the Lions.

Tactical sucker punches were soon replaced by the real thing. Davies piled in to an already uproarious melee only to be caught by van Heerden, intent on living up to his reputation. At the same time the Welsh number 8 was grabbed by the collar from behind and dragged to the ground by outside-half Vic Booyens.

The diminutive number 10 then proceeded to launch a kick straight into Davies's face, as though attempting to drill a ball from one try line all the way to the other. It was one of the most unsavoury incidents of a tour full of them.

Northerns levelled things at nine-all early in the second half through a third penalty from full-back Luther, only for Edwards and JJ Williams to lead the counter-reformation. They combined for a lightning strike, with the scrum-half's thrust and pass giving the winger just a fraction of space. Williams made it to within a yard of the corner and, as cover approached, he stepped back inside to find Neary catching up fast. The flanker took the pass and charged over.

The newly established 13–9 lead was soon cut to just a point thanks to Luther's fourth successful kick, and if Booyens had been half as sharp with an attempted drop kick as he was with his assault on Davies, then Northerns could have been ahead as they entered the closing stages. Their scrum had held up well, and they'd frustrated main man Edwards for the most part, meaning that they stopped the Lions at source. And while McGeechan was doing a fine job at outside-half under trying conditions, if ever a match showed just how valuable Phil Bennett was to the Lions cause, then this was it. They had missed his big game spark, and could only hope he'd be ready for the biggest game yet.

Luckily for the Lions, though unluckily for Milliken, another piece of outright thuggery gave them the chance to put the game to bed. The Irishman went charging down the left wing, only to be stiff armed by the airborne Northerns number 8 Oosthuizen. Today he'd be signed up as 'The Blue Bullet' or 'The Flying Dutchman' – a cert for stardom in the world of WWE wrestling. He took Milliken shoulder high, and left the tough as teak centre obviously shaken. A penalty ensued, and despite the touchline angle and distance, Irvine slotted home to make the final score 16–12 to the aggrieved but relieved touring side.

Of the big provincial teams, only Natal remained, but the most dangerous sides had been faced down. The unbeaten record was still intact, and after seven matches in the high country, the Lions were headed back to the coast. The African Leopards waited in East London, before the big showdown in Port Elizabeth. And the best news of all for the tourists? Bennett was back.

* * *

Following the perverse logic of the apartheid system, the rugby Leopards were the representative team of black South Africa. They had played against England in 1972 and had recently returned from a tour to Italy. As with the Proteas, the fixture either gave credence to the system as it stood, or presented a unique opportunity to build bridges, depending entirely on which side of the apartheid fence you stood. The match would attract a crowd of around 15,000, mostly non-white fans. No-one forced them to attend.

For young Mthobi Tyamzashe, the fixture proved to be a dilemma both in moral and rugby terms: 'I was for isolation in principle, and I was obviously against apartheid, but I still supported the Leopards, that's the interesting thing... South African communities were living so much apart at that time that you didn't know what was happening elsewhere... So we supported them.'

Was he naïve? Yes, in certain ways, by his own admission. But sides like the Leopards provided a grounding for administrators as well as players: 'First of all I thought that black rugby was so good that we would actually beat the white guys, so it was not seen as something we should not be involved in. Also, many of us who came to lead South African sport in later years were a part of those structures back then. It was a part of our background. So in my view a tour like the Lions tour was more than just a rugby tour. Remember, in those days we needed any kind of hope that things could change.'

There was another element to the tourists stay which meant something: 'They helped because they got publicity. They kept South Africa in the news, which to us was important, so that the world didn't forget us.'

Much of the rugby itself that day may have been forgettable, but the occasion was not. Tom David summed up the feelings among the squad: 'Beforehand we were very aware that we were a part of something important. But then once you start playing, it's just a game of rugby, and that's kind of the point isn't it... The colour thing didn't matter once you'd kicked off, because it was fifteen players against fifteen players, like everywhere else. And then afterwards you'd have a few beers with the guys as well, just like you'd do anywhere else. So just by doing our normal stuff, we were doing something important.'

With the Test looming, the Lions fielded a mostly dirt-track XV, bolstered by a smattering of first choice stars. Irvine started at full-back, with the in-form Grace and newbie Morley on the wings. McGeechan and Gibson partnered up in midfield, and Bennett was ready for a pre-Test run out. A niggle to Moloney meant that Edwards had to start too, hardly ideal, but Bennett at least would be glad of his presence. Carmichael, Kennedy and Burton could have been a first choice Test XV on any other tour, McBride stepped up alongside Ralston, with David, Ripley and McKinney behind them.

The pre-match entertainment, which consisted of long legged, baton twirling majorettes, made as much of an impression on the watching press pack as the game itself, but the Lions tried their best to maintain the entertainment level. Ten tries followed, the first of which was scored by Edwards in the opening few minutes. Grace kept up his hot streak with a hat-trick, taking his tour tally from four to eleven within the space of two appearances. On the opposite wing Alan Morley got a try on his Lions debut, while inside him Gibson bagged a brace.

The back row was playing host to a show-off competition, involving those two shy, retiring types, Andy Ripley and Tom David. Other than their enjoyment of the limelight, they were poles apart in terms of their personalities, as David found out when they shared a room together: 'The best parts of a tour are the parts people don't see, the banter, the friendships. We always shared rooms with boys who were from a different country, and one of the first blokes I shared with was Andy Ripley. And I came up from dinner one night and he had all this music going, waahh, waahh waahh... joss sticks smoking... Now I was from Ponty, I'd never seen anything like it. And he's saying; "This is good stuff for relaxation Tom," and I'm like; "Get that bloody stuff off, and put that bloody stuff out. Or you'll be out." He was a unique guy, a great guy.'

Other than their propensity for cradling the ball one-handed, Ripley and David each had their own differing playing styles, the Welshman looking to barrel through or over whatever stood in his way, the Englishman, like a twentieth-century doppelgänger of the great Southern Cheyenne warrior Roman Nose, always searching for the open ranges. Both got the chance to showcase their rampaging talents against the Leopards, and both scored tries. So too did Irvine, from a long distance kick and chase. Add penalties and conversions and the full-back's personal tally this time around would be twenty points, taking him past the hundred mark for the tour.

If the Leopards had plenty to learn in terms of the set-piece and defensive duties, they had certainly cottoned on fast to the 'take no prisoners' philosophy. Ralston took a hook to the cheek which left him unconscious. Blood flowed from his face, and he needed both stitches and an ambulance before he saw his team-mates again.

Tom David remembers that: 'Lurch was laid out, poleaxed, just crashed down horizontal like, with dust coming up everywhere around him. It was a four-inch cut, and it looked almost surgical, it was that clean, like a surgeon's knife. But at the end of the tour, I was presented with a scrapbook, and in it the player who'd hit him said he'd hit the wrong player – he was after me because I'd been pulling his shirt all game. I never told Lurch mind... In terms of the physical stuff though, you've got to remember, I played against Pontypool and Aberavon in the Seventies. It was just the same there, because they were dirty bastards. So it wasn't anything new... just a case of same shit different location.'

For once, the Lions refused to mete out their own unique

brand of vengeance, McBride deciding that this was neither the time or the place to be partaking of an on-field riot. Their generosity even extended to some lax defending near the end, errant enough at least to gift the Leopards a consolation try, scored with a spectacular pounce for the corner by winger Mgweba. The try's significance was not immediately apparent to the tourists, but it was to the Leopards players and their fans. This was a victory in itself. The mighty Springboks had failed to score a try against the Lions in two attempts so far. The lowly Leopards had now beaten them to that honour.

If Errol Tobias was the player who eventually emerged from that 1974 experience, the Lions players and press pack were convinced that the non-white player who was destined for greatness was Leopards talisman Morgan Cushe. The back row star went on to play for the first multiracial team to face an international side on South African soil. The officially sanctioned South African Invitation XV, as selected by Dr Danie Craven, beat France by eighteen points to three the following year at Newlands. Cushe, on the flank, was partnered in the back row by Dugald Macdonald and team captain Morné du Plessis.

Morgan Cushe passed away in October 2013. According to one South African newspaper report he was: 'Either the worst form of apartheid collaborator or a subsequently neglected trailblazer.' But among the many rugby men who expressed their condolences to the family of 'a fine man and a great rugby player' was SARU President, Oregan Hoskins. Those who knew Cushe say that he'd have loved being described by Hoskins as: 'A member of the South African rugby family' and as 'a great loose forward'. The man who'd impressed opponents and team-mates, players and administrators, black and white, would have appreciated being judged simply as a player, which of course was the whole point all along.

* * *

So just how would the South Africa team react to this latest indignity, a try scored against the Lions by a black side when the Springboks themselves had failed to score any so far? Well, they would come out fighting, of course. Literally so.

But not before they went through their customary round of 'pick the 'Bok', a popular pastime where the objective was to include at least half a dozen fresh faces in any given Test side. For the Third Test in Port Elizabeth, there would be eleven changes all in all, and six more new caps. Three came from the Orange Free State, centre Jan Schlebusch, converted number eight Gerrie Sonnekus at scrum-half, and 'The Cyclops', Johan de Bruyn in the second row. They were joined by number eight 'Klippies' Kritzinger, who had made an impression for both the Transvaal and the Quaggas in previous weeks, Polla Fourie, another back rower who'd shone for the Quaggas, and lock Moaner van Heerden, who'd made his own impression on a number of Lions in the blue of Northern Transvaal.

Tonie Roux hadn't featured at all for Northerns against the Lions, but he'd won his first cap against Scotland in 1969, and played at centre for the Springboks against England on that infamous day in 1972. He now came back into the international fold at full-back. So too did Peter Cronje of the Transvaal, who replaced Peter Whipp at centre. Cronje hadn't lost in his previous five Springbok appearances.

Gert Muller was fit – and back on the wing with the ever present Chris Pope, while Jackie Snyman was moved from centre to outside-half, meaning a swift exit for Gerald Bosch. Snyman's scrum-half partner was due to be Roy McCallum, harshly dropped after the First Test, brought back now, only to be injured after joining up with the squad.

Since the next pick, Paul Bayvel, had also been crocked playing for the Quaggas, the Springboks held what amounted to a three-way pass-off between Sonnekus, Barry Wolmarans of Boland, and Gert Schutte of the Griquas.

Schutte and Wolmarans had long flights home. That was

as close as Schutte got, he never did become a Springbok. Wolmarans waited another three years before winning his solitary cap, against a World XV. As for Sonnekus, well his selection by Johan Claassen proved to be one of the great positional blunders. Its modern-day equivalent came thirty-five years later when another South African coach, the much respected Nick Mallett, had his own moment of madness and picked top-class flanker Mauro Bergamasco at scrum-half for Italy against England at Twickenham. That too ended in disaster, but the stakes were nowhere near as high.

The other returnee for the 'Boks was 'Piston' van Wyk at hooker, between Marais and Bezuidenhout. Ellis was still there at 7, but the casualties included John Williams, deemed too nice for the dirty work ahead, and Morné du Plessis. Suffice to say that the Lions camp delighted in their absence.

I asked du Plessis, as a Capetonian and a Western Province stalwart, whether he felt there was any truth in the claim that the Springboks became increasingly Afrikaner in their mentality (and playing staff) as the series progressed. Whilst agreeing with the theory, he also accepted that someone had to be the fall guy: 'For me the prejudice stuff might just be a useful excuse for being dropped. I think they were looking for something better, and they felt it was out there – and if you're playing well enough you don't get dropped do you?... We'd just lost a Test match by an almost unthinkable margin, so someone had to go, you know.'

That said, the future Springbok captain also has an alternative theory as to his own omission and that of his back row partner Dugald Macdonald; 'Well, Dugald and I might have had a few too many beers on the Sunday after that Second Test match in Pretoria. That might not have gone down too well, either... So that might also have been a factor.'

While the Springboks were making wholesale changes, the tourists made just the one, but it was significant. Phil Bennett had to start, but his fitness was anything but guaranteed. The Lions needed a back-up place kicker just in case. With that in mind, Andy Irvine's proven record from distance, allied with his free running talent in broken play got him the nod on the right wing. Fellow Scotsman Billy Steele, who had done little wrong, was the unlucky player to miss out.

Irvine professed surprise at being selected: 'I'd started to play well, I was kicking the goals, and I was training well too, but I didn't really expect to get in because it's pretty tough to change a winning side. Billy Steele certainly wasn't playing badly, Billy had a very good tour... I think they were thinking about a long-range kicker.' JJ Williams felt there was more to it than that, and that Irvine deserved his promotion anyway: 'He was a much better player than Billy to be fair.'

The fact that they changed so little in terms of personnel was hugely important of course, but hugely discouraging for those with Test match pretensions. It was something which worried Syd Millar to the extent that he made a point of talking to the fringe players. He explained that these Lions were far from being a closed shop, despite the fact that it was difficult to change a winning team. After the tour, he would return to the theme of continuity, and continually praise those who hadn't made the Test line-up: 'There were people – I'd particularly single out Tony Neary in this respect, who was a magnificent forward – who were left out of the Test side. But the badge mattered to them. They all contributed enormously, and I think that was the key to the success of that side.'

Another component – however small – was some unexpected support from home. On a tour where they'd found friends to be at a premium, the Lions found themselves greeting familiar faces in Port Elizabeth – not the few dozen ex-pats that they'd seen up until now, but a group newly arrived supporters from Wales.

Phil Bennett was an avid writer of postcards: 'I'd be writing non-stop, but writing pretty much the same thing every time; "Weather lovely, having a great time, but missing a pint of Felinfoel [beer]." So we're in Port Elizabeth a few days before the Third Test and this bloke walks into the hotel with a Llanelli club badge on, and of course he's a mate of mine from home. So up he comes to my table and opens his case and pulls out two bottles of Felinfoel Bitter, and says; "You said in your card that you were missing it so I thought I'd bring you some." That's how daft it all was. But boy did it make you realise how important the whole thing was to people back home. And I think we were all glad of that feeling of not being alone any more.'

In the fight ahead, they would need all the support they could get.

* * *

Boet Eramsus, Port Elizabeth had already witnessed one eighty-minute pitched battle recently, but much had happened in the intervening weeks. The Lions had grown in confidence, grown stronger. The South Africans were in disarray.

On Saturday, 13 July, in front of a capacity 55,000 crowd, the Lions looked destiny in the eye once more. Cas de Bruyn was again in charge – a good sign – and what followed would, for better and for worse, become engrained in history. The Second Battle of Boet Erasmus was the whole tour in microcosm, and it would live on forever, in memory and in grainy archive footage, as the indelible image of the tour of '74.

Clem Thomas, chronicler of Lions history nonpareil, captured the absolute shock, the disbelief, as he watched events unfold: 'I must confess that this match is my biggest memory of the 1974 tour. I was never more astonished, as the game became the most violent Test match I ever witnessed.' Thomas had seen plenty, and taken part in a fair few, but nothing had prepared him for that Third Test in Port Elizabeth.

The Lions had a feeling that something was brewing as the teams emerged on to the field. 'You could see their eyes bulging' remarked JJ Williams years later, recalling the Springboks sprinting down the slope from their dressing room in the elevated grandstand. If only Ernest Hemingway, that ultimate exponent of the alpha male psyche, had found poetry in rugby instead of bull fighting, this would have been his perfect setting. 'In bullfighting they speak of the terrain of the bull and the terrain of the bullfighter' he wrote in *The Sun Also Rises*, 'As long as the bullfighter stays in his own terrain he is comparatively safe. Each time he enters into the terrain of the bull he is in great danger.' There was no snorting, no beating of hooves in Port Elizabeth, but the sight of those hated red jerseys challenging them on their own turf was enough of a trigger for South Africa's players.

Yet the Springboks had misjudged their foes once again. Hemingway had gone on to explain that the very best bullfighters 'worked always in the terrain of the bull'. It was the most dangerous place to be, but for those who aspired to greatness, the only place to be. The British and Irish Lions wouldn't take a step back, in fact they were intent on advancing right into the coming storm. Hemingway had essentially focused on the man alone, but even he might have been inspired by the collective on this particular day.

As always McBride led his side onto pitch holding the Lions mascot high above his head. And as always it was Andy Ripley who was waiting, like an autograph hunting schoolboy, to take it off his hands.

This says everything you could want to know about that particular relationship. Ripley the arch-individualist, yet the ultimate team man. Ripley who would joke that McBride: 'Never picked me in three and a half months' in order to hide his deep disappointment at missing out on the Tests. Ripley the ever ready, willing to take whatever burden the man he called 'My Leader' would throw his way. McBride did that to people. They would crawl over broken glass for him.

Those sentiments were echoed by the ultimate hard man – Bobby Windsor – in his own autobiography: 'Don't forget, this was a bunch of young, fit men – but grown men mind – who loved Syd and Willie John like their own fathers. If they'd have told us to go and jump off the Victoria Falls, we'd have done it.'

And now McBride would ask them to do it all one more time.

* * *

Jackie Snyman, the third outside-half in as many matches for the Springboks, did what his brother had done in the First Test by registering the game's opening points. Irvine responded with a siege gun kick of his own, from just inside the South African half. Some of his kicking towards the end of the tour was simply immaculate, especially considering that this match was back down at sea level. The player himself is as modest today as ever: 'I was in the side to kick goals.'

Irvine's attention was soon focused elsewhere, as the match erupted down towards his own corner. And if there was any need for a Hemingwayesque hero to take centre stage, then JPR Williams fitted the bill perfectly. Except that he was no matador, and this was no one-on-one encounter. This was more akin to the running of the bulls at Pamplona.

As the Springbok horde stampeded towards the Lions twenty-five-yard line Williams, the last line of defence, planted his feet, crouched, and prepared to be flattened. He was, but he'd stalled their momentum nonetheless.

As he lay prone on the ground he was well and truly trampled. Eight studs per boot, two boots per man, eight Springbok forwards planting everything they had on top of one defenceless player. Nothing new in that – it was the way of the southern hemisphere, it was to be expected.

But Moaner van Heerden had veered off his own path over Williams, specifically in order to land an extra size eleven on Lions number 11, Dick Milliken, another who'd been caught at the bottom of the rip tide. Roger Uttley saw what he did, and aimed a boot of his own at the Springbok second row. McBride too had noticed the stamp, and came out swinging. As both locks went head-to-head, others started to wade in, some ostensibly to break things up – but most, Windsor, Brown, McLauchlan included – simply seeing their captain in trouble and reacting.

No-one reacted with more fervour than JPR Williams. Having his back shredded had already put him in a fighting frame of mind, and seeing his captain in the thick of a brawl gave him an open invitation. He rose from the dirt and launched himself at the throng, targeting van Heerden in particular. The lock went tumbling backwards into the middle of the melee, ending up on the floor, but Williams kept on swinging at anything that moved in a green jersey. That essentially meant an assorted group of Springbok forwards, all considerably bigger and heavier than the Welshman himself.

He eventually found himself in a clearing, surrounded and outnumbered, and once again planted his feet ready to make his stand. This time though he did so with hands raised Marquis of Queensbury fashion, ready to take on whoever came his way. When no-one took up the challenge, Williams calmly dropped his fists, turned, and walked away from it all as though nothing had happened.

Moaner van Heerden walked away too after some treatment, but the Springbok enforcer wouldn't see out the match.

The whole unpleasant episode had lasted no more than fifteen seconds, but it helped build a legend. Williams was a fantastic player – a man of intense images. Whether they be bone crunching body-checks on flying Frenchmen, terrific Twickenham tries, desperate drop goals or coruscating counter-attacks – everyone who remembers rugby in the Seventies has his own favourite memory.

But they all remember South Africa, the white headband,

the man seemingly alone, defiant in a sea of green – JPR on Judgement Day.

The Lions may well have won the game anyway, but from then on there was no way they would lose. With a minute to go until the break, they had the Springboks cornered near their own try line. It was a defensive throw, and the line had been shortened. Gordon Brown, who had already scored some of the most important tries of the tour, now poached one more. It wasn't a rampaging charge in support of one of his backs this time, but pure grunt. He moved to the front of the line, and when the throw came, he snaffled it. The 'Boks had dropped their line-out expert Williams, and it came back to haunt them. As Cotton and Windsor on either side of him blocked for all they were worth, Brown hit the ground and flopped over the try line. It was his simplest try of the tour, and possibly his most valuable of all. It put the Lions 7–3 up at half-time.

Within six minutes of the restart, Irvine had exceeded his first-half effort by at least ten yards, nearer fifteen. That is to say, from way inside his own half. He had the wind at his back this time, but the kick was Thorburnesque in its distance. It sailed over, giving Irvine and his team-mates plenty of time to appreciate the majesty of the effort as it rose and rose. The Lions smelt blood at 10–3. Some were soon tasting their own.

Edwards box-kicked down the tramlines from just inside the Springbok half. He was jostled as he chased, and so put in the firmest of tackles when he finally nailed his man. Windsor, up supporting his scrum-half, was focused on the tackle area, and didn't see van Heerden coming. As the Welshman went to ground in an attempt to retrieve the ball, the Springbok number 5 hit him. There was no attempt to disguise the punch, just a stoop and a bang. Windsor was hurt to the extent that he didn't immediately get up and try to retaliate. Gordon Brown did that for him, charging at van Heerden, haymaking as he went. A right cross sent the Springbok staggering backwards, but as Brown pressed on he was hit by flanker Fourie. Mervyn Davies was also caught unawares and took a smack to the face – this was the '99' in reverse.

McBride had seen enough. He charged after van Heerden and the rest – not really caring who he hit, as long as he kept moving forward deeper and deeper into the Springbok throng. He seemed intent on taking on the whole South African team, the whole South African nation on his own, if need be. He was laying down the gauntlet, to his own men as much as the enemy, and at one point was surrounded by five green shirted forwards, each taking aim simultaneously.

That tore it. The trumpets sounded and the cavalry charged. First Davies, then Cotton and Slattery, and last but by no means least, Brown – all heading straight for the thick of the action, in support of their beleaguered leader. They got there just in time, although Brown took another hammering on the chin for his trouble – his second in the space of ten seconds – this time from Springbok number 8 Kritzinger.

Momentarily floored, Broon frae Troon was straight back up and after his man, only to be grabbed by the collar and flung to the ground yet again by Johan de Bruyn. The Scotsman would later describe the madness as: 'A slight altercation,' and yet it left one of his hands – his punching hand – in a real mess.

Where was the referee as all hell broke loose? Mesmerised – like everyone else not directly involved in the battle. Cas de Bruyn stood back and let it all unfold. In truth there was little he could have done anyway, and since both sides had been equally eager to get involved, he stayed calm, and carried on.

McBride finally fought his way clear only to look back and see JPR Williams joining the fray – all the way from full-back – and squaring up to the biggest Springbok he could find once again. It was that kind of afternoon. Forty years later, Williams recalls it like this: 'It's fight or flight isn't it? It's not rational, of course. If you thought about it at all, you wouldn't do it.

I found myself at that point running in from around forty yards to join a punch up, with Phil and Andy Irvine going the other way. It's funny but my son used to watch the clips all the time when he was younger, and it was his favourite bit of footage. And I'd genuinely look at it and think – is that really me? What the hell was I doing?'

He says all this with a smile though – and a shake of the head... Deep down one can't help but feel that he's still proud that he was there standing shoulder to shoulder with his captain: 'Well people don't realise that Willie John was a legend to us. We would do anything he said, follow him anywhere. That was one of our great strengths.'

While Williams was eager to show that no-one took a free swing at the skipper, Bobby Windsor took it all in his stride: 'I'd never seen anyone as big as these Springbok bastards. And to be fair they had plenty of heart to go with their muscle. But they looked at us and saw a bunch of fucking headcases. We had it over them in that regard you know. When van Heerden went off, they said he was injured. Total bollocks, he didn't know where in the fuck he was – Frannie Cotton had caught him as he tried to come through onto Willie, and he had it coming too.'

Willie John McBride chortles as he recalls van Heerden's exit in particular: 'I remember Bobby, who'd taken a few during that game himself, standing there by the touchline saying: "Bye, bye Moaner," it was a sweet moment.'

It came down not to the size of the dog in the fight, but to the size of the fight in the dog. The Lions had shown their mongrel side yet again – they simply would not be cowed. Next, they showed that they had pedigree too.

Cometh the hour, cometh Bennett, pumped up on painkillers and dropping the sweetest of goals to make it 13–3. Then came the Williamses, JPR and JJ, to remind everyone of just how great a side these Lions really were.

Gordon Brown, having taken every punch and taken a try-scoring opportunity as well, now won a vital line-out. Swift

265

ball was moved towards the open field, Edwards to Bennett to McGeechan to Milliken, each swinging their arms and hips in classic fashion – one pendulum, two pendulum, three pendulum, four. JPR Williams was up from full-back on the gallop, but Milliken went straight for JJ on his outside.

The winger looks back on that try now with immense satisfaction. It showcased their talent and training to perfection: 'I grew up in the valleys, passing, passing, passing, every training session passing, passing. Then the same with Llanelli, then with Wales, then with the Lions. I'd done a million passing sessions. Ian McGeechan would say the same, from Headingley to Scotland to the Lions, passing, passing, passing every day. So when you talk about slick passing, it was simply that when it counted we could do it. Skill at the vital moment shines through under pressure only if it comes as second nature.'

The winger raced into the South African twenty-five, before flipping the ball back inside to a still supporting JPR. As one Williams veered towards the outside with the ball, the other veered back inside without it on a scissors move. As the cover converged to cut JPR off, he executed almost exactly the same pass as his winger had seconds before, a flip back inside. JJ took it, and kept on dancing in-field, a step to the right and then a step on the gas. Past one, past two, over the try line and under the posts.

JPR smiles at the memory: 'We'd played together since we were fifteen, and you could see that. I just expected him to be there, and I still think today that it was a tremendous try.'

There were Springbok bodies strewn everywhere. Even Marais the captain had managed a last-gasp dive for Williams as he grounded the ball. The enduring images – still photographs of Williams scoring with the crowd as a backdrop, tell their own story. Behind him was the non-white corner, black supporters in their own cordoned-off kraal. The Lions had made a point of heading down there pre-match for their warm up, and now, as Williams touched down to finish off South Africa, that corner was united in jubilation.

The winger himself recalls that: 'We were aware of the non-white support from the very off. We'd always go down to the corner pre-match just to let them know we appreciated it, so we fed off each other. I'm not going to sit here and say that we changed anything radically, but I do think we did some good. By playing non-white sides, by meeting their players, by showing that the 'Boks could be beaten. I think that try summed it up in lots of ways.'

Peter Hain and others are right, those fans weren't celebrating the Lions specifically, they would have supported anyone laying waste to their oppressors.

But up to that point, they'd never had cause to celebrate, because no-one ever had. For the first time ever, a rugby team had steamrollered those mighty Afrikaners, right there in their own back yard.

One of those jubilant spectators, tucked away in the far corner of Boet Erasmus was twenty-year-old Mthobi Tyamzashe, who looks back from the distance of forty years and still chuckles as he remembers how he fell in love with those Lions players: 'It was a pleasure to watch them. It was like we were watching rugby for the first time... Now with me being a rugby person, it was about more than just beating the Springboks politically. I loved them for their style. I had never seen a player jinking before. When I saw Phil Bennett I didn't understand; "What's he doing, what's he doing?" and of course he was jinking, confusing the opposition. It was so unique, it was like a revelation to us.'

For a moment, at least, all questions as to the rights and wrongs of the tour were irrelevant. Nothing would change, conditions wouldn't improve. In fact, things would get worse before they got better, and some of those celebrating fans would pay with cuts and bruises post-match when they came across irate policemen and Afrikaner fans. But JJ Williams at least feels pride when he remembers that try above all others. That famous image, the touchdown, Marais clutching at air, hundreds of non-white supporters punching the air behind him, still hangs in a prominent spot in the Williams family home on the outskirts of Bridgend: 'Looking back now I still think we were better off going than not going. If we'd lost, then it would have meant nothing. But the fact we won, that we beat the 'Boks, I think that mattered in more than rugby terms. So when you ask now, forty years later if I'd do things differently, I say no, I'd still have gone. And if you want any justification look at that photograph over there. It mattered.'

Tyamzashe concurs: 'Remember that Hannes Marais's team was very strong and formidable. So for them to be beaten like that was huge. We wanted to knock sense into the white man. Rugby was seen as the Afrikaner's sport, his religion. We saw them as being responsible for apartheid, so anyone who beat them was supported by our community.'

Obviously the celebrations annoyed the white South Africans watching from their own stands. But that was a victory in itself. 'The more we realised they were getting annoyed, the more we celebrated' says Tyamzashe: 'The South Africans would see us and say; "Look at these Bantus", because that's how they'd see us. "The Bantus are cheering". It was our way of showing how we felt, showing where we stood. And that's why I remember that tour so vividly.'

As the non-white corner of Boet Erasmus came alive, in another corner of the ground the surreal strains of 'Sospan Fach', club song of Llanelli, adopted anthem of Wales could be heard. That travelling band of Welsh supporters, including JJ Williams's recently arrived brother, would also have memories to cherish for as long as they lived.

With Irvine's conversion, the Lions were up by nineteen points to three. Home humiliation was compounded when the mighty van Heerden had to leave the field clutching his ribs, finally admitting defeat after dishing out the rough stuff to no avail. To the credit of their captain and his players,

South Africa kept on playing, and kept on trying into the final quarter. Snyman slotted two penalties to narrow the gap, before the Lions closed in for the kill.

With five minutes to go JPR Williams collected a speculative kick inside his own ten-yard line near the grandstand touchline. By this stage the full-back had about him an aura of absolute invincibility. It was summed up by South African rugby historian Chris Greyvenstein: 'Every time he touched the ball... he sliced through defenders as if they did not exist. Williams, like Edwards, was the best player in his position in the world in 1974 and, again like his countryman, he was fully aware of the fact.' With his confidence sky-high, Williams started to run. A long pass across field found Dick Milliken, always eager to have a crack, and the Ulsterman drew two outside backs as he straightened. A pop outside and JJ Williams was away again, a yard of space soon becoming two. As he neared the halfway line he had centre Peter Cronje closing in, with wing Chris Pope and outside-half Snyman ahead. Williams, in full flight, dropped the ball onto his boot and sent it flying towards the Springbok twenty-five-yard line. It was no hoof this, and in a foot race there was only one winner, so it would all come down to the bounce.

Three green shirts, one red – Williams hesitated a fraction, forced to stoop slightly in order to collect the ball one handed. That cruel, unpredictable rugby ball, which often makes oafs out of the most talented – bounced perfectly into his outstretched right palm, but he collected Cronje at exactly the same time. He was still ten yards out, but even with the centre clinging to his shoulders, forward momentum carried Williams the rest of the way. As Windsor recalled decades later: 'JJ never got the credit he deserved for those performances. Not just as a player – but mentally – he was a winner. Out there he was amazing.' As the winger got up to be surrounded by team-mates, the whole Port Elizabeth crowd – not just one corner – rose to their feet and cheered, finally acknowledging that they were in the presence of greatness, that they themselves were privileged to be there.

For Williams that was the absolute pinnacle: 'Going back to halfway and listening to the applause was magic. For the first time ever, the whole stadium was on its feet clapping us. They recognise great rugby in South Africa, and they were letting us know they appreciated the way we played. For that one moment, time almost stood still, it was wonderful. Then of course the game started again and off we went.'

Andy Irvine remembers the countdown to the final whistle with immense satisfaction: 'We'd scored some fantastic tries, and there was really only one team in it. By the end the Springboks were punch-drunk, they just couldn't cope with it. If the game had gone on another fifteen minutes we'd have ended up with fifty points. It really was that great a performance.'

Was that the high-water mark for British and Irish rugby? Williams certainly thinks so: 'Yes, I do think it was. Three nil up in a series in South Africa, coming off the back of '71 in New Zealand... We'd stuffed them and played some fantastic rugby in doing so, but didn't get the credit for what we did outside of South Africa.'

Neither Phil Bennett nor Gareth Edwards garnered the headlines that day, yet both look back on the match with immense pride. Edwards, like his outside-half, had been carrying a knock, knew that he wasn't a hundred per cent fit, and yet played with supreme discipline and control throughout: 'I was so much on top of my game before the Third Test, I was so confident, but I'd strained a thigh muscle during the week and I just wasn't on top form. Benny was struggling too. But we had to play didn't we, so we just had to be disciplined. Ironically the South Africans were doing well until the big punch up in the second half, but it affected them more than us I think – it took their eye off the ball. Our experience, resilience, and attitude showed after that, and again we scored some fantastic tries.'

The final act was fittingly Bennett's. He knew that he wasn't the same player as he'd been just a few weeks before. He knew that the Lions had already seen the best of him, but on he went, at McBride's behest. Bennett would always feel uncomfortable having to pick up The King's mantle, but in South Africa he found his own way of embracing rugby immortality. A second drop goal, as sweet as the first, brought the curtain down. Twenty-six points to nine. The Lions had done the impossible.

The outside-half was spent: 'We'd done it, we'd proved everyone wrong. We'd beaten them in the mud and the rain and they'd said "Just wait until you get up to the Highveld". Then we destroyed them there too. And now we'd done it a third time. I was elated, just so proud, so thrilled, but I also knew that I was gone... shot to bits.'

As Milliken and McGeechen danced into each other's arms – brothers born in adversity – the players converged on their captain. Brown and Windsor hoisted McBride onto their shoulders. It made for a lopsided, comical sight, but no-one cared. There he stayed as one after another, McBride's boys came up and paid their respects – smiles, claps, handshakes – each wanting to be close, to let him know they'd done it for him.

But for McBride that wasn't enough. He steered those fifteen red-clad figures towards the stand, towards their non-playing team-mates. And there they all stood, shattered, victorious, high on emotion, and applauded. It was the greatest mark of respect, of leadership – yes of love – that one could have imagined. They applauded those men who had pushed them all the way, who had carried them at times, who had contributed so much to their own success. They were a team all the way.

Fran Cotton, one of the huddle at pitch-side, remembers that particular moment above all others: 'This was a thirty-man job. From day one we were all aware of that. And at that moment Willie just felt that it was a mark of respect. He felt it was really important to show the rest of the boys how much they meant. Remember he'd been in their shoes too. He knew how they felt. It was a huge moment that for all of us.'

Other than their team-mates, certain sections of the crowd celebrated with them. Just how good had they been? Good enough to leave an impression that's lasted a lifetime according to Mthobi Tyamzashe: 'In terms of excellence, even today when I see a good scrum-half, whether it be Will Genia of Australia, or our own Fourie du Preez, my immediate standard in terms of measuring his talent is Gareth Edwards.'

Before the celebrations there were the formalities, and one or two scores to settle. In his post-tour book *How The Lions Won*, Terry O'Connor remembered McBride, during his speech at Port Elizabeth's Town Hall, referring to: 'One British correspondent who has made a number of unfair comments before and during the tour.'

It was the one battle that McBride and Millar failed to win. Even in their moment of triumph, they were conscious of a cloud hanging over them. JJ Williams understands their frustration: 'Syd and Willie upset a few press men. They were Irish, rough and ready, and those journalists were very English. Carwyn was always good at that stuff, he had them eating out of his hand. He'd take them out, dine them – the press boys loved Carwyn. But there was never harmony in South Africa, and so we never really got the praise. Luckily by then the BBC had realised that there was something special happening, so at least people could see what we were doing for themselves on their TV screens back home. That made a difference, because when we got back home, the scenes were incredible.'

Having created history, having destroyed the myth, they celebrated as only a touring rugby team know how, and came pretty close to destroying Port Elizabeth's Marine Hotel. The Wreckers of 1968 would have been proud. According to legend, furniture was smashed, fires were lit, curtains were torched, empty cardboard beer boxes were added to the flames. Chief Fire Officer Bobby Windsor unreeled the nearest fire hose and proceeded to douse the fire and anything else that moved.

Forty years later, he is genuinely aggrieved that he is seen as the instigator-in-chief in terms of this episode: 'I seriously was trying to put the bloody fire out, because it was in danger of catching curtains and all sorts. It was only later, when the boss man complained, that I turned the hose on him.'

So if not Windsor himself, who were the budding pyromaniacs? 'Well they weren't Welsh, I can tell you that much... or English... or Scottish... But they were wild fuckers.' Half dressed, but fully inebriated, British and mostly Irish rugby players roamed the foyer and sparks flew. The hotel manager threatened to call the police.

McBride was woken from his bed at 3 a.m. Roger Uttley and Mervyn Davies suggested that he might be needed downstairs as there was a bit of trouble. McBride strode down, in his underpants, taking only his trusty pipe for protection.

As he surveyed the scene, he was accosted by a particularly unhappy South African: 'The manager was a mess and he told me he was about to call the police. Well, I thought the best thing to do was to delay him a wee bit, so I asked the first thing that came into my head; "These policemen... Tell me, will there be many of them?"'

The hotel manager could do nothing but laugh. No emergency call was made. McBride – the shepherd – calmly ushered his errant flock towards their beds, and an international incident was averted.

In the Lions' defence, these incidents were few and far between, and only really began after the tour was won. For the most part they were as professional as modern-day players, not drinking during the week, with the occasional blow out after a big match.

The following morning, manager Alun Thomas surveyed

the damage, and the claims for damages, then added them to the dozens upon dozens of champagne bottles, and the hundreds of empty bottles of Castle lager. This time there would be no quibbles, no questions asked. The bill was paid, and the Lions left the Marine Hotel still standing... just.

CHAPTER 19

Not All Who Wander
Are Lost

'Even victors are by victories undone.'
John Dryden, 'To My Honoured Kinsman, John Dryden', 1699

FOUR MATCHES REMAINED, and two weeks as a Lions touring party. If anything this was the hardest part. They had done all that had been asked and more. They had made history, done what couldn't be done. And now they wanted to go home.

When John Dryden, one of Restoration England's premier poets penned the words *'Even victors are by victories undone'*, his own example was Hannibal, scourge of Rome, a hero who eventually died defeated, and by his own hand. Earlier in the same work he references Alexander the Great: *'When the Persian king was put to flight, The weary Macedons refused to fight.'* After defeating his greatest enemy, the Persian King Darius III, Alexander kept on campaigning and drove on into India. Exhausted, and realising that their leader would take them all the way to the ends of the earth if he could, Alexander's soldiers eventually mutinied. Near the Ganges River, having come so far and done so much, they refused to go any further.

The Lions didn't refuse to go on, they had no choice. They were led by Willie John McBride. And besides, there was no Ganges to cross, just a plane to catch – bound for East London. That flight though did bring about a mutiny of sorts.

After an aborted take-off from Port Elizabeth, which took them out to sea and right back again after running into a flock of seagulls, Ralston, Windsor and McKinney decided they'd prefer to travel up the coast by car. The journey would take up most of their day, but they didn't care. The Lions were tired, emotional and very much the worse for wear. They were in effect 'undone'.

On Wednesday, they would be donning the red again, to take on Border.

* * *

Only four Test match Lions were asked to step up for that match. One of them, Edwards, had to since Moloney was still struggling. The Welshman would also captain the side, and according to the watching JBG Thomas, would try and take on too much himself: 'As he often did when not partnered by Bennett.' That was no reflection on McGeechan, again doing duty at 10, it was just that with Bennett outside him, Edwards knew that there was someone else good enough to play leading man. To be fair to McGeechan, he'd played eight of the nine matches since Rhodesia, including two Tests, and if anyone truly deserved a rest, it was the unassuming Scotsman.

The third Saturday starter was Roger Uttley, shifted to the second row. Gordon Brown had broken a bone in his hand, no great surprise to anyone who had come into contact with him during those infamous eruptions at Boet Erasmus. This presented Uttley's second row partner Chris Ralston with an opportunity to remind the selectors of his ability.

Irvine, the fourth Test match Lion, was sprightly enough to start at full-back. He would contribute another fourteen points to his tour tally that day.

Otherwise it was Grace and Steele out wide, Gibson and Bergiers at centre, Carmichael and Burton propping either side of Kennedy, with a back row combination of McKinney, Ripley and David.

Other than Irvine, no-one really functioned at the highest level that day, and they were lucky not to be playing a decent side. Besides the full-back's tally, Steele bagged a brace of tries before leaving the field with a rib injury, and Edwards crossed for one. On a windy day with little to enjoy by way of rugby, the 15,000 supporters raised their biggest cheer when Burton changed his shorts and mooned the crowd.

It ended twenty-six points to six, Border's outside-half Steenekamp landing two penalties. For the Lions it was simply a formality, another statistic, but there were a few more which needed to be marked. They had passed the mammoth tour tally of the greats of 1955, the side that had shown how rugby should be played. And Irvine had passed the all-time points' record for a Lions tourist in South Africa.

Their evening in East London was far more entertaining than their afternoon, and garnered a few more headlines to boot. There were plenty of trusted journalists on tour, from Chris Lander of *The Daily Mirror* to Terry O'Connor of *The Daily Mail*, but others, especially unfamiliar faces, needed to be treated with a certain wariness. Roy Bergiers and others learned this lesson the hard way: 'There was a little bit of naughtiness here and there, but what do you expect? Somewhere like East London for example, really just a frontier town then, things could get wild... But one female reporter had come and talked to a few of the boys, and then she'd printed a story along the lines of "Lions Leave Broken Hearts All Over South Africa". And she'd put my name up there in lights. Well, as it happened, a teaching friend of mine had come over to follow us for a few weeks, so that headline ended up on the notice board at school back home.'

Tom David just puts it down to youthful exuberance: 'We were young men... and we were away from home for three and a half months. What do you expect? Personally, mind you, I'd taken a big pile of books with me, so I'd be tucked up in bed by the time all this type of thing went on.'

He must have read the whole library by the time he reached East London, because that night, David was absent without leave – and paid a heavy price.

The Welshman's eyes glint at the prospect of a good story. There's no knowing wink to accompany the words, but there should be: 'I'd been turfed out that night... I must have been in a late night card school or something. So anyway, I went straight down for breakfast the following morning, and the team liaison came up to me and said that Syd, Alun and Willie wanted to see me. Well, it was three flights up, and I was quicker than JJ taking them – I'm thinking; "I'm in the Test side, I'm in the Test side". Of course I get up there, and Alun says; "Tom, we're not putting up with this kind of behaviour, it's just disgraceful". Well, I still had no idea – so then Willie said that my room wasn't there any more... that my bed was outside and three floors down. What can you do? I just said; "Boys, I may be dull, but if I'm going to wreck a room, it's not going to be my own."' When David did finally venture outside, he saw his own bed lying on top of the canopy above the main entrance of the team hotel.

But even that tale of excess took second place to the real headline grabber of their stay. The story broke in Afrikaans, but it was soon translated, and banner headlines including the words 'Lions', 'Girls', 'Nude' and 'Scrum' were bound to set tongues wagging. The '68 tourists had had a particularly boisterous time in East London, so there was form – the question in 1974 was just who's form? That remained a mystery.

According to Bobby Windsor, one or two of the front row fraternity may well have been willing participants in the frolics, but then again, so were the local ladies: 'I think there were thirty other halves who rang up from home during the following few days, and every one of the boys said; "It wasn't me". But the front row union were there, yes. What can you do, you know that a touring squad is going to attract attention. You're in the hotel bar having a few pints, some local girls start having a laugh and issuing challenges... It was actually hilarious... until it got in the papers.'

John Reed, writing for the *Sunday Express*, summed up the affair like this: 'The Lions have been involved in a traumatic week, what with the South African newspaper allegations of wild parties, drunken, naked players and women scrummaging in their hotel, a broken bed being thrown out of a window and damage amounting to £300 since their Third Test celebrations. All hotly denied by the management as greatly exaggerated or completely fabricated.'

The official version was that on a particularly warm night, a few towel wearing players had been locked out of their rooms. Those towels had then been spirited away by their fun-loving team-mates, leading to banner headlines. Where the equally disrobed girls fitted in, and how they came to be 'packing down' in the corridor, no-one quite knew.

One way or another, they'd shown East London plenty of Lions behinds. Now they were simply glad to be leaving East London behind.

* * *

They travelled to Durban on the day that Nelson Mandela celebrated his fifty-sixth birthday, his tenth as a prisoner 'for life'.

If the Lions were ignorant of Mandela's plight, they would at least meet one man during their time in South Africa who would become famous for voicing his concerns about the way the country was being run. He would go on to represent the liberal face of South African rugby, and play a crucial role in promoting the cause of black players. That man was Natal's captain, Tommy Bedford.

Durban was, and still is, a favourite destination for touring teams and their supporters. The sun shines, the sea is inviting, the locals are friendly. Bedford himself admitted that the province was seen as: 'The last outpost of the British Empire.'

He was a fascinating character, Thomas Pleydell Bedford, and the consensus was that if he had played a part in the previous three Test matches then things might just have been different for South Africa. He was a Rhodes Scholar, and Oxford Blue, an architect by trade and a number 8 by disposition. He'd won his first cap back in 1963, during the same series against Australia as Hannes Marais; he'd played all four Tests against the Lions in the 1968 series, and had gone on to captain the Springboks three times. He was thirty-two years old by the time he faced the Lions in 1974, but hadn't played a Test match for three years. He was seen, quite simply, as too much of a loose cannon.

Having experienced life in the UK, and taken part in the tour from hell in 1969/70, he had strong views on all aspects of South African life, including apartheid. He was outspoken too about the ills of the South African rugby system and about the perceived overlooking of his beloved Natal as a talent pool for the national side.

So Bedford was essentially a Springbok outcast, but a legend in Natal itself. He led a side that had lost in the previous months to Rhodesia among others, so they weren't expecting much this time around. It was ironic, therefore, that all of a sudden, this bastion of Britishness in the land of the Boer was, in Bedford's own words: 'Being put forward as South Africa's last hope.' In modern-day terms it was akin to the Welsh national team riding roughshod over Leicester, Gloucester, Bath, Saracens, Harlequins, Northampton and England, only for the RFU to turn to London Welsh as potential saviours of the nation's dignity.

Whatever the pre-match politics, there was little dignity to be seen on the pitch itself on Saturday, 20 July. But there was certainly plenty of excitement.

King's Park, Durban, was the venue, one of the greatest rugby stadiums in the world. And with 38,000 loyal fans there to watch, Natal came out all guns blazing. With only two provincial matches left, and an unbeaten record to protect, the Lions, like their predecessors in 1971, refocused and limbered up for one last concerted push.

And since this was likely to be a tougher match than the next, against Eastern Transvaal, they stacked the deck.

JPR Williams, JJ Williams, Milliken, Bennett and Edwards all started among the backs, with Morley on the wing and Gibson at centre. No-one was more pleased to be taking a seat in the stands than the dog-tired Ian McGeechan. The same could be said of Roger Uttley up front, who had put in a massive shift in recent weeks. The Test match trio of McLauchlan, Windsor and Cotton started, as did McBride, alongside 'Lurch' Ralston, who sensed that his chance had finally come. Behind them were Neary, Slattery, and Davies. It was formidable line-up.

The match was tight and fractious from the off, but Bennett kicked three first-half penalties to put the Lions 9–0 ahead at the break. Replacement wing Hannaford then pulled Natal back to 9–6 with two successful shots at goal. By then the atmosphere had become intense to the point of intimidating, after a huge flare-up involving Natal's favourite son.

The incident centred on a tackle by Bedford on JPR Williams. The full-back was hurled unceremoniously into touch, landing within feet of the crowd. Most reports told of an errant boot, reflecting that Williams had been kicked as he went down. But the player himself insists that: 'He pulled my hair. Well, somebody pulled my hair. So I hit him. It was just a reflex. But all hell broke loose then.'

Yes, Williams reacted by cuffing Bedford – hard – and more than once around the head. From the stands it looked completely unprovoked, and as their hero dropped and lay curled up on the sidelines, angry spectators took a hand, one physically restraining Williams.

With Bedford groggily back on his feet, things got worse. The number 8 was felled again in a subsequent dust-up, and this time the crowd reacted with a barrage of fruit, drinking receptacles and anything else that came to hand, which meant in one case a pair of binoculars. McBride took his team to the centre of the pitch, the only spot where they were safe, until the police calmed the situation and restored an element of order to proceedings.

JJ Williams remembers that the South African crowds always had a stockpile of ammunition: 'They'd been drinking since mid-morning there, because you got loads of warm up games before we came on. So they had plenty of empties ready, and they were coming from everywhere. So we just had to wait in the middle, the only place they couldn't reach, then wait until the cans were all cleared. Then we started again. All because of JPR.'

With ten minutes to go, the match was too tight to call, and too feisty for comfort. As he'd done throughout the tour when crisis called, Edwards turned the game. A dart down the blind-side, a pass to Irvine – on for the injured Morley on the wing – and the Scotsman was over in the corner.

Three more tries followed in quick succession, as did more kicks from Bennett. The outside-half was by now commanding operations – assured in his kicking, mesmeric from broken play – nigh on impossible to contain.

Despite his own concerns, as far as the rest of the world was concerned, Bennett was back to something resembling his best.

The home side was out on its feet, and had to endure not just the remaining ten minutes, but an extra ten on top due to the numerous injury breaks and stoppages. With the Lions scrummage in the ascendant, both Davies and Slattery took advantage of close range shoves to cross for tries. In between, Irvine got his second, again courtesy of a jagged cut through the heart of Natal's defence by the bamboozling Bennett.

All in all the Lions notched up a further twenty-one points during that protracted injury period, with the final score of thirty-four points to six making the whole afternoon sound academic. It had been anything but. Bennett was pleased with his eighteen points and a reassertion of his individual class. Irvine had again chipped in manfully, and the forwards had once again paved the way. But all the post-match attention focused on two men, Tom Bedford and JPR Williams.

Williams's wife had recently started working at a hospital in Durban. And on that particular Saturday afternoon, Dr Scilla Williams decided to go along and watch the game with some local friends. Needless to say they were unimpressed with her husband's behaviour, as were the fellow workers who greeted her in stony silence on Monday morning.

By that stage she had become used to defending her husband's honour. As JPR remembers it: 'I went into the Natal dressing room after the game and apologised, that's how it is between rugby players. But in the reception later on, Tommy's wife came up to me and started to give me some verbals. Well then Scilla naturally came to the rescue and stood up for me.'

The greatest irony of the day's proceedings was that JPR Williams was coming back to Durban to work alongside his wife after the tour ended. It took some time, but he won over the locals eventually. He, along with JJ Williams and Ian McLauchlan, would actually go on to play in the colours of Natal: 'I played for them against Eastern Transvaal, scored a try, and got a huge hug from the skipper – as you can imagine the crowd went wild.' Williams's captain on that occasion was none other than Tommy Bedford.

Bedford's post-match speech garnered attention for a number of reasons. To his credit he found time to poke fun at those recent newspaper headlines alluding to the Lions versus ladies late night scrummaging contest. Holding up one of the offending front pages, he explained that he now understood just where his own side had been going wrong. From his speech alone, it was easy to see why Bedford should be viewed as such a talismanic figure in some quarters.

And why he was viewed as such a dangerous figure in

others. If Bedford had been upset by the touchline incident involving Williams, he reserved his true wrath for the Springbok selectors, who had flown up to Durban in the forlorn hope of finding an answer to their woes.

Natal's captain made a point of expressing his surprise and gratitude that they had managed to find their way. He then adopted a gesture said to have originated among Welsh and English longbowmen during the Hundred Years War.

From Crécy to Poitiers to Agincourt, so dreadful was the toll exacted on the French by these archers that their capture prompted a particular kind of reprisal. Legend has it that if a longbowman was captured, his bowstring fingers, i.e. the index and middle ones, were cut off. And so, whenever the opportunity arose to taunt the French, these archers would hold up their two fingers towards the enemy.

The historical accuracy of that claim is still argued over today, but what is not in doubt is that Bedford employed the two-fingered salute in the post-match reception in Durban, and directed it towards the Springbok selectors. And so ended a distinguished international career, once and for all.

* * *

If the dust-up in Durban had been unexpected, the last provincial game of the tour, against Eastern Transvaal, was rich in pugilistic promise. Here was a side with history, and with a very recent record of violence towards visiting teams.

Willie John McBride in particular had vivid memories of his last visit to the town of Springs, about thirty miles to the east of Johannesburg. That was with the Lions of 1968. He wasn't playing that day, but he played a part in a particularly unsavory incident during the on-going and infamous 'Battle of Springs'.

Wales and Lions prop John 'Tess' O'Shea found himself in the middle of a rumpus that afternoon – one of many that had dogged the match. As the only red-shirted player in a blanket of white, he threw more punches than he landed, and as he kept three or four Easterns players engaged, the rest of their team got on with the business of scoring a try. When the referee finally noticed that he should focus his attention away from the try line and back up-field, he had no hesitation in sending O'Shea off. The Welshman became the first Lion to receive his marching orders for foul play. Oranges and beer rained down from the stands as the prop trudged from the field.

As though that weren't indignity enough, as he reached the tunnel, a smartly dressed, bespectacled gentleman, looking not dissimilar to former British Prime Minister Clement Attlee, approached from the other direction. Said gentleman then proceeded to land a punch of his own on O'Shea's jaw.

O'Shea was incredulous, and before he could get angry, he was ushered away by a posse of friendly faces. It was then that McBride appeared, suited as though preparing for a day's work at the bank, and looking almost as respectable as the assailant himself.

The Ulsterman launched himself fist first at the irate local, and continued to mete out his own form of justice until the supporter was dragged away by police.

So McBride had history in Springs, but then again so did most people. New Zealand legend Colin Meads had broken his arm, or had his arm broken, against Easterns in 1970. The opening ten minutes of that match were described as a full-scale war, and although Meads sustained his injury in the sixth minute of play, he stayed on the pitch, contributing one-handed throughout the remaining seventy-four minutes.

There were others, the Australians and French national sides had endured a torrid welcome to Springs too, and on the same weekend as the '74 Lions had been involved in the 'Battle of Boet Erasmus Part I' against Eastern Province back in May, the French club Tarbes had been subjected to the unique Springs custom of welcoming touring teams. Their match against Eastern Transvaal was abandoned with twenty minutes to go, the referee deciding that an hour's worth of running fight was enough for any sane South African.

So Eastern Transvaal came with an eastern promise, of fireworks guaranteed. And who did the Lions choose to take charge in this tinderbox atmosphere? Who could best keep a clear head and play the diplomat? None other than JPR Williams.

Yes JPR would captain the Lions for the first time and, as it happened, he did so admirably, in an unusually clean and free-flowing match.

Despite being a ferocious critic of the Lions back play in general, John Reason wrote afterwards that JPR: 'Had climbed such a pinnacle of performance on tour... He had been the most consistent of all the backs, even including Gareth Edwards. JPR Williams never had a bad game.'

When I asked JPR whether he was a better player in 1974 than in 1971, his response was unequivocal: 'Yes, absolutely. And to be honest I took that decision in terms of the captaincy by Syd and Willie to be a vindication of the way I'd performed. I'd never captained any senior side before... ever. For me personally it was a huge privilege.'

Sitting in his treasure-trove of a den, at his Vale of Glamorgan home forty years later, he showed me some of his prized possessions, the personal mementos of a star-studded career. Amidst the ties and the trophies, the programmes and photographs, there were reminders of London Welsh, of Bridgend, of Wales, and the Barbarians.

But it was an unfamiliar black and white still, pinned to the wall, that was the most compelling image of all. It showed JPR Williams, Lions captain, emerging from the tunnel of the PAM Brink Stadium in Springs to take his place in history.

And as personal milestones go, this one couldn't have gone much better.

Easterns had been warned pre-match that they couldn't afford another rugby bloodbath, which narrowed their options quite considerably, since their only player of note in pure rugby terms was Polla Fourie, the flanker who'd won his first cap in the Third Test. Even with the tour winding down, the all conquering Lions were still the hottest ticket in town as 25,000 came to see the 'dirt-trackers' make their last stand, and with honour, plus an unmatched record at stake, they proceeded to show their very best form.

Barring unforeseen injury, this would be the last game for ten of them, and they knew it. Bergiers at centre, Grace on the wing, Gibson and Moloney at half-back, the front row union of Carmichael, Kennedy and Burton, and the back row trio of David, McKinney and Ripley wanted to sign off in style. They knew that others hadn't even got this far, didn't have this one last chance – they relished the opportunity.

For Williams the skipper, Irvine, McGeechan and Uttley, there was one last challenge yet to come, and for Ralston, there was hope of joining them.

Traded penalties took things to six apiece before the Lions scored their opening try, through Tom Grace, and from there on in it was pure entertainment. David got the next just before half-time, and not to be outdone in the rampaging back-rower stakes, Ripley added the third just after the break. McGeechan notched his first try of the tour in his penultimate match, and it proved to be one of the most popular efforts of the whole lot. Clive Rowlands felt that the Scotsman's contribution throughout was crucial: 'He was another great thinker in the side. Good hands, good brain – could play outside-half too, which was crucial. Hell, he could have played scrum-half if needed. He was special.'

Grace rounded things off with his second of the match, his thirteenth of the tour, and the try that put him ahead of JJ Williams in terms of the record books. As the Lions relaxed, the home side entered into the spirit and ran everything. Deep into injury time, they tapped a penalty and scored through Fourie. It was a satisfying end for all concerned. Eastern Transvaal had maintained their honour and more importantly their dignity.

For the Lions, five tries, and another thirteen points from Irvine, made the last hoorah a worthy one, and the 33–10 scoreline was a wonderful way to sign-off. These days 'Tuesdays and Wednesdays' qualifies as the duration of a Shane Williams Lions tour, after the Welshman arrived in Australia on a Monday, played against ACT on a Tuesday and departed Warren Gatland's 2013 tour on a Wednesday.

Back in the day, 'The Tuesdays and Wednesdays' had real meaning. They had been a crucial factor in the success of the tour of 1971, and they proved equally inspirational three years later.

McBride had no qualms about JPR Williams leading the side into that penultimate battle, but it wasn't the Welshman who left a lasting impression on the tour captain at Springs. Williams, after all, had one more fight to get through.

For the likes of Andy Ripley, this would be it, and it was the Englishman who came to mind when I asked McBride about that match: 'He was so disappointed that he didn't get that Test jersey, but the opportunity just didn't arise... I'll never forget his last game up in Springs. He came to my room beforehand for a chat, and I told him that the next day would be a big one for him. And I remember him telling me; "Skipper thanks, I've had a great time." And my response was; "Well let's finish the job then. Finish it in a big way." And you know what, that following day in Springs he had an outstanding game, immense. And, of course, that was his last game for the Lions.'

Roy Bergiers was another who had plenty of reason to feel disillusioned. But when I asked him how he kept going to the very end despite missing out on a Test spot, this was his response: 'The honour – the absolute honour – of being a part of an amazing team. And we felt a part of that team all along. You had Ripley for example, a free spirit, a rebel, in his Dunlop tyre home-made flip-flops, and make no mistake he was bitterly disappointed too. He felt he was better than Mervyn. And yet there he was, there we all were, still giving our all. We gave it everything in midweek, and then we'd be in the stand cheering the boys on when it was their turn. They did the same for us too, mind. So we were with them all the way to the end of the line.'

For Bergiers and half the squad, the tour was now over. For the rest, the Springboks lay in wait one last time.

CHAPTER 20

Homeward Bound,
I Wish I Was

*'I firmly believe that any man's finest hour, the greatest
fulfilment of what he holds dear, is that moment when he
has worked his heart out in a good cause and lies
exhausted on the field of battle – victorious.'*
Vince Lombardi, Head Coach, Green Bay Packers, 1959–67

THE SPRINGBOKS WOULD employ yet another secret weapon
for the Fourth Test, and this one actually had a galvanising
effect. They even managed to keep their personnel for the most
part. There were only three changes from the starting line-up
for the Third Test. Paul Bayvel was fit and back at scrum-half
again, the only player to come into the back division. Another
wise decision was the re-selection of John Williams at lock.
The third change saw Kleintjie Grobler of the Free State come
in at number 8, with Fourie dropped and Kritzinger moved to
the flank. Marais, Ellis and winger Chris Pope would be the
only three to play every one of the four Tests, but at least this
time – for the first time – there was a sense of continuity, of
familiarity.

The Lions had that in spades of course, which was one
of the reasons for their success. For the Fourth Test they
resisted the urge to include Mike Gibson at centre and
made only one, enforced change. Brown's right hand had
not healed, and one break led to another – 'Lurch' Ralston

getting a chance he could never have foreseen in the preceding weeks.

Brown was deflated, as was his skipper. Together the Scotsman and the Irishman had played five consecutive Lions Test matches in tandem, and had not been beaten once. Now McBride would have to face his last battle without the man he had come to know, trust and depend upon in the most trying of circumstances. Ralston was good, but this was a blow nonetheless.

As for Brown, having failed to see the job through to its conclusion, he chose to seek solace somewhere he knew well enough – on the fairway. In terms of putting Troon on the international map, Brown was second only to the famous golf course, and he was as comfortable with a club in hand as a rugby ball, even if that hand was thoroughly well-bandaged.

During those decades, years which saw South Africa cast into the sporting wilderness, golfer Gary Player was the country's acceptable face on the world stage, winning golf's four 'majors' before he was thirty years old. A man of unimpeachable honour, immense talent, and a uniquely South African appreciation for hard graft, Player was loved wherever he went.

He had just returned to South Africa after a spectacular few months. In April 1974 he had won the US Masters at Augusta, Georgia, his second Green Jacket victory.

Then in July, on the same weekend as the Lions were bashing the 'Boks in Port Elizabeth, Player swept all before him at Royal Lytham & St Annes in Lancashire, to win the Open Championship for a third time. He would go on to win nine majors all in all, and to be considered as one of golf's all-time greats. In the year 2000, he was voted as South Africa's 'Sportsman of the Century'.

Less than two weeks after winning the Open in July 1974, he was back in Johannesburg, playing golf with Gordon Brown, Gareth Edwards and Mike Gibson at the Killarney

Club. The diminutive Player was a genuine rugby man, and was more than happy to spend an afternoon in the company of some of his own sporting heroes. As he explained years later: 'I was a scrum-half at school, and I was still a huge rugby fan... Gareth Edwards was at the very top for me. I looked at him, this small guy playing against giants, getting elbowed, kneed, chinned, and the more they gave him the more he came back. That's what I loved, a man that could compete, no matter what his size.' Kindred spirits then, and the admiration was returned in equal measure.

So much so that decades later, when asked to nominate his own hero – the person he would most like to meet – for a television series, Gareth Edwards chose Gary Player. Their second meeting was as fascinating as the first. Player was by then touching sixty, but still kept up his daily regimen of sit-ups and push-ups, insisting that mental toughness and dedication was the foundation of all good things.

It was his other admission that caused a stir though. Edwards had heard the rumour, but never had it confirmed. Now Gary Player looked him in the eye and told him that yes, he had ventured into the Springbok camp before that Fourth and final Test, and given South Africa's team-talk.

After his round with the Lions, he had decided he needed to do something for the Springboks. Stern, patriotic, and a perfect example of the tough as teak South African mentality, he pulled no punches. He left those players in no doubt about where they were currently, and where they needed to be. Their country expected, but more than that – he expected: 'There we were, such a great rugby nation, and the Lions were beating us like a drum... I wanted to contribute just a little bit, and boy did I let them have it. I called them a bunch of ninnies, and I said that what I'd really like was for them to go out there and try to die; "I want you to put such an effort in that you're going to feel like you might die. If one of you dies, I promise I'll take care of your family for the rest of their lives. So you've got no concerns, just go out there and put something extra into it." And they went out there and did it.'

And so it was that the Springboks found themselves at Ellis Park on Saturday, 27 July 1974, motivated by a master, and ready to die for the cause. Seventy-five thousand people crammed into an already creaking stadium that day, meaning more temporary scaffolds, more ridiculously dangerous vantage points and, more to the point, world record takings for the Transvaal Rugby Union.

There are famous black and white photographs taken by Charles C Ebbets which depict workers at rest during the construction of the Rockefeller Centre in Manhattan during the early 1930s. The stands at Ellis Park may not have been skyscrapers, but looking at pictures of those steep banks, covered with a seething mass of humanity, seemingly structures with a life of their own, gives one that same queasy feeling as those Ebbets pictures. Smile for the cameras and don't look down.

What a venue to play out the final drama. Fathers told sons that on a clear day, from the highest point at the back of the stand, you could see all the way to the Cape. The capacity crowd was still considerably lower than the 100,000 who had turned out at the same venue to watch the 1955 match between South Africa and the Lions. But Ellis Park had changed in the interim, and anyway that was the First Test. This was the last, and their side – their own heroes – had been comprehensively beaten three times already. And still they came. It said everything about the effect these Lions had on their hosts. They were simply a must see event in themselves.

But by now those Lions were mentally on the plane. Jaded, emotionally drained and physically spent, another afternoon of gut-busting on the Highveld was asking too much. That, combined with a pumped up home side, made for a miserable afternoon. A dirty one too, Bobby Windsor suffering a huge gash to the head early on, and spending the

293

rest of the afternoon swathed in bandages. The Springboks, as was their wont, made the early running, and got points on the board through a Snyman penalty. Then referee Max Baise, back again after a two-Test absence, made the first of two crucial, controversial calls, which would prove to be the match's enduring legacy.

From a defensive five-yard scrum, the Springbok pack was weakened and wheeled by the force of the Lions eight. The ball shot back on South Africa's side, but scrum-half Bayvel, under immense pressure himself from Edwards, could barely tap it away. The ball bobbled back towards the try line, almost in slow motion.

With the scrum skewed sideways, parallel to the line, the player nearest the ball was Lions flanker Roger Uttley, who disengaged himself from the tangle to see the opportunity of a lifetime within his grasp. Blind-side winger Chris Pope reacted quicker though, and the 6' 5" Uttley, with further to fall and with fifteen gruelling matches already under his belt, felt in that split-second that he was going to be too late. He dived anyway, his giant frame unsighting Max Baise as he did so.

The next thing the referee saw was Gareth Edwards, directly in front of him, jumping arms aloft in celebration. Edwards was by then the dominant on-field character of the tour, so influential that some South Africans, including Hannes Marais, accused him of refereeing big matches himself: 'I never played against a better scrum-half... If I had one criticism of Edwards, it was the way he constantly baited the referees' wrote the Springbok captain later.

The Welshman's triumphant turn towards the referee must have had a subliminal effect. Despite the fact that it was Chris Pope who sat up with ball in hand, Baise awarded the try.

As they had in previous matches, the watching crowd reacted with fury. Oranges once again poured down from the stands as the Lions retreated towards halfway. The crowd on that far side had spotted exactly what had happened, and what Baise had missed. They had seen Chris Pope clearly touch the ball down, with Uttley failing to lay a finger on it.

In the heat of battle, Edwards was convinced, or had convinced himself, that Uttley had grounded first. And in that same furnace, the flanker had allowed everyone else to think so too. Small margins, big decisions, moments that change lives. Did Edwards buy a try for his team? 'I certainly didn't think so at the time. My reaction was that Roger had scored. A split-second, there's no time to think. So I didn't try to deceive Max at all, it was simple instinct; "Yes. We've scored!" Of course you see it back later and you know we didn't.'

Years later, Uttley would admit to being ashamed of his actions, of not drawing the referee's attention to the truth of the matter. Max Baise, who carried the weight for decades afterwards, called it simply the biggest mistake of his life.

With Bennett's conversion, the Lions led by six points to three. That lead was soon snuffed out by another Snyman penalty, only for McBride's men to inch their noses back in front again with a second try.

This time there was no controversy, just a clinical finish. Edwards protected at the base of a scrum inside the Springbok twenty-five. He picked up, sprinted blind beyond the back row cover and directly towards winger Muller, who instinctively came inside to challenge. As Edwards took the hit, he slung out a pass to Irvine, who simply had to catch and waltz over. The Scotsman accepted the gift with open arms. By that stage Irvine had well and truly won his Lions' spurs. His contribution and his talent left a lasting impression on team-mates and locals alike. He was described by watching journalist Chris Greyvenstein as: 'A player of exceptional talent... his eclipse of Gert Muller, a wing so feared by the 1970 All Blacks, underlined not only his skill but also his courage.'

It was 10–6 to the Lions at the break, and the 'Boks had to replace their prop Nic Bezuidenhout with another new cap from the Free State, Rampie Stander.

But that first half had undoubtedly been their most impressive showing of the tour so far. In his report for the *Sunday People*, legendary Lion Bleddyn Williams wrote that: 'The South African forwards, with Ellis and Williams the stars, were on the rampage. The backs too, spearheaded by the splendid half-back pair of Snyman and Bayvel, were prepared to run the ball.' The second half would bring more of the same, as the home side came out fighting, both literally and figuratively. In so doing they showed their best and worst.

A line-out on the Lions twenty-five was palmed at the back by Grobler to Ellis on the peel.

The flanker passed straight to centre Schlebusch in midfield, and he straightened, drew Milliken and set loose a stampeding Chris Pope. Some sight in full flight, the big winger arced outside JJ Williams, outstripped the covering McGeechan and Slattery, and had only JPR Williams left to beat – death or glory.

The full-back planted his feet as he had done so often, and waited for the hit. Pope was rocked sideways, but still managed to get the ball away in-field. JJ Williams overran it, so did a desperate Mervyn Davies. Schlebusch, Kritzinger and Grobler also arrived only to see the ball elude each and every one.

As it came to earth and settled a yard from the line, McGeechan and Bennett converged to cover the threat, but they were beaten to it by Peter Cronje.

And so the Transvaal centre, the Johannesburg native, donning the Springbok green for what would turn out to be the last time, scored his country's first try of the series. His country's only try of the series. It had taken almost 300 minutes of Test match rugby, in which their opponents had scored ten unanswered tries, but finally the Springboks had breached the Lions line. Ellis Park erupted, giving those hardy souls clinging to their neighbours high up in the gods reason to be fearful for their lives. Never mind seeing all the way to the Cape, they could surely hear them celebrating in far off Cape Town, such was the noise.

Soon 10–10 became 13–10 to South Africa after a third Snyman penalty, and suddenly the Springboks were within sight of victory.

That was the good. The bad and the ugly were never far behind. Grobler, who's palm had instigated the Springbok try, now put his hand to use again, in the form of a fist.

JPR Williams had taken his usual punishment, without complaint – in fact with a certain amount of relish. But after taking his umpteenth high ball of the series and being enveloped once again by a green backed horde, he took a knee to the head. Moaner van Heerden, once again intent on proving that Boer manhood would stoop to any level to make a point, caught the full-back flush in the face. Max Baise missed it, Ian 'Mouse' McLauchlan didn't. Presented with van Heerden's back, he took aim at the only target he could, and booted the lock in the backside.

At the same time Windsor, another who had seen van Heerden's latest trick, firstly pointed Max Baise in the direction of the crime and the culprit. Then, having had no joy whatsoever, he took matters into his own hands. The hooker launched himself from ten yards out, and was fully airborne by the time he reached van Heerden – it was effectively the only way his punches could have connected with the second row's chin. The Springbok reeled backwards. In the meantime another Lion went down. McLauchlan, having literally 'kicked arse', was now rubbing his own cheek after a well-aimed haymaker from Grobler: 'These things happen in rugby football' was the Scotsman's matter of fact recollection: 'You just got on with it.'

The South African number 8 kept retreating, face to the enemy, as amazingly, Milliken and Irvine set off in pursuit. Thankfully for them and the game, their animosity extended only as far as a few pointed fingers and choice phrases.

They turned back towards their own ranks, but any offer

of rapprochement as the series wound down was well and truly off the table.

Irvine exacted his own revenge by bringing the Lions level. The bag of nerves from the first few weeks of the tour was absolutely nerveless by now, and slotted a penalty to go with his earlier try. Forty years later, Irvine still regrets that his efforts weren't enough, and that the Lions didn't round the tour off as they should have: 'The pressure was off, we were ready to go home, we had a couple of injuries, we were tired, but I think if we'd have had to win that last Test we would have... And I don't want to make a big thing of it, but I think we did actually win it.'

The Lions went into the last few minutes of their South African odyssey drawing their last match, at thirteen points all. They were almost encamped on the Springbok line. They wouldn't lose, but they might just win. With seconds to go JPR Williams set off on a mazy midfield charge, beating one man, two, three, tearing into the home twenty-five and towards the posts. He was surrounded, stopped, smothered, but still managed to get the ball away to the ever present Slattery. Despite taking the ball standing still, the flanker had less than five yards to go and so gathered himself for one last surge. He had JJ Williams calling outside, but in the winger's own words: 'He was a greedy bastard, Slatts.'

Head down he heaved towards and then over the try line. Standing in his way was Peter Cronje, the man who'd scored the Springboks' try. His last act for his country was the most important of all. He embraced Slattery firmly, and took the full momentum of the hit. Cronje fell backwards, Slattery forwards, the ball sandwiched in between.

They hit the ground with Cronje still wedged below the Irishman, but as more bodies piled in on top of them, Slattery somehow managed to wriggle the ball free and downwards, between his thighs to the ground.

Yes, he did. He got it down. He grounded the ball. What's more he knew he'd grounded the ball. Cronje knew he'd grounded the ball. McGeechan, Bennett, JJ Williams, Milliken, all celebrating around him, knew that he'd grounded the ball.

The Lions had done it at the very last.

Except they hadn't.

Max Baise didn't know that Slattery had grounded the ball.

The referee had arrived to find the flanker under a pile of bodies, on top of Cronje. From where he stood, it seemed to Baise that the South African centre's legs were underneath the ball. He was positioned in the worst possible place to judge. Scrum called.

Swiftly followed by pandemonium. JJ Williams pointed Baise to the ball, but to no avail. He turned away in disbelief.

Even the unflappable Bennett was outraged; he stood hands on head, and let out a cry of frustration. Seconds later it was all over, and Baise was running for the safety of the tunnel.

As he did so JPR Williams let him know exactly what he thought, while Bennett came across to remonstrate again. For a split-second Baise flinched, as though expecting to be physically confronted by the only man on the pitch smaller than himself. The Lions number 10 followed him all the way down the field, still appalled by the final act of the final Test: 'I was tamping mad, because I was sure we'd scored. But you look back now and think OK, on any tour the last Test is the hardest. You've been shopping for your wife, your kids, you know that you're going to be home in a few days. And in our position it was so different to the Second and Third Tests. So yes, we should have won, but they'd improved a great deal, and Max Baise had to stay and live there in South Africa long after we went home.'

So it ended in a draw, 13–13. To the Lions it felt like a defeat, to the Springboks it felt like a victory. That pretty much said it all. Hannes Marais, who'd led his team to a three-nil series defeat, was hoisted on the shoulders of his comrades and cheered off the field. Willie John McBride, who'd led his team to a three-nil series victory, was treated to one last piece of unwanted South African hospitality.

As he left the field through the throng of eager fans, one of them saw him coming past and left a leg trailing. The crude attempt at a back-heel trip had been intended to send McBride sprawling to the ground. Instead he took it in his stride and kept on jogging.

Then he stopped... and turned. McBride, who hadn't taken a backward step throughout the tour, wasn't about to start now. He stalked over to the denim clad culprit and gave him an almighty shove. As the young man reeled away into the crowd, McBride resumed his journey.

McBride, as always, had stood firm. He had seen off all comers to the very end, to the very last act of the very last match of his long and illustrious Lions career. Now, he trooped off towards the tunnel, towards the darkness.

The 1971 Lions had drawn their final match as well. It secured them an historic two-one series win. The 1974 Lions had drawn a match they felt they'd won, and they ended their tour downcast despite their staggering achievement.

Was it a try?... Yes... Is it history... Yes? JPR Williams summed it up nicely: 'My wife told me afterwards that it was only Slatts and myself that wanted to win that game. She didn't mean it disrespectfully to the rest of the boys. But you could tell that for the most part we were shot, we were on the plane. I think Fergus and I still had something left – and we gave it all.'

So was it a let-down, that final result? 'Yes. It's daft because it wasn't even failure really. We didn't lose a game all tour. But it would have been so much nicer to have won every game. That said, they were such good hosts that I was glad in the end that they'd got something to celebrate.'

It took a while, but their minds eventually cleared, the hurt ebbed away, and the sense of injustice lessened. After all, the Lions had happily accepted Max Baise's wrongful award of a first-half try, so in a sense there was an element of justice being done. The Springboks had deserved their draw, the Lions hadn't deserved to win.

But did they deserve the ultimate accolade?

After three months away from home, after twenty-two matches unbeaten, after breaking individual and team records for points and tries scored, after destroying the myth of Springbok invincibility – the first side to do so – and after carving out their own unique place in rugby history, did they in fact deserve to be considered 'The Greatest'?

CHAPTER 21

Lies, Damned Lies
and Statistics

'Painting is poetry that is seen rather than felt,
and poetry is painting that is felt rather than seen.'
Leonardo da Vinci

FOR LEONARDO AND his contemporaries, and for centuries afterwards it was painting and poetry. But in the twentieth century sport managed to combine the best of both worlds, because at its very best sport could – and still can – be felt as well as seen. How many batsmen have been described as maestros, how many goals as masterpieces, how many moves as poetry in motion? The canvas can be blank, or broad or narrow, depending on a team or player's development. And the poetry can range from being uplifting, ground-breaking and romantic, like the 1971 Lions, to being by turns epic, staccato, brutal and breathless, like the Lions of 1974. Both examples can be termed as great, just in different ways.

To put the achievement of Willie John McBride's Lions into some form of context, it would be another twenty-two years before Sean Fitzpatrick's awesome All Blacks registered New Zealand's first series win on South African soil. By then the ground breaking Lions of 1974 would be long established as rugby legends.

And so to those wonderful, impossible, pointless, irresistible comparisons, in all their odious glory.

Critics, *The Daily Telegraph*'s John Reason foremost among them, were quick to write off the achievement of the Lions of 1974, especially in relation to the astonishing feat achieved by their predecessors three years earlier in New Zealand.

Reason was in no doubt as to which Lions were the greatest: 'Unfortunately, the Lions' management went to South Africa thinking that the task of winning would be much more difficult than it turned out to be... In fact, of course, the 1974 Lions were nothing like as good as the 1971 Lions... In New Zealand in 1971, the pressure never ceased. In South Africa in 1974, it never even started.'

Some of Reason's arguments are solid enough. In terms of provincial rugby, New Zealand in 1971 was generally acknowledged to be the harder tour.

But there is a caveat even here. That estimable chronicler of New Zealand rugby Terry McLean wrote a book titled *Goodbye To Glory* in the aftermath of the All Blacks tour to South Africa in 1976. That tour began just weeks after the outrage of Soweto, and would prove a breaking point for many in terms of the 'special relationship'.

It was also a shock in terms of the rugby.

New Zealand not only lost the Test series 3–1, but lost provincial matches to Western Province, Northern Transvaal and Orange Free State. They were pushed mighty close by Transvaal and The Quaggas too, just as the 1974 Lions had been.

McLean summed up the experience with these words: 'South African rugby at provincial level... was immeasurably stronger than [that] which the team of 1970 had so effortlessly overcome. To put the matter in perspective, and bluntly, the Big Four of South Africa's provinces – Western Province, Orange Free State, Transvaal and Northern Transvaal – would on their form against the '76 All Blacks beat any province in New Zealand decisively. Transvaal would simply crush any New Zealand provincial pack.'

That assessment came just two years after the Lions

had gone through the whole of their South African tour unbeaten. Might it be possible that the strength of South Africa's provinces in 1974 has been underestimated, which once again would mean the Lions achievement being played down?

The achievement of their backs almost certainly was. The back division of the 1971 Lions, including Barry John, Mike Gibson, John Dawes, David Duckham and Gerald Davies were indeed in a class of their own – they were unsurpassed. But what about the class of '74?

JPR Williams, perfectly placed to judge, and a man who admired his 1974 team-mates unreservedly, concedes that: 'The 1971 backs were better. I'm reluctant to say that almost, but that is the case. And Barry, whatever anyone says, was a better outside-half than Phil. He did it with poor ball – that was the difference. The forwards in '74 were so dominant that the backs weren't eulogised as much as the '71 backs. Remember though that it was a totally different scenario. In New Zealand we were living off scraps, so we had to move every ball... But it's a joke to say that we didn't play rugby in South Africa, because some of our back play was exceptionally good.'

Even Gareth Edwards, another giant of both tours, felt compelled to defend the honour of the 1974 backs in his own autobiography: 'Some have criticised the 1974 Lions for not being as enterprising as their 1971 predecessors. I would put one simple statistic before those critics – the 1974 tourists in the Test series scored ten tries to one, the 1971 Lions scored six tries to their opponents eight in the Tests. Lacking in enterprise? I don't think that is fair.'

When I asked Edwards about the criticism recently, his response was even more forthright: 'This isn't about John Reason. I'm not interested in revisiting all that. Everyone had their opinions. Could we have played a more expansive game? Yes, I suppose so. But I was more than content, as was Phil, as was Syd, as was Willie, to work along the lines of; "Don't give them an inch. Not one inch, not one chance." For the first time in history we had a pack of forwards who were every bit as good if not better than South Africa. We felt we could control the game, not give them a peep. We'd have been mad not to utilise that. Now you start spraying the ball around willy-nilly, yes it's lovely to look at, until they get their hands on the ball. Give them an opening and they'll take it, so why give them that opportunity? ... There's a lot of water gone under the bridge so I don't feel aggrieved about it anymore. I'm not upset, and I don't feel the need to justify anything either. We've got nothing to answer for or to prove. We scored more points and more tries than anyone before in the Tests and provincial matches. We beat South Africa by five tries to none in Pretoria, their own back yard. And they were bloody sensational tries too. I can't really see what more you need to say.'

JJ Williams is another who's more than happy to stand up for his side's credentials: 'The backs never got their due. Without a doubt that's true. Especially the centres. The '71 boys always got the praise, people say they were better. Well we scored far more tries than them, and plenty were just as good – there were some fantastic tries scored... Plus New Zealand in the early Seventies didn't have a clue about back play, so it was easier for the '71 boys behind. The 'Boks, to be fair, had some decent players behind. So we still haven't had the acclaim, not as individuals... On a personal level I think maybe I have by now, because the tries have been shown over the years, and people now appreciate the fact that I'm the second highest Test try scorer for the Lions behind Tony O'Reilly. That's not bad going is it?'

So some of the criticism hurt, and some of it still does. Some too was completely unfounded. John Reason's contention that: 'The 1974 forwards were about on a par with those of the 1971 team' for example elicited the same response from every one of the 1974 Lions I spoke to: 'Really?'

Critics also claimed that South African rugby was at an all-time low, with the Springboks already beaten in Johannesburg by England two years previously. In riposte one could present the argument that England also beat New Zealand in Auckland in 1973. So they beat the All Blacks two years after a victorious Lions side had done so, and the Springboks two years before the Lions would do so, proving... absolutely nothing.

And for those who continue to argue for the relative strength of New Zealand and weakness of South Africa at the start of the Seventies, here's another tour statistic. When the All Blacks toured to the northern hemisphere in 1972/73, a year after the Lions had won in New Zealand, they lost to Llanelli, North Western Counties, Midland Counties, the Barbarians and France, whilst also only managing draws against Munster and Ireland. Hardly a fearsome record.

So, the weaknesses and strengths of South African rugby when compared to New Zealand can be chewed over ad infinitum, but in essence it all proves very little, or it proves what you want it to prove.

Yes British teams had won in South Africa during the nineteenth century, yes, the French drew in Cape Town and won in Johannesburg to win a two-match series back in 1958. But in terms of the relative might of South Africa and New Zealand, how's this for a statistic:

South Africa won a three Test series in New Zealand as far back as 1937. It took their All Black counterparts until 1956 to win any series against the Springboks, home or away, and they had to wait until 1996's historic series win to redress the balance in South Africa itself. That win also finally brought them level in terms of head-to-heads, with twenty-two wins apiece.

In fact, despite New Zealand's clear superiority in recent decades, until rugby went professional, the Springboks were leading the All Blacks in head-to-heads by twenty-one wins to eighteen. Take the argument further – as many in South

Africa are happy to do, and you'll notice that before isolation took its toll, that record was even further weighted towards the 'Boks.

Until apartheid finally faced its sporting reckoning – and South Africa was cut adrift in terms of sporting links – there was clear blue water between those two fierce rivals and rugby superpowers. In the sixty years between their first meeting in 1921 and the last before the boycott in '81, New Zealand played South Africa thirty-seven times, eighteen times in New Zealand and nineteen in South Africa. Of those matches two were drawn, the All Blacks won fifteen, and the Springboks won twenty. The rivalry was the lifeblood of South African rugby, as evidenced by the legendary Springbok Boy Louw's contention before the 1949 series that: 'When South Africa plays New Zealand consider your country at war.'

Any attempt to put the strength of the opposition into context in terms of the Lions tours of 1971 and 1974 is difficult therefore. New Zealand themselves toured South Africa in 1970 and lost the series by three Tests to one. They toured South Africa again in 1976, and lost the series by three Tests to one. Any contention that the Lions took on New Zealand at their peak, but just happened to catch the Springboks at a rugby nadir, is pretty difficult to back up, and impossible to prove.

Any further balance – if needed – is provided by Clive Rowlands, who toured New Zealand as Wales coach in 1969 and travelled as a selector to South Africa to watch the Lions three years later. His view: 'I know the likes of John Reason and others said that South Africa was easier. I think it's the other way round. Did New Zealand come close to winning a series over there in the Seventies? No, they were stuffed – twice… If anything, the Lions in '71 were quite lucky in terms of timing. The New Zealanders were on the wane, and they caught them at the right time.'

The contention that sporting isolation had taken its toll is another factor. It's true that the South Africans could have been more battle hardened going into the 1974 series, but they faced equally unpromising situations before and after, and always managed to find an answer.

Here are just a few examples. In 1965, South Africa went on tour to Ireland and Scotland. They lost four matches, including both the Tests, and drew one. They then embarked on a two-Test tour to Australia, and lost both matches. They then travelled to New Zealand, and lost that series 3–1. The All Blacks then cancelled the return series in 1967.

If ever there was a case of a poor South African side, if ever there was a case for them suffering the effects of political isolation and dreadful form, surely this was it. They had no rugby and no reputation. Yet the Springboks defeated the British and Irish Lions of 1968 by three Tests to nil.

And yet so much is made of their poverty in 1974. There was the political minefield of the UK tour of 1969/70, followed by the England debacle of 1972 and the fact that they missed out on another date with the All Blacks in 1973. But the 1974 vintage had in fact out-played New Zealand in 1970, had beaten both France and Australia in 1971, would beat France again in 1974 and 1975, and would once again beat New Zealand 3–1 in 1976. That record does not point to a side on the wane, or a poor side.

For the Springboks, as for the Lions of 1971 and 1974, continuity was the key. Just as a reference point, the 2013 Lions used forty-four players over the course of a ten-match series in Australia. They used thirty players in three Test matches. The 1974 Lions used thirty-two players over a twenty-two-match tour, and only seventeen over four Tests. Modern-day apologists will argue that the game has changed beyond all comprehension, that these figures mean nothing. But Derek Quinnell's take on this is interesting. Luck, conditioning, selection and the very make-up of the men involved all play a part according to the three times Lions tourist: 'We were lucky in '71 in New Zealand to have continuity. The '74 side was just the same. In 1968 the Lions lost Barry [John] early and their plans went west. In 1980 we didn't play the same set of half-backs in any of the four Tests, that's how bad the injury situation was. With time to gel at a premium, continuity is a massive help.'

While the Lions picked seventeen players in 1974, the South Africans fielded thirty-three players across four Tests. Twenty-one of them were new caps. Those players were unfortunate that their international baptism came against one of the best sides ever to walk the face of the earth. The experience would certainly stand them in good stead though, according to Morné du Plessis: 'There are two fundamental issues here. The first one is that we were up against one of the greatest teams in rugby's history. Every one of them, in every position, was a world-class player. Now we didn't have that. We had some who had been world-class players, we had some who would become world-class players, but at that particular time, we just didn't have enough of them – we weren't world class in every position – they were. Secondly, the selectors saw fit to change the team after every Test match. Therein lies the problem.'

And what of the country's rugby isolation? In terms of the tour of 1974, du Plessis feels it's been overplayed: 'We beat the All Blacks in 1976, we beat the Lions in 1980, so we can't blame isolation for the '74 defeat really, can we? It's purely a cyclical thing, a rugby cycle in many ways. The big problem was that we couldn't accept that. It was the fundamental mistake. After that First Test we couldn't just face the fact that the other side was better than us, then work on how we would be able to counter that superiority. Instead the selectors thought that there was another fifteen men out there that could do better, and then another fifteen, so they kept changing.'

When he talks about the series victories of 1976 and 1980, he's talking from personal experience – du Plessis played in both those series wins. The beating of New Zealand in 1976 – only two years after the Springboks had been demolished by the Lions – is a case in point.

That All Black side featured all-time greats such as Bryan Williams, Grant Batty, Sid Going, Ian Kirkpatrick and Andy Leslie. The Springbok side that won the First Test against them in Durban contained no less than eleven players who had faced the Lions two years earlier. Morné du Plessis himself was captain, creating history by following in the footsteps of his father Felix, the man who'd skippered the Springboks to victory over New Zealand in 1949. He was joined by Oosthuizen, Whipp, Germishuys, Bosch, Bayvel, Stander, Williams, van Heerden, Coetzee and Jan Ellis – still going strong! If not for Dawie Snyman's pre-match injury, that figure would have been twelve. Those very same players had failed to beat the Lions in four attempts, yet they were good enough to beat the All Blacks three times in the space of a month and a half.

At the end of that series South Africa led New Zealand overall by nineteen victories to thirteen, the largest gap that had ever existed between the two nations, and the All Blacks' worst win-loss ratio ever.

Ian McIntosh remembers that 1976 tour well: 'They were a really good nucleus of players, as they had been for the Lions two years previously. Selection was poor in '74, but the players themselves weren't. They were vindicated in 1976 against New Zealand.'

Edward Griffiths is now chief executive of Saracens Rugby Club. He was at one time chief executive of the South African Rugby Union and, as such, is the man widely credited with helping to unite the country behind its team as they built towards their momentous World Cup win in 1995. Griffiths feels that the weakness of the 'Boks has been overplayed, as has their isolation. By the same token he feels that the Lions themselves are undervalued at home: 'They are certainly not underrated in South Africa. Of all the teams that have played against the Springboks, they are still the most admired. They stand apart – Afrikaners thought they were the best, and the non-whites were in awe.'

Morné du Plessis highlighted the fact that between 1976 and 1980, South Africa's rugby team suffered further isolation. Those Springboks didn't play any international rugby of note at all during that period, not one Test match against a major nation in four years. That was before they welcomed Bill Beaumont's Lions in 1980. South Africa won that Test series 3–1.

For younger readers there is another, more recent example. The Lions tourists to South Africa in 2009 were a well-prepared, well-led and multi-talented squad. They were confident of adding another Springbok scalp to the British and Irish totem pole. And yet they contrived to lose a series they could – and quite possibly should have won. Ian McIntosh is right, there is no such thing as an easy ride in the land of the 'Bok. In fact, the very sight of the Lions' red invariably brings out the best in South Africans.

Prior to that 2009 tour, as the excitement built, there were columns and polls in British newspapers discussing the best ever Lions XV. *The Daily Telegraph* chose the following:

15 JPR Williams (Wales)
14 Gerald Davies (Wales)
13 Brian O'Driscoll (Ireland)
12 Mike Gibson (Ireland)
11 JJ Williams (Wales)
10 Phil Bennett (Wales)
9 Gareth Edwards (Wales)
8 Mervyn Davies (Wales)
7 Fergus Slattery (Ireland)
6 Richard Hill (England)
5 Martin Johnson (England)
4 Willie John McBride (Ireland)
3 Graham Price (Wales)
2 Keith Wood (Ireland)
1 Fran Cotton (England)

That XV consists of only one player who toured New Zealand in 1971 but not South Africa in '74, the supremely gifted Gerald Davies. There are six included who made it onto both tours: JPR Williams, Mike Gibson, Gareth Edwards, Willie John McBride, Fergus Slattery and Mervyn Davies, although Gibson didn't play a Test in '74 while Slattery didn't play a Test in '71. There are three players in the fifteen who didn't tour in '71 but did shine in '74 – JJ Williams, Phil Bennett and Fran Cotton. So the Lions of 1974 outweigh the Lions of 1971 by two players.

A more recent poll, run by *The Guardian* newspaper prior to the 2013 tour to Australia, came up with something similar, and again the 1974 tourists came out comfortably ahead. In a list of the top twenty Lions of all time, fourteen had gone on one or both of those tours. Barry John and Gerald Davies had gone in 1971 only, Gareth Edwards, Willie John McBride, JPR Williams, Mike Gibson, Mervyn Davies, Ian McLauchlan and Gordon Brown had gone on both tours, while JJ williams, Ian McGeechan, Andy Irvine, Fran Cotton and Phil Bennett had gone on the latter.

It's all subjective of course, but interesting nonetheless. Equally interesting is the choice of Phil Bennett as opposed to Barry John at outside-half in the first of those two surveys.

The Daily Mail also put Bennett ahead of John in their list of the 'Top Ten Lions of All Time' (Cotton, McGeechan, Millar, JPR Williams, Edwards and, of course, McBride at number one also made it onto that illustrious list).

Now in a straight vote for the best outside-half ever, most rugby people would opt for John, not only above Bennett, but above everyone else who played before or after. Barry John is acknowledged worldwide as the ultimate rugby number 10, much as Pelé is in football. But there are always those who prefer Cruyff, or Maradona, or Zidane, or Messi.

In rugby terms, Gareth Edwards matured alongside Barry John – partnered him for both club and country. Yet he eventually went on to play more games for Wales alongside Phil Bennett. He's been asked the question hundreds of times over the years. Can you separate them?

'Well I haven't been able to do it. Maybe it's suited me not to over the years, mind you. It was easier not to think about it too much, and not to compare them. But the longer it went on, and the more I started to ponder the whole thing, I realised that I actually didn't need to separate them. I achieved so much in tandem with both, they were both absolutely outstanding in their own individual ways, that I never felt the need to compare... If you think of it in terms of a football analogy, Argentina have had two of the all-time greatest number tens – right up there with the very best in history – in Messi and Maradona. But they came generations apart. You can argue the toss 'til the cows come home about who's better. What you can't argue about is that they both did the same job, both so far above anyone else as to make them unique, and yet they both did it in very different ways. Now we in Wales were lucky enough to have Maradona and Messi in the same era. That's the point people can't grasp. Phil was everything Barry wasn't and Barry was everything Phil wasn't. They were different personalities, and they played the game differently, but each was a top, top player, and each achieved pretty much all you could ask in the game. I was just lucky to get the best of both.'

Others who toured with Bennett feel equally strongly that he deserves his place among the greats. Andy Irvine was once quoted as saying that: 'Pound for pound Phil Bennett is the best stand-off we've ever seen.' When I asked him about the remark recently he was glad to reiterate: 'Yes, I would still say that. The two guys for me that could beat anybody – on a sixpence – were Benny and Gerald Davies. Now it was slightly different in that Gerald always had a wee bit more space, and further out. Benny was always under pressure... I used to love training with Benny, we'd play touch rugby and you'd be really chuffed if you could touch him because he was just so quick off the mark. And although he wasn't the biggest boy in the world, he was a reasonable tackler for his size too. But it was really his game-management that I admired most... I loved playing with him because from a full-back's point of view he involved you so much. He did things with a quiet authority, he wasn't bossy, he wasn't big headed... he was wonderful to play with, just fantastic.'

Willie John McBride, who played with both Bennett and John, admitted once that he would choose Bennett simply because: 'When something wanted to be done, he could do it.' Forty years on, when I asked him to clarify the remark, or in fact whether he wanted to change his mind, he told me that there was no doubt in his mind: 'Benny or Barry? Yes, it would still be Phil. Two great players – the greatest – and I played with both. And Barry was fantastic, just phenomenal. But the difference between the two was that Benny was a team man. Barry was an individual whereas Benny was a team man. To me that made a huge difference... And one more thing. Benny would take the rough stuff too.'

Of course there are plenty of other players, and there are countless other lists and surveys that put Barry John way out in front on his own. But when it comes to comparing the greatest tours, and the greatest Lions, nothing it seems is clear-cut, not even the coronation of The King.

Clive Rowlands coached both John and Bennett, knows each well, and is proud to call them friends. He is superbly placed to answer that all-important question about the contentious Number 10 jersey. So his response when I put the question to him was unexpected to say the least: 'Who was the best? Barry or Phil... Good question. The answer – neither... Cliff Morgan was better than both of them.'

* * *

As for the greatest side, well the South Africans themselves were in no doubt. Dr Danie Craven, who'd seen them all come and go, loved the Lions of 1955 above all others for their dash and romance. He wrote in 1959 that: 'With the Lions, rugby is still a game where adventure, enterprise and initiative form as great part of a player's outfit as his physical attributes.'

In 1974, Dr Craven proclaimed that year's Lions vintage simply: 'The Greatest team to visit South Africa.'

The majority of his countrymen seemed to agree. John Gainsford, another Springbok great, summed up the Lions of 1974 this way: 'They were mentally tougher, physically harder, superbly drilled and coached.' Journalist Chris Greyvenstein of *The Cape Times*, another respected rugby man, was fulsome in his praise, calling the Lions: 'A team without weakness from the front row to full-back.'

Morné du Plessis, from the distance of four decades, still holds that side in the highest regard: 'Those Lions are simply legends in South Africa. Twenty-two matches and three months... Our public got to know them so well – almost better than they did our own players, because they were always in the papers, every day. They became a part of the social fabric. Then you add to that the fact that they beat us. Then you add in the way they beat us, that they were brilliant players. All that gives you the makings of a legend. And they are a legendary team.'

As if to prove his point, he begins to reel off the names – and continues through each and every one of them, in every position. Then he starts on the players who didn't make the Test side: 'You just look at the bench, the likes of Tony Neary and Andy Ripley in the back row, my position. They couldn't even get a Test cap – that's a frightening thing. So I can still give you the names, I can reel them off. Now I couldn't do that with the recent rugby championship, for example. That I can still remember something from forty years ago so vividly – that says everything.'

A number of the 1974 Lions had also toured with the ground-breaking 1971 team to New Zealand. Their thoughts on the respective achievements, and the respective strengths of both sides are fascinating. Ian McLauchlan for example sees them as two distinct entities, facing very different challenges, and yet they're linked by a common thread, the very backbone of the side: 'In 1971, a team went out to New Zealand and did something incredible, they won a Test series. Now the core of that team was retained for '74. A lot of the guys who were very good in '71 were exceptional in '74, and that's the difference between the two tours.'

When I ask him to name names he gives me three in particular: 'I was very much a better player by 1974, I'd realised what it was all about by then. Edwards was great in 1971, but he was absolutely sensational in 1974. Mervyn was immense on both tours, but again took a step up in South Africa, where he was just superb. He never courted publicity Mervyn, so never got the credit he deserved. But there is no praise high enough for that man.'

McLauchlan could have added JPR Williams to that list too. For his part the full-back, the bedrock of both the 1971 and 1974 sides, went along with the assessment of the incomparable Clem Thomas: 'Perhaps if you had the 1971 backs and the 1974 forwards, you would be close to creating the perfect Lions team.'

For Williams, it came down to enjoyment: 'South Africa was enjoyable. Hard grounds, good weather, dominant pack. Also the welcome was great, and you could escape now and again, the place was big enough and varied enough. New Zealand was small, cold, wet – and everyone lived for their rugby, even the old ladies who stopped you in the street. New Zealanders have that chip on their shoulder too – it was a tough place to go, a tough place to enjoy. So I enjoyed South Africa more, but the achievement was greater in New Zealand.'

These thoughts mirror those of another player who anchored both the triumphs of 1971 and 1974, the player Ian McLauchlan valued above all others – Mervyn Davies.

The number 8 summed up his feelings on the two tours

in an interview years later: 'One was hard, one was easy. In South Africa the sun shone, the grounds were hard... and we had the nucleus of the team from '71.'

So New Zealand for Davies was the tougher tour. He would expand on these thoughts in his autobiography *In Strength and Shadow*: 'In the imagination of modern-day rugby fans, the 1974 Lions have usurped the feats of '71... Were we the best Lions? Perhaps. Was it our greatest achievement? I think not. The record books insist that it is, but ask the men who toured in '71 and '74 to compare both feats and I am sure they will say winning in New Zealand was the pinnacle of their rugby careers... But perhaps to consign the '74 Lions to second place so quickly is to do a grave disservice. To begin with we had to deal with something the '71 squad never encountered – expectation.'

For Mervyn, and for others, those anomalies could happily coexist. The greater achievement need not necessarily have been accomplished by the greatest side.

Of all the Lions I spoke to for this book, no-one carries his greatness more humbly than Gareth Edwards. He'll say it's something he learnt from Gary Player, noticing how the South African dealt with well-wishers, autograph hunters, time wasters – with infinite patience and a self-deprecating manner. But it goes deeper than that.

There is no pretension, no self-aggrandizement, nothing aloof or superior in Edwards. He treats all comers with respect and expects the same in return. He is also the one who thinks longest, and chooses his words most carefully when it comes to the difficult questions. He doesn't want to be misunderstood, or misconstrued. In some ways no-one has more to lose when comparing the best with the best. Edwards, as he did when playing, feels loathe to let anybody down.

When I asked him to talk about the relative strength of the 1971 and 1974 tours, I began by asking about his own contribution. Was he a better player in 1974 than three years previously? 'Yes, absolutely. I was fit, I was more experienced and I was behind one of the best packs of all time, so I was on the front foot all the time.

So what of those two touring parties? As a man with a foot in both camps, which way does Edwards lean?

'It depends on which day and in which company I get asked. Someone will make a case for '71 and quite often I won't disagree. Then someone else will make the case for '74 and I can't help but agree with them when that happens. Every point put forward for one is balanced by an equally strong point in favour of the other... Of the boys who went again in 1974, I think you can say that we were better players. But 1971 was a remarkable tour and a remarkable achievement because it was the first time ever we'd won as Lions. And we played some amazing rugby too. Then again we had no choice. When we got ball we had to use it... In '74 we were in complete control, we dominated. So every time I think about how good the '71 side was, it's countered by '74. What I do think sometimes is that the '74 side's achievement has been dismissed too easily, that we never got the credit such a fine team deserved. People have talked about the quality of the rugby, the 'Boks being weak, the provinces being weak, all that stuff – all rubbish. Then throw in the expectation levels after the '71 win, the fact that the South Africans couldn't underestimate us, couldn't be complacent, and it's some feat. I think when you look at the history books, and see twenty-one wins, one draw, and an unbeaten team – that tells its own story.'

Fergus Slattery, honest and abrasive in his opinions as he was on the rugby pitch, is another who can find greatness in both sides, and both achievements. He wrote after the 1974 tour that although: 'During a major tour of New Zealand you play against stronger provincial teams than in South Africa... Overall I think that the thirty players who went to South Africa were better than those who went to New Zealand.' He added that there was less pressure on the Lions of 1971, since they'd lost their opening match in Australia: 'In 1974 we were under pressure throughout, defending an unbeaten record.'

Ian McGeechan didn't play in '71, but his Lions record over the decades makes him a voice, and an opinion, to be reckoned with. His feelings were presented in his autobiography: 'I have always admired the 1971 Lions, but I am in no doubt that the 1974 team are the greatest Lions, and I cannot see their achievements being repeated.'

Phil Bennett beat the All Blacks three times, in 1972 with his club Llanelli, in 1973 with the Barbarians, and in 1977 when he skippered the Lions to victory in the Second Test at Christchurch. As ever, he is modest, diplomatic and even-handed in his thoughts: 'You can only play what's in front of you. All I can say is that every game in South Africa was a battle. Whether we were breaking records or scraping through in the last few minutes, they were all physical, hard, and brutal. It was war to them really... I remember looking at the 'Boks coming out for the Third Test and being terrified by what I saw – seriously. Now maybe they weren't the greatest side, and maybe we did catch them on the hop, but don't tell me they were no good... And I can also say this with my hand on my heart, having toured New Zealand with Wales in 1969, I think the '71 boys caught New Zealand at a good time. They weren't at their strongest.'

And what about the perception that the Lions of 1974 didn't play rugby to compare with their predecessors? 'The '71 tour had Gerald and Barry and Duckham, and I think maybe they were seen as being more glamorous than us. But I think we played some great football, and we ran them off the park at times... But more than that, we had character in buckets, there were no superstars, just team-mates. And we had Willie, the greatest Lion ever as captain... No-one will ever achieve that again.'

In terms of glamour, the 1971 Lions were indeed untouchable. Davies, John, Duckham and the rest had that

X factor in spades. But even Gerald Davies himself can appreciate that glamour – the X factor – is just one factor.

In terms of comparing the two sides and their respective achievements, I asked him whether it was fair to say that the 1974 Lions failed to live up to the standards set by the '71 Lions, and whether the comparison would always be weighted in favour of his own side.

From the man who turned down the chance to tour in '74, the response was remarkably even-handed and generous: 'You can't do that. The '74 Lions, as we had done in 1971, managed to do something really special. They did it in the best way that they thought possible. They scored some brilliant tries, you only have to look at the record, the way Phil played, the way Gareth played. But the point in South Africa was always that if you didn't match them at forward, you weren't going to win... I saw it there as manager in 2009, so it's still true today – you've got to hit them psychologically and physically, in the scrum. It's an iconic phase of the game for South Africans, they don't expect anybody to beat them there. The '74 Lions began there and defeated them where they thought they were strongest... New Zealand and South Africa are different in where their emphasis lies. New Zealand have never emphasised the scrum. It's the ruck, the maul, the back row and break down. So there is a difference in approach... In '74 they attacked South Africa where they needed to be attacked. They had to win that battle first, which is what Syd Millar and Willie John McBride did superbly... They were terrific.'

JBG Thomas, who went on both tours, not only called his post-tour book *The Greatest Lions* but began it with it these words: 'The 1974 Lions will be known as the greatest, although long may be the argument among rugby men.'

Terry O'Connor, another who chronicled the success of both the '71 and '74 Lions, explained that: 'There was little to choose between the two teams, but I would opt for the 1974 side because they were that much more successful at winning. And that is what sport is about.'

So why do some of the '74 vintage still feel a touch hard done by? JJ Williams expands on the perceived bias of certain Fleet Street scribes: 'There were some journalists that were very much '71 orientated. They were public school, Oxbridge types. They loved the London Welsh boys, but then John Dawes, Gerald, Geoff Evans, JT those boys were also a part of that same set at the time. Then I come along – straight out of the valleys. Phil was the same, and Bobby too – it just took us longer to get the respect we deserved.'

The Lions of 1974 were blessed in many ways according to JPR Williams: 'Blessed with great captaincy, great forward coaching, good management and a true team spirit. There were a lot of world stars there, we made a few more along the way, and most of all we were driven by a hard core of winners.'

Bobby Windsor, one of that hard core, struggles with the very idea that there are doubts about the 1974 side's standing at the top of the pile: 'We've never really had that recognition, and I suppose politics comes into it doesn't it, because if you look at it in purely rugby terms, then you're looking at the best ever. That simple.'

Tom David points to the record books for a definitive answer: 'I was lucky enough to catch the end of the '71 tour, because I'd managed to get out to New Zealand on cheap flights through work. As you can imagine that really fired me up, and to follow those boys was amazing. But if you're asking which was the best... My opinion? South Africa. There is no doubt about it, and I've got no problem saying it. New Zealand were a great side, but twenty-two games unbeaten? In South Africa? How anyone could even make a comparison I'm not sure, because only one side did that, only one went unbeaten. So it'll always be the '74 Lions.'

The Greatest Lions? Better than those of 1971 even? Absolutely according to Fran Cotton: 'We weren't playing against dummies out there – they were absolutely top-class players. The Springboks had never lost a series like that to anyone at home before. So you've only got to look at the record books to get your answer. The stats tell you that the '74 Lions were the best team we've ever produced. I do genuinely believe that the 1974 Lions were a better all-round team than the '71 boys as well. More than that, we were stronger all over, throughout the squad.'

Those sentiments were echoed by JJ Williams when I asked him the inevitable question, which side was the best?

'We were unbeaten. You could not beat the '74 team. That team was a brilliant team. Yes, we would have beaten them [the '71 side]. We would have stuffed them up front, and we had boys behind who could go for the kill. JPR was better in '74, so was Gareth. Benny was just incredible, those boys in the centre, Milliken and McGeechan were on fire. Andy Irvine is an all-time great, and I wasn't bad either was I? These boys scored more points than on any other tour, and more tries, and were never beaten. What more could you do?'

Finally, after forty years, Williams believes that the opinions first expressed by the likes of Clem Thomas, JBG Thomas and Terry O'Connor back in the Seventies are being accepted as the truth: 'How do you determine the great sides. It's if they win. It's in the record books. You can only go by facts and figures. Those facts and figures speak for themselves... We were the greatest Lions team ever, because we won almost everything. We never lost. That's a fact... Would we have beaten the 1971 team? I think we would have, yes. And I think we sit at the top of the tree, I really do believe that.'

The final word on this subject should really go to the man who led those undefeated Lions. Willie John McBride was another who straddled both legendary tours. I'd read years ago that he considered '74 the stronger team, and that he saw the victory in South Africa as his: 'Single greatest achievement in rugby football.'

But does he still hold those views? And if he does, is there an element of annoyance that the 1974 Lions have had to live in the shadows for so long? McBride exhales deeply, and chooses his words carefully: 'Look these are things that are beyond my words. I can't tell you that. What I do know is that I have the satisfaction inside my chest. That for me is good enough... And I know that all those guys who travelled with me, they gave me a little silver memento that I keep. All it says on it is; "Willie John, it was great to travel with you". Now that means more to me than anything that has been or is written by anyone else.'

So Willie John, which is 'The Greatest' Lions side?

Now McBride is seen as such a key figure on both tours that I expect this answer to be equally diplomatic, equally careful. Here is the man who strode across the playing fields of Dunedin, Christchurch, Wellington and Auckland with the superstars of 1971, giving their stellar backs enough possession to shine. And the same man who battled his way from Cape Town to Pretoria, through Port Elizabeth and Johannesburg with his undefeated band of brothers three years later.

But it turns out that for McBride, the answer is simple when it comes right down to it: 'Well it has to be my team.'

MY team, the Lions of 1974. A long, loud laugh follows, as though he can't quite believe that he's saying these words out loud, being so forthright, so bold, so undiplomatic. Then this: 'We had better forwards, we would have dominated them. And what's more there was much greater depth in 1974 than in 1971... I'll tell you there's one simple way to sum it all up. We were never beaten... We were never beaten. I think that answers your question.'

CHAPTER 22

To Good Friends
Living Large

*'I can never remember whether it snowed for six days and
six nights when I was twelve or whether it snowed for
twelve days and twelve nights when I was six.'*
Dylan Thomas, *A Child's Christmas in Wales*

As DYLAN THOMAS remembered the ghosts of Christmases
past, so those Lions remember their exploits in South Africa.
In a collective memory bank full of rugby highlights, that tour
is still their Christmas Day. Context fades, faces dim, names
and matches become blurred. Whereas for Dylan only the
snow remained, for the Lions only the glow remains.

They became known collectively as 'The Invincibles', and
in 2014 they will gather again to tell their stories, to remind
each other of those unimaginable highs, to relive the punches,
the kicks, the tries and the ultimate glory. They are older,
though by their own admission not all wiser. They still meet
like this because they share something that no-one else can
understand, and their bond allows them to relax, to forget
about the outside world, their public personas and their
reputations. They can be themselves. 'It is one of the blessings
of old friends that you can afford to be stupid with them'
goes the old saying. They've seen you at your weakest, your
strongest, your most vulnerable and your most endearing.
Much is forgotten, all is forgiven, the hugs, the smiles – and
yes the tears – will be genuine and heartfelt.

On meeting them certain things stand out. Their unfailing politeness and hospitality, their honesty, their good humour, their patience, their sense of time and place. And that far away look as they capture a certain moment and relive it, a look that tells you they have seen things, done things, shared things that most of us can only imagine. They are aware that they are part of a select band. And that's why seeing each other means so much.

JJ Williams for one is looking forward to catching up: 'It was a special part of my life. They were a very special bunch of people and it was a privilege to be a part of their achievement. We became great friends, some of my best friends are still among those boys. We won't see each other for a year, but then we catch up and just fall back into it. Old stories, old jokes, old memories. I shared a room with Mike Burton in Cape Town for about two weeks, and it was the best two weeks of my life. Some will say that we're just living in the past, but they don't understand. They weren't there. Success has a lot to do with it. We won together. There are no stars among us, just the boys.'

Roy Bergiers admits that the three months he spent in South Africa put him on such intimate terms with some of his fellow tourists that they became a surrogate family: 'It was the experience of a lifetime, and my feelings for those boys have lasted for the rest of my life. I felt closer to them than to my own family at times. We were essentially an extended family, we shared personal things, whether highs, lows, triumphs, disappointments, or even homesickness... Shed tears at times together too.'

For Andy Irvine, that tour still defines his rugby life: 'If I had to pick one moment from the whole of my rugby career, it would be the seconds after that final whistle [in the Third Test] when we were cheered off and the series was won. To be a part of it was a magnificent feeling. But what I would say is this – that group of guys, whether it be the Saturday team or the Wednesday team, there was a very close bond. Obviously those lads from the Wednesday team were disappointed that they weren't playing in the Test match, but they never showed it... It's a strong man that doesn't show that, who rallies and supports the lads who are on the field. There were a lot of lads in that Wednesday team who would have been Test players on any other Lions tour. But the calibre of player was so high that it was just so difficult to get in. There was a tremendous spirit and camaraderie – that we were all in this together – and that was one of the strengths of that side. And to this day there's still a very strong bond.'

As their fortieth reunion nears, even Tom David can celebrate his part in the success of the 1974 Lions without that nagging element of regret: 'I remember Roger Uttley saying at a dinner recently that prior to my injury I was in the Test team, which was a lovely thing of him to say. And looking back now, I am just so pleased and proud to have been a part of it all. If you'd have said to me; "Tom, you're going to play nine games on a Lions tour – the greatest Lions tour, the most successful tour ever – and you're going to score five tries, and you're going to contribute to that amazing success, and you're going to come back unbeaten", well I'd have been there like a shot.'

Fran Cotton saw other battles, other victories and defeats with the Lions. But those few months will forever be the ones that stand out: 'You feel like you've been to war with people. You've been through so much together... That tour was the highlight of my rugby life. It was life-changing for everybody that went on it – it was absolutely marvellous. I look back now and feel privileged to have been one of them.'

Willie John McBride will insist it was his privilege to lead them: 'We were thirty players who were together throughout. No superstars, no cliques. Just loyalty to each other. That's the word. Loyalty. To each other, to me as a captain, and to Syd as a coach. They were outstanding. And these weren't professionals remember, these were just thirty guys, away from home for a long time. They had all the pressures of the tour itself to deal with, and then the ordinary pressures of life. You know Benny is a man who can get homesick, others had problems back home, everyone there had to deal with their own issues in one way or another. But when one was down, or one had said something stupid, they were never just left, sitting in their rooms. It counted you know.'

If they are bound together by shared experiences, they are bound too by the Lions code of honour.

It's a code which some feel has been disrespected by players from more recent tours. With the lure of easy money from ghosted newspaper columns, some Lions have broken ranks, publicly criticising and openly questioning certain aspects of tour life and management decisions. This was particularly apparent on the 2001 tour to Australia. The players who cause the ructions are invariably the players who aren't being selected for the Test side.

Roy Bergiers didn't play a Test match for the Lions, but he finds this attitude, a perceived lack of respect for tradition particularly upsetting: 'I played ten games for the Lions, I'd have liked to have played a bit more. But to think that so many great players haven't made it onto a Lions tour, I can always say that I was on not just a successful one, but a great one. I still feel very proud and honoured, so it gets on my nerves when I see people like [Matt] Dawson and [Austin] Healey moaning that they should be in the side instead of someone else. It's not a divine right. You've got to earn the right to put on that jersey. No matter how disappointed you are, you get behind those who are out there if you are a team man.' The Lions of 1974 were team men to their core.

Bergiers's mate Phil Bennett agrees: 'Even the great Cliff Morgan and Jeff Butterfield and Tony O'Reilly only managed to draw out there in South Africa... We came home as we'd left, unbeaten, united. No superstars, just a partnership of equals and everyone feeling that they were a part of the success. It was unique I think in that way – I don't think it was the case so much in 1971 from what I gather. And then when we got back to Heathrow, Willie John shook us all by the hand, and used his usual line; "Men, it's been great to travel with you", no hugging, no kissing, no crying. It was sad, but it was done with dignity.'

And now, decades later, Bennett is still being reminded of those halcyon days: 'I was at an airport in Toronto a few months back, and I saw this giant making his way towards me. And I knew, just knew – grey hair, square shoulders, big belly, checked shirt, red face – he just had to be a Boer. And you know Afrikaners can be awkward buggers at times. But this chap comes up, shakes my hand and says; "Boy, you murdered us… just murdered us… Can I buy you a beer?" And that kind of thing says it all really. Forty years later even the 'Boks are still shaking your hand.'

* * *

And yet old wounds still fester. And for some there will never be a rapprochement. Peter Hain went on to become Secretary of State for Northern Ireland years later. He appointed Willie John McBride to a commission at one point: 'Because I thought he was the best man for the job.' Yet the matter of the 1974 tour still rankles. When I ask him about his feelings four decades later, Hain is still vehement in his condemnation of what those players did: 'Quite simply they were collaborating with the worst racial tyranny the world had ever seen.'

So can he understand why some might still view them as heroes?

'Of course I can. They were a great rugby side… In that sense of course they're heroes… just like George North or Leigh Halfpenny today. I understand all of that. But what I cannot accept to this day and what I will never accept is people who refuse to take responsibility for what was actually their complicity in sustaining a system which excluded anyone who wasn't white… Anyone who doesn't understand that in retrospect seems to me to have a serious moral vacuum.'

But what of the non-white crowds cheering on their Lions heroes?

'Black spectators cheering for the Lions? I've had it put to me that this was a good enough reason for their going. Well, frankly that's bollocks. Black African rugby fans, of whom there were many, cheered anybody who beat the Springboks.'

And what of the oft-told tale of Nelson Mandela sitting in his cell on Robben Island in 1974, listening to the irritation of the Afrikaner guards, and celebrating that small victory over his oppressors. Didn't that count for anything?

No: 'Nelson Mandela always had a phrase which I think is relevant – forgive but never forget. I'm not sure if I'm quite in forgiving mode even now. But one thing's for sure, I'll never forget that tour.'

Of course there are those who are happy to take issue with Hain's views. Gary Player was in no doubt about the righteousness of the tour when he met Gareth Edwards decades later. Did the tour help at all he was asked: 'It depends' came the reply, 'It depends on your standpoint. If you're militant you'd probably say no. If you are a man who believes in communication, like I do, then yes.'

Mthobi Tyamzashe appreciates both sides of the argument, agreeing that isolation was an important weapon in the battle against apartheid, yet seeing the Lions as a force for good too: 'People like Peter Hain did a huge amount to contribute to the changes that happened here. What they were championing was right. Being on the outside they had a particular view, a better view maybe... and I support that view wholeheartedly. But I am still proud to have been there supporting the Lions as well. One would think that it's a past we would be embarrassed about, but we are not. To me it all comes back to those small beginnings, so I don't see any conflict, I don't think we were different in our ultimate objectives.'

But maybe they were different in the way they saw those objectives being achieved:

'Remember that for anything to happen, there must be some level of engagement,' says Tyamzashe: 'To me, although we didn't want them to come, once they were here they were our champions. That's really what the tour was about... These were the building blocks that were essential in what was to follow. So I'll always have a soft spot for them because I felt they were there when we needed them.'

Morné du Plessis, figurehead of multiracial Springbok rugby during the mid-Nineties, is another who appreciates both views: 'I still believe that sporting isolation was one of the major factors in forcing our eventual move towards a normal society. So you must give credit to the guys who stood their ground – Peter Hain, the Watson brothers, the Mthobi Tyamzashes of this world. We didn't like them at the time because they were interfering with our lives. But they were right in the end.'

But du Plessis, like Tyamzashe agrees that the profile of the 1974 tour helped to keep apartheid in the news internationally: 'I just have another take on that, in that it gave the anti-establishment campaigners a chance to voice their opinions on a global scale. If the Lions had not been here, there would have been nothing to report. So it gave a platform, in terms of the British press and the world media. It gave the protest movement a valuable stage, which they used well.'

JPR Williams points to the disparity in the treatment of the 1974 tourists and those of 1980 in the context of their decision to travel: 'I disagree with Peter Hain totally. You think about the 1980 tour – no-one talks about it. But of course they lost. We won, and for some reason that rankles.'

Tom David puts his argument simply: 'Forty years on, I'd still go. Sport is a wonderful thing, and a wonderful way of building bridges. I think by going we highlighted the problems, people became more aware. There were a lot of things we didn't like – awful things, but I wouldn't have known that without going.'

When I talk to Fran Cotton about Peter Hain's views on the tour of 1974, he has this to say: 'Peter Hain has his own view on these things, and in the end I'm not sure his actions were right. Who had the bigger influence? The Lions, by going and playing sides like the Leopards, and by demonstrating that the Springboks could be beaten, or someone who threw tacks on a rugby pitch to stop a game being played. Which was the more important? I've talked since to black administrators out in South Africa who remember that tour, and they all say how important it was to them. There was no huge, sudden swing, but we'd begun to chip away at the psyche of the white South African mentality. That's something isn't it?'

Whilst interviewing Peter Hain, I asked if he thought any of those 1974 Lions might have changed their perspective over the years. Did any of them feel a sense of guilt or remorse? His answer: 'Maybe one – Gareth Edwards.'

When I put this to Edwards he doesn't disagree: 'Yes, he's right. I've thought about it a great deal since. I met Nelson Mandela. By now I understand and respect everything that he – and they – fought for and suffered for. There's no point me saying I've no regrets, but you can't turn the clock back. I've had a love affair with South Africa from the very first time I went there as a youngster to play. The country, their rugby, their hospitality – it's always been a special place to me. But over the years I did come to realise what we didn't grasp as young men. I came to understand how much propaganda we'd been subjected to whilst out there, how we'd been used as well maybe. The portrayals of Mandela as some kind of bandit, a villain, a terrorist, well you come to understand as you get older that you've been duped I suppose. Hindsight is a wonderful thing, isn't it?'

So Edwards respects Hain's views, and can understand his long-standing antipathy towards the tourists: 'I'm not going to dismiss Peter Hain's views at all. He was brought up in apartheid South Africa, he'd seen what went on first-hand. We only saw it from afar, and you certainly weren't going to see any of the really bad stuff on a Lions rugby tour were you? But we did have chances to speak to local people and invariably they said they were glad we'd come... I remember talking to a number of black South Africans while I was out there, and I've spoken to any number since. And I always asked what they thought, did we do the right thing by going? And I don't remember any saying no, we shouldn't have toured... The bottom line is that I went. I can't say that I look back on it with sadness because it was an incredible experience, a huge part of my life and I don't want to be a hypocrite. What I can say is that I'm sorry that I didn't understand enough about it back then. If I knew as much about it then as I know now, I wouldn't have gone.'

Edwards told me this, and talked about his meeting with Nelson Mandela just a few weeks before South Africa's most iconic figure died at the age of ninety-five at the beginning of December 2013.

* * *

Nelson Mandela was never a rugby man, but he certainly understood the game's importance in terms of the Afrikaner psyche. On his eventual release from prison in 1990, on South Africa's reintegration into the international rugby fold in 1992, on his inauguration as president of the newly democratic South Africa in 1994 – an election that caused fear and outrage among thousands upon thousands of unreconstructed and terrified Afrikaners – Mandela was very much aware of the game as a means to an end. And so one of the indelible images of Mandela's life, and possibly the indelible image of rugby's long, often illustrious and sometimes embarrassing history, is Nelson Mandela wearing the Springbok jersey on 24 June 1995.

On that day, after taking part in – and hosting – their first ever Rugby World Cup, South Africa beat New Zealand in the final to become world champions. And there, at Ellis Park, Johannesburg, in the heart of Afrikanerdom, presenting the trophy to an über Afrikaner captain in Francois Pienaar, Nelson Mandela wore the skipper's number 6 jersey – the enemy jersey. Mandela thanked the Springbok captain for what he had done for their country. Pienaar's response: 'No, Mr President, thank you for what you have done for our country," came to symbolise the new South Africa.

Edward Griffiths was the man credited with conjuring up the all-inclusive and inspirational 'One Team, One Country' slogan. Black winger Chester Williams was the player who gave the words a public face, but Nelson Mandela was the man who gave the words true meaning.

For all the propaganda, for all the harsh truths that emerged in the aftermath, Mandela's gesture of reconciliation, of forgiveness and support was genuine, as well as being a truly inspired piece of political thinking. 'What we saw that day was a revolution' said Desmond Tutu. Pienaar himself was moved to say years later that: 'When the final whistle blew this country changed forever.'

So in the end it wasn't the Springboks or any other team that brought South African rugby into the light, it was Mandela.

Francois Pienaar was among a number of Springboks past and present to offer their tributes in the days following Nelson Mandela's passing. They were not alone. Political commentators described him as a secular saint. President Barack Obama said simply: 'He no longer belongs to us. He belongs to the ages.'

* * *

At the end of July 1974, the victorious Lions went their separate ways. Fortunes fluctuated thereafter, and the fellowship started to dwindle. South Africa itself endured the multiple tragedies of Soweto, Biko, decades more of Mandela's incarceration, and a nation's continued oppression.

The Gleneagles Agreement of 1977 isolated the country even further in terms of sport, and yet the Lions toured again in 1980. For some reason that tour never seems to make the headlines, never seems to engender such polarised emotions or opinions, never seems shrouded in so much controversy. As JPR Williams was quick to point out, the Lions lost that tour.

The Springboks themselves travelled to New Zealand in

1981 on the most contentious tour of them all. Errol Tobias's tour, a tour of cancelled matches, of riot police, of barbed wire and baton charges. The tour made famous forever by a flour-bombing plane. This was the tour that finally put an end to official All Black/Springbok relations for the foreseeable future. Those barren, non-contact years would last for over a decade.

Still other tours followed, with England officially playing the Springboks as late as 1984. Next came the rebel tours – with unsanctioned rugby and cricket sides heading for South Africa and the lure of a small fortune for each player involved.

In terms of putting the tour of 1974 into a political context, those subsequent tours make for an interesting comparison. According to Mthobi Tyamzashe, there is a world of difference between McBride's Lions and the cricket tours led by Graham Gooch and Mike Gatting in later years for example: 'Are they seen differently? Yes. Why? Because one, and only one, was seen as having done some good.'

Tyamzashe understands the bitterness, even forty years down the line, but from the standpoint of someone who stood on the terraces and danced when the Lions scored, he can also remember the joy, the hope that those Lions engendered:

'If it was an evil, it was a necessary evil, and in a strange way it was a positive towards the eventual integration of South Africa... That's why there are people who can still look back on that tour with affection... Someone like Fran Cotton for instance, why would I keep a name like that in my mind, or Willie John, or JJ... Afterwards you'd see youngsters playing in the street and when they'd catch the ball they'd say "JPR", or "JJ". The way they played meant that our young players had role models – and I'm talking about black boys here not white.'

And did that legacy last? Well yes if the fans who were thrilled by them went on to administrate at the highest levels. As Tyamzashe recalls: 'I've seen so many rugby Tests after that, Rugby Championships, Rugby World Cups... Remember there have been Lions tours after that which have not left any mark on me… But I even remember the headlines in the paper back in 1974; "The Pride of the Lions". That sums up their impact.'

Some of that 'pride' continued to serve the cause with distinction over the years as players, coaches and managers. Irvine, McGeechan, Gibson, JJ Williams, Brown, Cotton, Neary and Windsor himself, alongside Bennett as captain, travelled to New Zealand in 1977.

That tour is considered a disaster, yet they lost only four games out of twenty-five in New Zealand, and didn't lose once to those mighty provinces. They won one Test and were so dominant up front in the last that the All Blacks eventually resorted to a three-man scrum, so dire was their predicament. It came down to a single point in the end, 10–9 to New Zealand, and those are the fine margins that make Lions either legends or lummoxes.

Andy Irvine went back to South Africa in 1980, as did Fran Cotton, both on their third tours.

Syd Millar went back to South Africa in 1980 too, as tour manager. McBride toured New Zealand as manager in 1983. Both lost.

Cotton managed the Lions in 1997 in South Africa, Irvine did so in 2013 in Australia. Both won.

Roger Uttley and Ian McGeechan coached the Lions to a win in Australia in 1989, McGeechan won again in South Africa in 1997. Add New Zealand in 1993 and 2005 (assisting Sir Clive Woodward) and South Africa again in 2009 and you have possibly the most outstanding Lions record of all.

Some Lions prospered, others did not. Dr Sydney Millar eventually became chairman of the International Rugby Board.

The two English props, Burton and Cotton, went on to found multi-million pound business empires, but not before Burton had gained a certain notoriety by becoming the first English player ever to be sent off in an international match – against Australia in 1975.

JJ Williams returned to a hero's welcome in his home

village, Nantyffyllon, and changed direction completely: 'I went back to Maesteg and we were paraded through the town, it was bedlam. And at the function afterwards I remember speaking to one county councillor who said; "See, I voted for you to go John." And I told him; "Everyone I speak to says they voted for me, so who voted against me?" Of course it had been unanimous that decision, they'd all voted against!' Williams decided enough was enough. He set up his own painting and decorating business soon afterwards. The company flourished, as did he.

Roger Uttley remained a teacher, and went on to become Director of Physical Education at one of England's most famous private schools, Harrow.

Gareth Edwards and Phil Bennett brought the curtain down on Welsh rugby's 'Golden Era' together. They both retired in 1978 after inspiring the national team to its second Grand Slam in three years. It was secured in epic fashion against France at the Arms Park, with Edwards contributing yet another crucial, booming drop goal on the run during a masterful display. Phil Bennett captained Wales that season. Against France, in his final international, he scored two typically jinking, scampering, dummying, career-defining tries, the second of which was set up by the combined efforts of Edwards and JJ Williams. For the two legendary half-backs, there was no better way to take their leave. In the immediate aftermath of that victory, each told the other of his decision to retire. Neither had said anything beforehand because the focus had to be on the team, the match, the performance. That summed them up perfectly.

It would be another twenty-seven years before Wales achieved a Grand Slam again.

Flanker Tony Neary became a highly successful and a very wealthy solicitor. Yet in 1998 he was sentenced to five years in prison for theft. The headlines screamed that he'd 'plundered' a close associate's trust fund.

Sportsmen, especially those who reach the peaks, seem particularly prone to clinical depression, what All Black legend

John Kirwan described in open, inspirational terms as 'The Black Dog'. A number of those Lions players have found themselves battling depression, including Clive Rees and Roy Bergiers. Mervyn Davies lived under the cloud too in those years after his career ended so prematurely. Alcohol also played its part in the troubles of Davies and others, as did that deadliest of foes, cancer.

Bobby Windsor lost his first wife to the disease, and considered suicide years later, so bad was his depression. Today, tanned, fit and based for the most part in Majorca, 'The Duke' has: 'Sixteen grandchildren, six great-grandchildren and another on the way.' He can finally appreciate the good things again.

Alun Thomas went on to become president of the Welsh Rugby Union. No-one who was there ever forgot his welcoming speech to the Fijian tourists of 1985, when he referred to the Welsh missionary tradition in the Pacific Islands and concluded: 'And to think, a hundred years ago you were eating us.'

Thomas was the first of the 1974 Lions party to pass away, in 1991. Mervyn Davies lost his battle against cancer in 2012 – and days later, as Wales clinched another Grand Slam against France in Cardiff, a whole stadium, a whole nation – rose in salute to say its final farewell.

Gordon Brown, who always saved his best training – and subsequently his best rugby – for Lions tours, was forced out of the game by injury and suspension.

In December 1976, he became embroiled in a vicious fight while playing in a match for Glasgow against the North-Midlands at Murrayfield. Opposition hooker Allan Hardie was alleged to have grabbed hold of Brown's hair and kneed him full in the face. As though that weren't bad enough, the assault continued with a stamp on the lock's face as Brown went to ground. It was far worse than anything he'd suffered during those bruising Lions tours to the southern hemisphere. Brown rose to his feet and chased the perpetrator, finally catching him and meting out some retribution of his own. Both were banned, Brown for three months, Hardie for sixteen, and the feud extended down the decades. Brown never played for Scotland again.

Andy Irvine was sitting in the Murrayfield stands that day, and still remembers the episode with distaste: 'My recollection is that Gordon was on the deck and that Allan Hardie saw him and basically put a boot into his face... Gordon was so incensed that when he got up he actually chased him, and when he got hold of him he started to swing... Most people had sympathy for Gordon because although admittedly he was retaliating, he had bloody good reason to retaliate. I think the fact that he chased him didn't help his cause. Had he just hit him straight away, well... But he was banned for months after that.'

It was a testament to the man and his Lions pedigree that Brown was still picked for the Lions tour to New Zealand in 1977, and starred once again in the Test matches. He would eventually be banned from the game one final time, for – of all things – writing a book and making himself some money. Such were the amateur ways.

He went on to make a name for himself as an after dinner speaker and television pundit, giving the rest of the rugby world a glimpse of the charm and character that had beguiled his team-mates all those years ago.

At the turn of the millennium, Gordon Brown was diagnosed with cancer. He died in 2001, aged just fifty-three. His passing left a gaping hole in the hearts of his fellow Lions. Many have written about the man, his courage, his humour, his charm. But his own words told it best, and if he told the story often, it never lost its resonance.

Before the third, decisive Test match in Port Elizabeth in 1974, Willie John McBride had turned to his companion and exhorted him to put his body on the line just one more time: 'Broonie,' he'd said: 'Tonight you must be able to look me straight in the eye.' Hours later, having put everything on the line, having followed his captain through the swinging arms and the punching fists, and having emerged victorious on the other side, Brown went to sit next to McBride, hoping to spend some time with his friend: 'In the wee small hours, I went and found him, and I said; "Willie, can I look you straight in the eye?" And he looked at me and said; "Broonie, for the rest of your life."'

Nine years later, in June 2010, another Lion lost his longest, toughest battle, as cancer took Andy Ripley. Ripley the superstar, Ripley the chronicler, Ripley the conscience, Ripley the unlikeliest of disciples.

It was Ripley who captured the very essence of what those Lions had done and how they'd managed it. 'Show us the broken glass Willie,' he wrote in his brilliant opus *Ripley's World* – he would still have willingly got down on his hands and knees and started crawling over the shards decades later, if only McBride had asked it of him. Even Alun Thomas would have been proud of his rebellious number 8, for Ripley, the man who loathed the blazer and the tie, would wear them proudly at 'family' reunions over the decades to come.

Ripley had visited townships, had talked to agitated students, had met Helen Suzman, the great liberal activist and politician whilst on tour. He never bought into the theory of the Lions having – in his own words – given: 'A morale boost to the black population.' In fact he referred to such talk as 'guff'. Over the subsequent years he asked the hard questions, questions that some didn't want to hear, and didn't want to answer – whether they'd been used, whether they should have gone at all, why had they done what they did, and how had they achieved so much in the end?

He came to his own conclusion, an answer that sat uncomfortably with some of his gruffer colleagues… Love. They did it for love, love of one man – William James McBride. Ripley himself tackled this very issue honestly when he asked the question 'Why did we love Willie so much?' Of course he'd thought long and hard about the answer. Ripley explained that it wasn't because of McBride's considerable ability, or his leadership qualities, or even his vast experience. All those factors counted, but there were a number of others who could claim to have those admirable attributes as well. No, what made Willie John McBride a man apart according to Ripley was that: 'He knew about disappointment, about rejection, about feeling unloved, and that's why he never let us feel any of those things in South Africa.'

I finally plucked up the courage to put this theory to the captain of the 1974 Lions himself. To ask the gruffest, toughest of the lot, this five-time Lions tourist, this conqueror of New Zealand and South Africa, the greatest Lion of them all, about love.

And when I did eventually ask McBride whether he could appreciate that those players had given everything they had, and accomplished so much, because they simply loved him, there was an embarrassed pause, a hesitation.

Then laughter. Then an acknowledgement: 'Yes, maybe... I suppose so, if you're talking about that tour. But I think that was just something that was in this team. We had this feeling, this thing for one another that you can't really explain. It hasn't gone away either. When we'll meet up soon for the fortieth, and I'll walk into that room, well you just can't begin to describe it, that bond – but it's there all right.'

And is that one word, 'Love', the difference between the tours of 1971 and 1974, what sets one apart from the other? 'Yes, I think that's probably right.'

So Ripley nailed it, no matter how uncomfortable an admission it was. When the number 8 had been at his lowest in 1974 – a Test match reject, deemed not good enough, it was McBride who'd consoled him, who'd encouraged him, who'd made him feel he still had a huge role to play, who'd made him understand that the team meant each and every one of them.

In one winning post-match function McBride had asked his team to stand and be recognised. Fifteen players got sheepishly to their feet. 'No', said McBride: 'I want the team to stand up... All of them.' And that's when Ripley understood. McBride loved them all, and they loved him back. So when McBride led his Test side out to battle, holding that Lions mascot aloft, who should be there – waiting to take the burden off his hands – but Andrew George Ripley.

Years later, when fighting his most famous battle of all, the Englishman would happily confess that when it came to McBride: 'I loved him forever.'

When troublesome journalists ask Ripley's team-mates for their tour memories, to recapture the essence of those long lost glory days, the giant number 8 is always one of the characters who raises a smile. And they all remember that iconic T-shirt, bold, brazen, challenging and amusing, 'I'm So Perfect It Even Scares Me'.

Perfect?

The funny thing is that in rugby terms, for a brief moment in time – twelve weeks and twenty-two matches over one long South African winter in 1974 – he pretty much was.

Then again, so were they all.

Acknowledgements

MY STARTING POINT in terms of the 1974 Lions was in fact a television programme on their illustrious predecessors. In 2011, I produced a documentary on the 1971 Lions to celebrate the fortieth anniversary of their epic series win in New Zealand. Not only was the core of that party Welsh, but it was Welsh speaking – Carwyn James, Barry John, Gareth Edwards, Gerald Davies, Delme Thomas, Derek Quinnell and Geoff Evans all came from a small circle of villages in west Wales. I felt as though I had been brought up with them, knew them and admired them as more than just players. They were the rugby romantic's dream team.

Afterwards my thoughts turned to the next big Lions milestone, the fortieth anniversary of the 1974 tour. I soon realised that I knew very little about these Lions in comparison with the giants of '71, despite the fact that their own achievements in South Africa seemingly surpassed those of the New Zealand tourists three years previously. That got me wondering why.

It quickly became apparent that the story of the 1974 Lions – and what those history making players accomplished – hadn't really been explored in any depth over the following decades. The controversy surrounding the tour in terms of apartheid added another complicated, fascinating dimension to the story. There were moral as well as rugby issues to contend with.

As ever with the Lions, the first port of call in terms of research was *The History of the British and Irish Lions* by Clem and Greg Thomas. They whetted the appetite, and from

342

then on the trawl was long and thoroughly enjoyable despite the relative scarcity of in-depth reportage.

In fact there were two fascinating accounts of the tour, written in its immediate aftermath. Both were by well-respected rugby journalists, both of whom had travelled with the Lions and knew the players. Yet both offered startlingly differing perspectives on the tour and its characters. So JBG Thomas's *The Greatest Lions* and John Reason's *The Unbeaten Lions* formed the basis of my research. They also underlined the fact that this was a tour which polarised opinion in almost every way. From there I took in biographies, collected memoirs, newspaper archives, rugby magazines, online articles, players' personal collections and the DVD documentaries that offered valuable video archive of the tour.

There isn't much footage, but what does exist is precious. *The Invincibles*, *The Lions Roar of '74*, the BBC's *The Lions Roar* and the rarely-seen *Glorious Victorious*, made by another tourist, BBC producer Dewi Griffiths – these all helped in terms of putting the story into context and bringing the tour alive.

Of course, in that regard, nothing brought the story of the '74 Lions to life as vividly as the words of the people who experienced the tour, and its complicated genesis, first-hand. Mostly that meant the players themselves. I can never thank them enough, and can only hope that I have repaid them for their time and trust by doing them justice.

I am grateful in particular to Gareth Edwards for his kind words and encouragement, to JPR Williams, Tom David and Roy Bergiers for letting me pore over their amazing collection of photographs, cine-footage, slides and tour memorabilia. Roy's vast collection of newspaper cuttings from South Africa proved particularly illuminating. Thanks are also due to librarians, administrators and to genuinely supportive publishers for their faith and enthusiasm. Finally thanks to the family for their infinite patience, constant encouragement and the occasional well-timed 'sws'.

Bibliography

Richard Bath – *The British and Irish Lions Miscellany* (2008)

Phil Bennett/Martyn Williams – *Everywhere for Wales* (1981)

Phil Bennett – *Phil Bennett – The Autobiography* (2003)

David R Black/John Nauright – *Rugby and the South African Nation: Sport, Culture, Politics and Power in the Old and New South Africas* (1998)

Mike Burton – *Never Stay Down* (1982)

John Carlin – *Playing the Enemy: Nelson Mandela and the Game That Made a Nation* (2008)

Mick Cleary/John Griffiths – *Rothmans Rugby Yearbook 1996–97* (1996)

Mick Cleary – *Rampant Pride – The Lions in Australia 2013* (2013)

Jeff Connor/Martin Hannan – *Once Were Lions – The Players' Stories: Inside the World's Most Famous Rugby Team* (2009)

Fran Cotton – *My Pride of Lions: The British Isles Tour of South Africa 1997* (1997)

Saul David – *Zulu* (2004)

Mervyn Davies/David Roach – *In Strength and Shadow – The Mervyn Davies Story* (2004)

Gareth Edwards – *Gareth – An Autobiography* (1978)

Gareth Edwards/Peter Bills – *Gareth Edwards – The Autobiography* (1999)

Chris Greyvenstein – *Springbok Saga: A Pictorial History from 1891* (1977)

Peter Hain – *Don't Play with Apartheid – The Background to the Stop the Seventy Tour Campaign* (1971)

Peter Hain – *Outside In* (2012)

Peter Hain – *Ad and Wal: Values, duty, sacrifice in apartheid South Africa* (2014)

David Harrison – *The White Tribe of Africa – South Africa in Perspective* (1981)

Andy Irvine/Ian Robertson – *Andy Irvine – An Autobiography* (1985)

Barry John – *The Barry John Story* (1974)

Barry John/Paul Abbandonato – *Barry John – The King* (2000)

Stephen Jones/Tom English/Nick Cain/David Barnes – *Behind the Lions – Playing Rugby for the British and Irish Lions* (2012)

Frank Keating – *The Great Number Tens – A Century of Rugby's Pivots and Playmakers* (1993)

Ian Knight – *Zulu Rising – The Epic Story of Isandlwana and Rorke's Drift* (2010)

Denis Lalanne – *The Great Fight of the French Fifteen* (1960)

Nelson Mandela – *Long Walk To Freedom* (1995)

Nelson Mandela *Conversations With Myself* (2010)

Willie John McBride/Peter Bills – *Willie John – The Story Of My Life* (2004)

Ian McGeechan – *Lion Man – The Autobiography of Ian McGeechan* (2009)

Stewart McKinney – *Voices from the Back of the Bus: Tall Tales and Hoary Stories from Rugby's Real Heroes* (2009)

Stewart McKinney – *Roars from the Back of the Bus: Rugby tales of Life with the Lions* (2012)

Terry McLean – *Goodbye to Glory – The 1976 All Black Tour of South Africa* (1976)

Donald R Morris – *The Washing of the Spears* (1966)

John Nauright – *Long Run to Freedom: Sport, Cultures and Identities in South Africa* (2010)

Peter Oborne – *Basil D'Oliveira – Cricket and Conspiracy: The Untold Story* (2005)

Terry O'Connor – *How the Lions Won – The stories and skills behind two famous victories* (1975)

Thomas Pakenham – *The Boer War* (1979)

Thomas Pakenham – *The Scramble for Africa* (1990)

John Reason – *The Victorious Lions – The 1971 British Isles Rugby Union Tour of Australia and New Zealand* (1971)

John Reason – *How We Beat The All Blacks – The 1971 Lions Speak* (1972)

John Reason – *The Unbeaten Lions – The 1974 British Isles Rugby Union Tour of South Africa* (1974)

Wallace Reyburn – *The Lions* (1967)

Trevor Richards – *Dancing on Our Bones – New Zealand, South Africa, Rugby and Racism* (1999)

Simon Richmond/Alan Murphy/Kim Wildman/Andrew Burke – *Lonely Planet: South Africa, Lesotho and Swaziland* (1993)

Andy Ripley – *Ripley's World* (2007)

Quintus van Rooyen – *SA Rugby Writers' Rugby Annual 1973* (1973)

Quintus van Rooyen – *Rugby Writers' Annual 1975* (1975)

Anthony Sampson – *Mandela – The Authorised Biography* (1999)

Clem and Greg Thomas – *The History of the British and Irish Lions* (1996)

JBG Thomas – *The Roaring Lions* (1971)

JBG Thomas – *The Greatest Lions* (1974)

346

David Tossell – *Nobody Beats Us: The Inside Story of the 1970s Wales Rugby Team* (2010)

Marian Wallace – *A History of Namibia: From the Beginning to 1990* (2011)

Frank Welsh – *A History of South Africa* (2000)

JPR Williams – *JPR Williams – An Autobiography* (1979)

JPR Williams – *Given the Breaks – My Life in Rugby* (2006)

Bobby Windsor and Peter Jackson – *The Iron Duke: Bobby Windsor – The Life and Times of a Working-Class Rugby Hero* (2010)

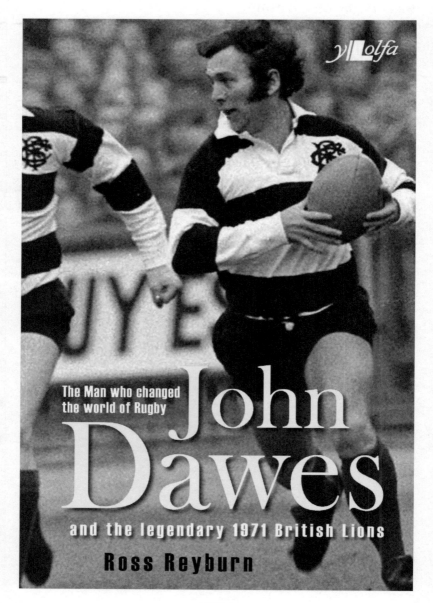

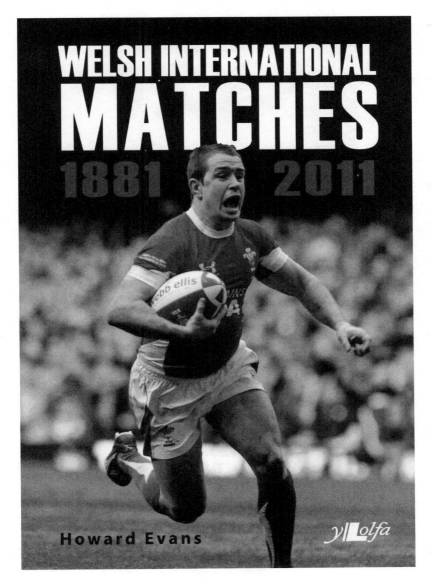

WELSH INTERNATIONAL MATCHES 1881 2011

Howard Evans

y Lolfa

£14.95

LYNN DAVIES

hard men
of WELSH
RUGBY

y Lolfa

£7.95

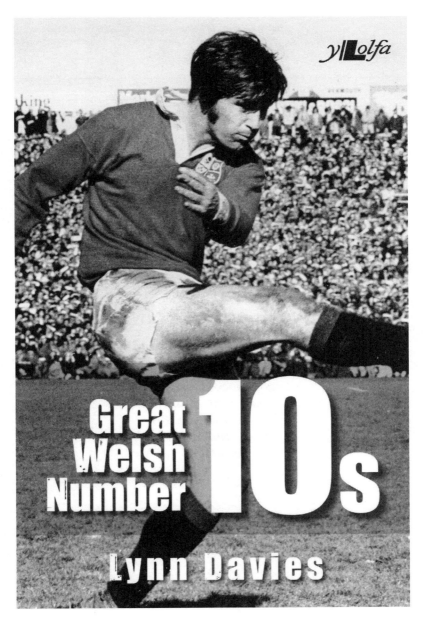

Great Welsh Number **10**s

Lynn Davies

£9.95

y Lolfa

y Lolfa

TALYBONT CEREDIGION CYMRU SY24 5HE
e-mail ylolfa@ylolfa.com
website www.ylolfa.com
phone (01970) 832 304
fax 832 782